ENGINES OF ANXIETY

ENGINES OF ANXIETY

Academic Rankings, Reputation, and Accountability

Wendy Nelson Espeland
and
Michael Sauder

Russell Sage Foundation
New York

The Russell Sage Foundation

The Russell Sage Foundation, one of the oldest of America's general purpose foundations, was established in 1907 by Mrs. Margaret Olivia Sage for "the improvement of social and living conditions in the United States." The foundation seeks to fulfill this mandate by fostering the development and dissemination of knowledge about the country's political, social, and economic problems. While the foundation endeavors to assure the accuracy and objectivity of each book it publishes, the conclusions and interpretations in Russell Sage Foundation publications are those of the authors and not of the foundation, its trustees, or its staff. Publication by Russell Sage, therefore, does not imply foundation endorsement.

Library of Congress Cataloging-in-Publication Data

Names: Espeland, Wendy Nelson, author. | Sauder, Michael, author.
Title: Engines of anxiety : academic rankings, reputation, and accountability / Wendy Nelson Espeland and Michael Sauder.
Description: New York : Russell Sage Foundation, [2016] | Includes bibliographical references and index.
Identifiers: LCCN 2015041225 (print) | LCCN 2015042663 (ebook) | ISBN 9780871544278
(pbk. : alk. paper) | ISBN 9781610448567 (ebook)
Subjects: LCSH: Law schools—Ratings and rankings—United States.
Classification: LCC KF272 .E836 2016 (print) | LCC KF272 (ebook) | DDC 340.071/1073—dc23
LC record available at http://cp.mcafee.com/d/FZsSd2gs739J5xxUQsEIFzDztPqtPhO-qekTDAPhOrjKqenPhOCYqekm3qtPhO-qekTDCkjqadT3hOUOMYyrlSdLfG2E
QQz_00jsqqh_w09J0sqetI-U_R-josu73KLsKCO_vDSbIFTVqWdAklrzD-l3PWAp
mU6CQjq9K_9Tspu76zAs-UrKr01DSJ3zWSUzkPytQnXI8FFLCXkGS2zWSUzk
Orpv7fCMnVClfgd40A6xoQg8rfjh0Xm9Ewd78VWXMV5ZxxcsYrpodX7UDjenD

The paper used in this publication meets the minimum requirements of American National Standard for Information Sciences—Permanence of Paper for Printed Library Materials. ANSI Z39.48-1992.

Text design by Genna Patacsil.

RUSSELL SAGE FOUNDATION
112 East 64th Street, New York, New York 10065
10 9 8 7 6 5 4 3 2 1

This book is for our families.
Bruce, Sam, and Esther
Jean, Claire, and Ben

Contents

About the Authors |

WENDY NELSON ESPELAND is professor of sociology at Northwestern University.

MICHAEL SAUDER is associate professor of sociology at the University of Iowa.

Acknowledgments |

OUR BOOK HAS been collaborative in all of the best senses. As authors, we two often no longer remember who wrote which parts. We start by thanking the many people who agreed to talk to us, including the deans who gave us access to their schools and the many faculty, staff, students, and lawyers who agreed to confide in strangers about personal and controversial aspects of their jobs and professions. We can't name those we interviewed or their affiliations, but you know who you are—and we hope that you also know how very grateful we are for your trust, patience, and expertise.

This project evolved from an idea for a short article on rankings into a broader and much more protracted venture, one culminating in this book. It started with the American Bar Foundation, where Jack Heinz planted a seed about why law school rankings would be a fruitful example for studying the effects of rankings more generally. Along the way this seed was generously nourished with support and community, both material and intellectual, from other wonderful institutions. The Russell Sage Foundation deserves special mention because it was there where, happily, we met our accomplished and very patient editor, Suzanne Nichols. Suzanne, in turn, found conscientious and insightful anonymous reviewers whose detailed comments made the book better. Thank you.

Early support for both of us came from the MacArthur Collaborative Research Grant (Department of Sociology, Northwestern University) and a decisive research grant from the Law School Admission Council.[1] For Wendy, additional fellowships and support came from the Lochinvar Society; the Regulatory Institutions Network, Australian National University; the Alice Kaplan Institute for the Humanities, Northwestern University; and the Sciences Po Centre de Sociologie des Organisations. Year-long residencies at the Russell Sage Foundation, the Radcliffe Institute for Advanced Study at Harvard University, and the Institute for Advanced Study Berlin (Wissenschaftskolleg zu Berlin) offered time to think and write, along with enduring friendships that deeply shaped this work.

For Michael, support was provided by the Robert Wood Johnson Scholars in Health Policy Program, Harvard University; the Obermann Center for Advanced Studies, University of Iowa; the Career Development Award, University of Iowa; and the Department of Sociology, University of Iowa. Our findings do not reflect the views or policies of our funders.

We also appreciate the many institutions that invited us to present our work to them. Between us, we gave many talks about this work, and we cannot identify all the audiences who helped us so much in developing our ideas. But because educational rankings have been such a fast-moving and globalizing technology, it was especially helpful that these audiences spanned many disciplines and locations. And we thank our departmental colleagues at Northwestern and Iowa for providing such stimulating and collegial intellectual homes.

Our book is possible because of the support we received from friends and colleagues. We wish we could single them all out for thanks, but there are too many. We would be remiss if we did not mention—among the many who read parts of the manuscript, talked through pieces of it with us, or helped make it possible to conduct our research—the following people: Gabriel Abend, Fabrice Bardet, Bruce Carruthers, Elspeth Carruthers, Mary Carruthers, John Carson, Jeanette Colyvas, Alan Czaplicki, Raine Daston, Emmanuel Didier, the late Alain Desrosières, Bryant Garth, Kathy Hall, Tim Hallett, Terry Halliday, Carol Heimer, Tong Lam, Michèle Lamont, Ryon Lancaster, Jean "Littlejohn," Stacy Lom, Freda Lynn, Jeff Manza, Andrea Mennicken, Sally Merry, Peter Miller, Bob Nelson, Jahnavi Phalkey, Damon Phillips, Ted Porter, Woody Powell, Mike Power, Tanina Rostain, Debra Schleef, Peter Seigelman, Susan Silbey, Mitchell Stevens, Art Stinchcombe, Jessica Thurk, and Berit Vannebo.

We are also grateful for the expert research assistance we received from Lauren Buxbaum, Ana Campos, Corey Fields, Cassandra Malik, Chad McPherson, Amanda Mitchell, Emma Sherman, Sasha Tuzel, Vernon Woodley, Leah Woods, and Sophia Yang.

We have been more than lucky in having family who sustain us. Wendy thanks especially Anne and John Mitchell; Mark Espeland and Anne Boyle; Janet Greenhow; Elspeth and Gladys Carruthers; and Mary Carruthers. Esther M. Espeland continues to inspire her. Michael thanks his parents, Mike and Judy Sauder, as well as Minta Colburn and Troy Cummings. He would also like to express a special note of appreciation for his grandmother, Wilma Sauder, who never failed to ask about the progress of the book.

We dedicate this book to our partners and children because, after all this time, it is theirs as much as ours.

Chapter 1 | The Transparency of Transparency Measures

It's one of the real black marks on the history of higher education that an entire industry that's supposedly populated by the best minds in the country—theoretical physicists, writers, critics—is bamboozled by a third-rate news magazine.... They do almost a parody of real research. I joke that the next thing they'll do is rank churches. You know, "Where does God appear most frequently? How big are the pews?"
—Leon Botstein, president of Bard College

WE LIVE IN an era when individuals, organizations, and governments face pressing demands to be accountable.[1] Not only do we expect actions to be transparent, we also expect them to be demonstrably transparent: the general public has the right to see disinterested evidence of performance, competence, and relative achievement. Quantitative measures seem to offer the best means to achieve these goals. They have the patina of objectivity: stripped of rhetoric and emotion, they show what is "really going on." Even more, they can reduce vast amounts of information to a figure that is easy to understand, a simplicity that intimates that there is nothing to hide, and indeed that nothing can be hidden.

Consider, however, three recent controversies:

An inspector general's review of a Veterans Affairs Health Care System hospital in Phoenix, Arizona, found that administrators had doctored records to make the wait times for medical appointments appear shorter than they actually were.[2] In the face of an agency goal of thirty-day wait times for initial appointments—a goal to which bonuses and salary increases were tied—administrators misreported the wait times for some veterans and placed as many as 1,700 others on unofficial

1

"secret lists" until appointments could be made for them. Veterans on these unofficial lists were not included in the hospital's official statistics and therefore did not affect the hospital's mean-wait-time statistic.[3] The report states that this sort of gaming was not limited to the Phoenix hospital, but is a "systematic problem nationwide."[4]

The *New York Times* reports inconsistencies with the Medicare rating system of nursing homes, which is based on awarding up to five stars for different aspects of the care offered.[5] This rating system, designed to make quality distinctions among nursing homes, is used not only by consumers making decisions about elder care but also by referring doctors and insurers. Key components of the ratings, however, are self-reported, and the *Times* investigation shows that there is clear evidence of gaming. Homes manipulate their scores by temporarily hiring more staff before scheduled annual surveys, providing an inflated representation of their true staffing levels. They also misreport their quality measures, knowing that these data are not easily auditable. This means that even recognizably poor facilities can score well on the ratings. Advocates of the rating system claim that these numbers have led to improvements in the nursing home industry, but others point out that results are "implausible" and lead to a "false sense of security."[6]

Facing the threat of sanctions, humiliation, and possibly even the closure of their school as a result of poor test results, teachers—by all accounts dedicated and otherwise conscientious—at Park Middle School in Atlanta admitted to systematically changing student answers on tests that determine whether schools are meeting the federal standards outlined by No Child Left Behind. Investigators later found that cheating by teachers in this district was rampant and attributed it to "a culture of fear, intimidation and retaliation that [had] infested a district" that was using data "as an abusive and cruel weapon to embarrass and punish." This is by no means an exceptional case: Rachel Aviv reports that the Government Accountability Office found comparable instances of cheating in forty states.[7]

These three high-profile news stories provide glimpses into the unexpected problems that public measures designed to assure transparency and accountability can create: despite their appearance of objectivity and impartiality, measures are often the product of political processes and contain biases. Detailed investigations of how measures are constructed and implemented often make one less, rather than more, confident about their validity and reliability; the production of measures necessarily entails subjective decisions about how the measures are chosen, assembled, and weighted.

Measures create new incentives and power dynamics. Jobs and jobholders come to be defined by the numbers of their office or organization. As the pressure to chase better numbers increases, the quest for numerical improvement can be used as a weapon by those who are dissatisfied with specific outcomes or desire change. This pressure to produce the best numbers possible also motivates those in charge of the numbers to cheat. Numbers can be gamed and measures subverted, especially when financial or other motivating incentives are involved. Short of cheating, quantitative assessments drive people to "teach to the test," focusing their attention on improving the numbers instead of the qualities the numbers are designed to represent.

Accountability measures do not produce transparency simply, or simply produce transparency. Although most do make some aspects of social processes more apparent, they are complicated constructions—often more complicated than we give them credit for—that have the tendency to transform the phenomena they are meant only to reflect. Even more, they nearly always displace discretion rather than expose what is hidden about social processes and phenomena. At worst, they create new forms of obfuscation, forms that pose new dangers because it is difficult to discern precisely how measures are constructed and what kinds of information are left aside. There is a deep irony here: transparency measures themselves often lack transparency.

Concerns about accountability measures are especially relevant because quantitative evaluation has come to permeate social life. If it seems difficult to escape talk of accountability and assessment, it is because these ideas are now far more common than in the past. Google's Ngram Viewer shows a steep increase in the use of the words "rankings," "transparency," "accountability," "audit," "performance measures," and "metrics" during the last two decades. These new forms of evaluation, along with the surveillance and discipline that go hand in hand with them, are applied to an astonishing range of organizations, from churches and schools to insurance providers and philanthropies, and permeate the activities within them. Increasingly, we even apply these principles of accountability to ourselves as new devices allow us to carefully measure and assess our fitness, mood, and sleep in an attempt to produce a "quantified self." We are truly awash in the numbers that are used to provide evidence of accountability, transparency, and efficiency.

This book aims to develop a better understanding of this new culture of evaluation by thoroughly scrutinizing a single set of numbers and their consequences. Specifically, we examine the *U.S. News and World Report* (hereafter, *USN*) rankings of law schools and the sweeping changes these rankings have produced in legal education. We have spent more than ten years studying the *USN* rankings, conducting over two hundred in-depth interviews with law school students, faculty, and administrators; collecting observational data at schools, job fairs, and professional meetings; and combing through decades of school statistics, newspaper reports, online bulletin boards, and organizational documents. We contend that a close case study of this type is necessary to understand the full extent of these measures' effects in terms of the pressures they generate, the psychological changes they induce, and the organizational behaviors, patterns, and routines they alter. The amount of work needed to unpack the complexities of a seemingly straightforward and simple numerical evaluation is itself a telling illustration of what numbers obscure: only through an intensive examination such as this one can we make the effects of transparency measures more transparent.

Our title, *Engines of Anxiety*, is meant to highlight two of the central points that this book makes about rankings and reactions to them. The first is the fear of falling in rank that dominates the consciousness of those subject to them. Nearly everyone we spoke with lived in dread of the inevitable day that new rankings would come out showing that their school had dropped to a worse number or tier, and many of the changes caused by the rankings can be directly traced to this fear. The second point is that rankings are structured to constantly generate and regenerate these anxieties and reactions. In much the same way as sociologist Donald Mackenzie documents the ways in which quantitative models actively produce financial markets in *An Engine, Not a Camera*, we show that rankings are constitutive rather than simply reflective of what they are attempting to measure.

RANKINGS

Rankings are a compelling example of accountability measures both because they are so common in contemporary society and because their precise comparisons generate intense competition among those being evaluated, a competition that makes the rankings' effects easier to see. Rankings—of sports teams, cities, schools, police departments, doctors, lawyers, and so forth—are seemingly everywhere; there appears to be no limit to our demand to know who is the best and where we stand in relation to one another. We are so accustomed to rankings that they have become a naturalized way of making sense of the world. But while we often express doubts about the results of rankings—about where our team or city or school lands on a particular ranking—we rarely question the legitimacy of rankings per se or ask whether they are a productive way of evaluating the people or things they rank.

With the possible exception of sports teams, the ranking of schools is the most popular and influential form of ranking in the United States. A school's rank serves as a status marker and a signal of what a degree might be worth. *USN*'s law school rankings, much like educational rankings of other fields, create a very public hierarchy among schools, one that overwhelms other conceptions of how schools might be compared to one another. Within this ranking universe of educational institutions, legal education is unique: in this field, one ranking entity has a monopoly on public perception, and all accredited law schools are ranked together according to the same metrics. These characteristics of law school rankings make it easier to directly connect school action to particular criteria used in the rankings and to see variations in how schools respond to the rankings. (Other fields in which rankings have a powerful influence, such as those of business schools and world universities, either have multiple rankers assessing schools in different ways or have schools divided into subgroups according to their characteristics and missions.)

Moreover, given the hyperimportance of status in the legal field[8] and, at least in our experience, the tendency of lawyers to speak their mind, the legal field provides an ideal opportunity to document the anxieties produced by rankings for students, faculty, and administrators; the range of protest and criticism leveled at this form of public assessment; and the shockingly extensive efforts adopted by schools to "do something" to surpass—or often just to keep up with—peers and rivals. Our subjects were often very forthcoming and eloquent about their concerns about rankings as well as their battles with each other and *USN*.

All of these factors led us to focus our attention on how rankings have affected legal education. We emphasize, however, that while legal education provides a particularly clear window into the effects of rankings, the dynamics created by rankings are very similar in other contexts. As we show in chapter 7, the patterns of evaluation and response created by rankings in legal education, as well as the patterns of effects they produce, are apparent not only in other forms of educational rankings (of undergraduate institutions, medical schools, business schools, graduate programs, and world universities), but also in nearly every other form of public quantitative assessment: from the ratings of doctors and hospitals to the management of crime statistics; from the measure of "hits" newspaper articles receive to international indices of corruption and well-being.[9] We are confident that the dynamics we document here—the redistribution of attention and effort, the gaming strategies, the anxiety—will be familiar to everyone in higher education and the many other fields now subject to rankings and other accountability metrics.

EMPIRICAL AIM

The empirical aim of this book is to meticulously document the effects, both intended and unintended, that rankings have had on the field of legal education and to demonstrate how they have changed law schools, influenced the people who work and study within these schools, and altered the perceptions of the external constituents who play a powerful role in directing the future course of these schools. In the following chapters we carefully trace the influence of rankings through legal education, showing how rankings affect prospective students, admissions, deans, faculty, career services, alumni, and employment. This approach allows us to demonstrate the extent to which rankings have permeated the decision-making of schools from the bottom to the top of the status hierarchy.

Broadly, we argue that rankings produce a new status system that reorganizes how law schools are stratified. This broad change in legal education influences how law schools define their goals, admit students, and deploy resources, and how employers evaluate candidates. These kinds of changes affect who gets to be a lawyer, what kind of lawyer he or she becomes, people's sense of their own status, and the ways legal jobs are allocated among schools and persons. Because rankings are standardized algorithms applied to all schools, they promote a single, idiosyncratic definition of what it means to be a "good school" and punish schools that do not conform to the image of excellence embedded and embodied in the rankings.

The practical consequences of rankings, as will be made apparent throughout the following chapters, are wide-ranging and often disparate. Our data show that rankings have altered how people in all types of law schools make decisions, allocate resources, and think about themselves and others. Nearly everyone would agree with the dean of a school ranked outside the top fifty who said, "[Rankings] are always in the back of everybody's head. With every issue that comes up, we have to ask, 'How is this impacting our ranking?' " At the same time, our data also demonstrate that although the rankings are a force with which all law schools must constantly contend, not all law schools are affected—or choose to respond—in the same way. Even more, the pressures that rankings exert on schools change over time and in light of current events. Take, for example, the turmoil created by an event like the Great Recession and its aftermath. The downturn transformed the economic environment and was accompanied by a severe constriction of the legal job market and a steep decline in law school applications.[10] This upheaval changed many aspects of legal education, but it did not diminish the attention schools paid to rankings or the efforts they made to achieve a higher rank; it only mediated these effects. As highly ranked schools were much less affected by these events, improving rankings once again became an expedient answer for schools looking to fill classes or ensure future employment for more of their graduates.

It is challenging to catalog such diffuse effects, but we have been able to identify three particularly powerful categories of transformations produced by these measures: they transform the power relations within schools, day-to-day organizational practices, and the ways professional opportunities are distributed. These categories provide perspective on the changes created by rankings while also pointing toward the types of unintended consequences that the implementation of other accountability measures can produce generally.

THEORETICAL AIM

In addition to documenting the practical effects of rankings, our study of the consequences of rankings on schools provides new insights into how we understand the nature of quantitative measures and the changes they engender. First, we develop an explanation of *how* rankings generate the far-reaching and transformative effects we describe throughout the book. We argue that the "reactivity" of social measures is a key reason for the changes generated by rankings. In the case of law school rankings, for instance, "reactivity" refers to the fact that the measures do not simply reflect an underlying social hierarchy but in fact play a crucial role in creating this hierarchy by changing how people think about and react to law school and legal education. This new cognitive map of the field of legal education powerfully influences how quality is defined and which aspects of legal education are prioritized. We believe that reactivity is a key component of all social measures and is often responsible for the unintended consequences these measures produce. In chapter 2 we take a close look at the mechanisms that contribute to this reactivity—commensuration, self-fulfilling prophecies, narrative, and reverse engineering—and explain why this process is so potent.

Second, our work provides new insights into how numbers create accountability and, importantly, specify the distinctive type of accountability they create. We argue that the accountability produced by quantitative assessments like rankings is best characterized as "selective accountability," meaning that these assessments hold people or organizations accountable on some dimensions while obscuring other aspects of the processes they measure. These biases are often overlooked not only because numbers are useful simplifications of complex social realities, but also because they are granted a great deal of cultural authority. We tend to see numerical measures as objective and legitimate because we associate them with technical efficiency as well as mathematical and scientific rigor.

Finally, our detailed examination of the effects of rankings provides a rare opportunity to explore the often-ignored moral aspects of public measurement. Moral assumptions—such as about what is a good school, what is a good student, what is valuable about education—are embedded in the measures, but these assumptions tend to become invisible in the face of quantitative authority. In this book we hope to draw attention to the ethical dilemmas that quantitative assessments create for those who must manage them, the culture of cynicism that the mind-set of "playing to the test" promotes, and, most generally, the importance of distinguishing between the inarguable usefulness of quantification and the moral implications of creating elaborate measures of everything.

In examining these broad questions, we draw on and contribute to traditions in the sociology of culture and organizations. Like other sociologists, we see cultural processes as instrumental in creating, reinforcing, and redressing inequality.[11] Rankings have changed the stratification system of higher education by transforming shared understandings about what education is for; who should have access to it; what it means to be a good student, faculty member, scholar, or administrator; and what excellence is. Even more profoundly, rankings have replaced a system of loosely structured meanings and symbols with arbitrary precision that erases ambiguity while also eroding the authority of professional expertise in favor of calculation and numerical facility.

Along these same lines, rankings also change the categories and schemas through which people and schools are classified and evaluated. Categories are a form of symbolic boundary that allow us to make distinctions between what (or who) should be included and what (or who) should not.[12] As we show, rankings directly change how we categorize schools: we now focus on a specific numerical rank or tier instead of on earlier, more nuanced definitions of what qualifies as a worthy school. In doing so, rankings reorient how both insiders and outsiders conceptualize where schools stand in relation to one another and how the field of legal education is structured. In short, these cultural changes have transformed not only the traditional meaning of legal education but also the values that define this field.

This book also speaks directly to organizational research by demonstrating the distinctive effects of performance measures on organizations and the fields in which they operate. Throughout the book we document the many ways in which these measures impose organizational change: rankings have clear effects on organizational behavior, policy, and strategy. One reason that rankings generate such extensive change is that they override the strategies organizations normally use to manage external pressures. As many scholars have pointed out, organizations often respond to external threats or interference by developing symbolic responses that leave their core activities untouched. New regulation, for example, often results in the creation of formal departments or committees that take on the appearance of compliance but effect little change: organizations may create offices, put ineffective programs into practice, or develop policies that may never be implemented in order to appear responsive.[13] This "buffering" of the organization from external efforts to influence it is circumvented in the case of rankings. Rankings make symbolic compliance harder to achieve by allowing outsiders to easily scrutinize the organization, by creating powerful inducements to try to game the rankings, and by providing insiders with incentives to both adopt the goals implicit in rankings and internalize rankings as a form of professional identity. Accountability measures like rankings are often simultaneously coercive and seductive, and this is what makes them such powerful agents of transformation.

These more general questions about how social measures work and the nature of the accountability that they produce both contextualize our findings and, more important, provide a framework for understanding the ramifications and limitations of rankings, ratings, and accountability measures. With these broad implications in mind, we now turn to the details of the numbers for our particular case, explaining the history and construction of law school rankings.

A BRIEF HISTORY OF RANKINGS

Rankings of U.S. universities date back more than a century. James Cattell's *American Men of Science*, published in 1910, ranked schools on the basis of the number of eminent scientists they produced.[14] In 1911, the United States Bureau of Education created an evaluative system that divided hundreds of American colleges and universities into one of five tiers, but this ranking was never published owing to the outcry of college officials who believed their school's quality was not fairly represented in the assessment and were fearful of the reaction of their constituents.[15] Raymond Hughes is credited with creating the first rankings of graduate programs in 1925 and, in conjunction with the American Council on Education, again in 1934.[16] These early evaluations and others that followed were prepared for and mostly used by academics. It was only much later, in the 1980s, that popular media regularly began producing rankings of colleges and graduate programs intended for consumers rather than educators. *U.S. News and World Report* helped pioneer media rankings when it published its first issue ranking colleges in 1983.[17]

When Mort Zuckerman acquired *U.S. News and World Report* in 1984 and became its editor in chief, it was a lackluster news weekly overshadowed by its more successful rivals, *Newsweek* and *Time*. Zuckerman hired a new group of editors to enliven and distinguish *USN*, one of whom was Mel Elfin, the former Washington bureau chief for *Newsweek*. Earlier, *USN* had published the results of two simple surveys in which college presidents named the best college and universities. Elfin recalls that it was Zuckerman's idea to expand these rankings and issue them annually as a way to solidify *USN*'s reputation as the magazine providing "news you can use."[18] As editor of special projects, Elfin was charged with figuring out ways to do this, and he quickly became a driving force behind rankings. He remembers feeling skeptical and daunted by the task that his bosses "dropped on his desk," wondering if it was possible to get the right kind of information, whether they could make sense of it if they did get it, and, finally, whether anyone would notice.

They did notice. After publishing initial surveys in 1985 and 1987, *USN* produced revised college rankings in 1988, incorporating statistics collected from colleges, public sources, and results from a survey of college administrators. After 1988 the college rankings issue was published annually. Readers bought it in droves.[19] In 1990, *USN* built on its success with an annual issue dedicated to rankings of graduate schools (the magazine had published a more rudimentary version of graduate rankings once before, in 1987). Among those ranked were schools of law, medicine, business, education, and engineering, as well as graduate programs ranging from chemistry to music. The first law school rankings were derived from a simple survey sent to deans asking them to name the 10 best American law schools. Deans from 96 of 183 accredited schools responded, and Elfin's staff culled from their responses a list of the "Best Law Schools."[20] This admittedly crude early model spawned enough interest to warrant further development. In 1990, when *USN* began ranking law schools and other graduate programs annually, they used more sophisticated rankings that combined survey data on reputations with statistical measures.

The man in charge of designing and implementing this more complex ranking methodology was Robert Morse, the responsive and quietly passionate director of data research at *U.S. News and World Report*. Morse has worked at the magazine since 1976; he now presides over *USN*'s rankings empire from a small office in a corner of the magazine's Washington headquarters. Morse has been described by one boss as "the brains of the operation, the heart and soul of the engine," as "Mr. Rankings" by colleagues, and as maybe "the most powerful man you never heard of" by a reporter for a college magazine.[21] Morse oversees the production of the *USN* college and graduate school rankings. According to Morse, law school rankings have been the most popular and controversial of the graduate and professional school rankings.[22]

In launching their annual rankings of law schools in 1990, *USN* invoked the language of the marketplace to frame rankings—perhaps borrowing from the example of *Consumer Reports,* a respected magazine that had been evaluating products for consumers since 1936. *USN*'s law school rankings provide consumers with useful information about a specialized product market: legal education. Mel Elfin told readers, "The sad truth is that those who face the daunting prospect of raising upwards of $75,000 to finance a legal education often can find out more information on the relative merits of two $250 compact disc players than on the relative merits of law schools."

Over time, the rationale for rankings was adapted to new uses and linked to new concerns. Students and parents are not the only ones who are concerned with the quality of educational products. Employers also care deeply about the schools their employees come from. It seems unlikely that when the editors at *USN* launched their rankings issues they imagined law firms would one day be using them to screen candidates; but as they became aware of this practice, the magazine elaborated its framing of rankings. Elfin, speaking in 1998, explained that law firms and their clients should also care about rankings: "People want to know, when they walk into the hiring partner's office, what does it mean when it says X school on your résumé, and what does it mean when it says Y school? This is part of the thing you're buying."[23]

With the advent of vibrant "accountability movements" spanning many countries and institutions—health care, government, business, philanthropy, and especially education—rankings are now advertised as addressing even more fundamental concerns. Rankings, the publishers suggest, offer ordinary people the means for holding powerful organizations accountable to those who use their services or buy their products. Robert Morse's blog quotes approvingly from a speech made by Margaret Spellings, U.S. secretary of education, to a group of education accrediting officials on December 7, 2007. She praised her audience for their oversight of education. As evidence of the public demand for accessible information about choosing and paying for college, she enlisted the example of *USN* college rankings: "If you ever doubt the need or appetite for your mission, consider the *U.S. News* college rankings. It's been called the 'Swimsuit Edition' of postsecondary reporting. Within 72 hours of its release, the *U.S. News* website was viewed 10 million times. There's a reason why this magazine is so popular." Morse wrote in his blog:

> U.S. News and U.S. Secretary of Education Margaret Spellings share an important goal. We both believe that there should be considerably more transparency at colleges and universities so prospective students and their parents can be informed about the costly and very important decision of which college to attend. In fact, U.S. News has been a leader in the drive for increased accountability among higher education institutions, and our rankings have been one of the factors that have pushed schools to publish more evaluative and consumer-friendly information about themselves.[24]

Rankings illustrate a general pattern in innovation and diffusion. As a new idea or technology becomes available, and as new groups begin to use it, the meaning of the innovation changes, including the nature of the problems it is designed to solve. As Michael D. Cohen, James G. March, and Johan P. Olsen suggest, problems, solutions, and decision-makers need not be aligned; successful "solutions" often go in search of new problems to which they can be applied both inside and among organizations.[25]

In offering consumers better information about making their college investment, rankings respond to dramatic changes in higher education in the United States, many of which began after World War II. After returning soldiers and, later, their baby boomer children began entering colleges in large numbers, the meaning of higher education changed. The federal government has invested enormously in expanding higher education and making it accessible and affordable for students who, a generation previous, would never have considered it.[26] As colleges expanded, proliferated, and provided social mobility, the field of education was transformed. Once higher percentages of Americans routinely began attending college, *that* one had attended college was no longer enough: *where* one attended college became increasingly important, and stratification among colleges and universities sharply increased.[27] This shifting stratification quickly began to shape career trajectories and income. Those who attend a selective college can clearly benefit from the institution's status and the robust social networks that this selectivity affords, and they may enjoy higher incomes than those who attend less selective schools.[28]

The stratification of schools is also closely associated with another important trend: the nationalization of the market for higher education. As late as the 1960s, most people went to college near where they lived, options were fewer, and it was easier to learn about the various alternatives through informal processes. Even Ivy League schools were still largely regional colleges, and most who could pay their tuition were admitted.[29] In the 1950s, Harvard admitted 60 percent of its applicants, whereas in 2015 it admitted just 5.3 percent of a much larger pool of applicants.[30] This pattern of greater selectivity shifted most prominently in the 1960s as part of an emphasis on merit rather than class or legacy in admissions decisions.[31] One result of these changes is that competition for admission in the top schools also increased dramatically, beginning in the early 1980s.[32] This places enormous pressure on upper- and middle-class applicants and their parents, who are well aware of the social and economic stakes involved in getting into the "right college." Patricia McDonough argues, "This knowledge, however tacit, is a bone-chilling wind blowing through suburbia where the dread of downward mobility is very real."[33] She reports that parents no longer feel as though their experience is helpful to their children; many view college admissions as an "erratic, chancy game" over which they have little control.[34] Such anxiety and insecurity is also fueled by a glut of media stories on the competition, high stakes, and travails involved in getting into a "good" college.[35] Emerging from all this uncertainty and competition is what McDonough describes as a "college admissions industry" that includes private admissions counselors, test-preparation companies, a proliferation of guidebooks of all sorts, and, of course, media rankings.[36] Most of these trends in undergraduate education apply to law schools and other professional schools as well as to colleges and universities. Most salient for our purposes is that students applying to law schools in the last decade have grown up amid this hysteria over admissions, and that magazine rankings are a direct response to these changes.

With the stakes higher, the competition fiercer, and the choices more elaborate, the appeal of rankings for applicants and their families is easy to understand. Accessible information that simplifies important decisions filled a void for people who felt overwhelmed by the complexity of college admissions, and this helps to explain the popularity of the rankings. As David Webster has pointed out, in their eagerness to market themselves in the best possible light, the information that colleges (or law schools) produce is self-serving.[37] Students know they are objects of sophisticated marketing campaigns; after enough photos of bucolic settings populated by beautiful, diverse students, it is easy to become skeptical of the PR.

But there are other reasons for the popularity of rankings. Webster and other commentators make note of Americans' "mania for rankings."[38] It is difficult to pin down the origins of this penchant, but a quick perusal of magazines testifies to its breadth, and it is clear that the media both cater to and cultivate our taste. Theodore Porter suggests that there has long been a peculiar relationship between quantification and populism in the United States, especially surrounding politics and administrative culture;

how policy is scrutinized and defended, Porter argues, sheds light on our ambivalent relationship to elite power and expertise.[39] Perhaps this trait reflects America's fascination with the self-made man or a political culture that idealizes the wisdom of the common people. Perhaps it is because we are especially wary of some forms of elite discretion, yet nonetheless believe fervently in progress and the importance of expert knowledge in improving our lives. Or maybe we fancy rankings because they are embedded within a vibrant popular culture dedicated to self-improvement, social mobility, and knowing how one compares to the competition; the widespread fixation on sports rankings in the United States lends support to this view. Whatever the precise origins of this collective fascination with lists and rankings, it is so familiar and extensive that we enjoy mocking our obsession. The genre of the top-ten list, made famous by the comedian David Letterman, now appears regularly on T-shirts and websites, in bar-room debates, and, as we ring in the New Year, in newspapers and magazines everywhere.

Given these big changes and widespread predilections, it is perhaps not so surprising that Mort Zuckerman's hunch paid off. In creating rankings he was tapping into a broad anxiety about important shifts in the stratification of schools and the evolving role schools play in mediating social standing more broadly. Rankings became extremely lucrative for *USN* and are now, in today's parlance, so fundamental to its "brand" that it is hard to imagine *USN* without them. According to Mel Elfin, rankings "became, essentially, our franchise."[40] "As the editor," he says, "I am very proud of [rankings]. It kept the magazine in the game. When you talk about colleges the first thing that comes to mind for many young people is *USN* rankings."[41]

HOW *USN* CALCULATES LAW SCHOOL RANKINGS

USN law school rankings are made up of four general indicators. Reputation accounts for 40 percent of a school's score and is based on surveys sent to academics and practitioners. Selectivity determines 25 percent of the overall score and is calculated using student Law School Admissions Test (LSAT) scores and grade-point averages (GPAs) and the school's acceptance rate (the ratio of students accepted to those who applied). Placement success accounts for 20 percent of the overall ranking and is based on the percentage of students employed at graduation and nine months after graduation and the percentage of students who pass the bar exam. Finally, "faculty resources" represents 15 percent of the overall ranking and is composed of four separate measures: expenditure rate per student (for instruction, library, and supporting services), student-faculty ratio, "other" per-student spending (primarily financial aid), and the number of volumes in the library. These factors account for 65 percent, 20 percent, 10 percent, and 5 percent of the faculty-resources indicator, respectively. To compute the final ranking, each school's score is standardized. These scores are then weighted, totaled, and rescaled so that the top school receives a score of 100 and other schools receive a percentage of the top score.

Along with these composite rankings, *USN* evaluates eight specialty areas. These specialty rankings are derived from surveys sent to legal educators, who pick the top fifteen schools for the designated specialties. Recently, *USN* evaluated specialties in clinical training, dispute resolution, environmental law, health-care law, intellectual property law, international law, tax law, and trial advocacy. The magazine has changed how some components are constructed, but the basic structure has remained the same. In adapting its rankings, *USN* has made them more comprehensive and precise over time.

USN treats law schools differently than other professional schools. Whereas in the other professional fields only the top twenty-five or top fifty schools are ranked, since 1992 the magazine has ranked every law school accredited by the American Bar Association (ABA), the accrediting body for U.S. law schools. For most of this period, law schools were divided into four tiers: the top tier listed the fifty highest-rated programs, by ranking, with other schools divided into the second, third, and fourth tiers and listed alphabetically within each tier. Beginning with the 2004 rankings, *USN* expanded its ordinal rankings by reporting the top one hundred law schools by rank and dividing the rest into the third and fourth tier, again listing these schools alphabetically. Now, they rank the top one hundred fifty schools and only leave the fourth tier—approximately fifty schools—unranked. Because *USN* publicly evaluates *every* school, not just the most elite schools, the influence of rankings has become pervasive in legal education.

Each year *USN* asks schools to prepare an elaborate report to supply the information the magazine uses to compile rankings. Initially some schools refused to comply, so the magazine estimated the missing information. Administrators doubted the validity of these estimates. They suggest that estimates are almost always conservative, punishing schools that did not provide information to *USN* by ranking them lower than they would have been had they submitted the information. Some administrators complained about providing what they see as an unwarranted subsidy to a for-profit firm. Generating the information for *USN* remains tedious and time-intensive, but *USN* forms have evolved to conform more closely to the statistical reporting requirements of the ABA; this has made the reporting process less laborious for schools and easier for *USN* to verify.

Many law school administrators and faculty are highly skeptical of rankings methodology, and their criticisms have helped fuel the controversy over rankings. While our focus is not on evaluating rankings, many researchers have criticized *USN's* methods strenuously. Several papers have outlined the weaknesses of each measure employed by *USN*.[42] A study by Stephen Klein and Laura Hamilton, commissioned by the Association of American Law Schools, presented a scathing critique of *USN's* methods.[43] The authors depict the twelve measures used by *USN* to construct their rankings as deeply flawed, but their most eye-catching finding is the disproportionate influence of LSAT scores in determining the differences in rank among schools.[44] Klein and Hamilton conclude:

> About 90 percent of the overall differences in ranks among schools can be explained solely by median LSAT score of their entering classes and essentially all of the differences can be explained by the combination of LSAT and Academic reputation ratings. Consequently, all of the other 10 factors US News measures (such as placement of graduates) have virtually no effect on the overall ranks and because of measurement problems, what little influence they do have may lead to reducing rather than increasing the validity of the results.[45]

Brian Leiter, a law professor at the University of Chicago and the creator of an alternative set of rankings, the "Educational Quality Rankings of U.S. Law Schools," criticizes *USN* rankings for excluding information about scholarship and for harboring biases against large public schools.[46] Michael D. McGuire's analysis of college rankings highlights the volatility of rankings, showing how small adjustments in the weights attached to various components generate wild fluctuations.[47] He also criticizes the weights attached to components as reflecting the judgment of editors rather than being informed by empirical research.

Legal educators from schools across the rankings spectrum have also emphasized the important qualities that rankings ignore. For example, a letter published in 1997 by the Law School Admissions Council (LSAC), the organization that administers the LSAT, and signed by nearly every dean at accredited law schools was sent to every prospective law student for years. It lists twenty-two factors that students identified as "among the most important in influencing their choices of law school."[48] Among these factors not included in *USN* rankings are the quality of teaching, the accessibility of teachers, racial and gender diversity within the faculty and student body, the size of first-year classes, the strength of alumni networks, and tuition.[49] In an unpublished study, Richard Lempert, a sociologist and law professor at the University of Michigan, characterizes rankings as "pseudo-science" and describes every rankings factor as deeply flawed.[50] Judith Wegner, past dean of the University of North Carolina's law school, depicts *USN*'s methods as "so seriously flawed that it makes any thinking person despair [of] journalistic ethics."[51] But not all deans feel this way. David Van Zandt, the former dean of Northwestern Law School who became the president of the New School for Social Research in 2011, believes that rankings are useful, if imperfect, measures and simply formalize reputations that were already widely known.[52]

Our focus is on law schools, but the patterns we describe here are not unique to them. Accountability measures such as rankings simplify complex and dynamic institutions, but they are rarely the neutral technical feat we sometimes imagine them to be. Because people are reflective and reflexive, they tend to react to being measured in unanticipated ways. People scrutinize rankings, worry over them, invest in them, and act differently because of them, and these behaviors change the institutions that rankings evaluate. In short, measures are hard to control. So it is important that we understand the results of our efforts to create accountability. To do so, we will need to examine numbers as they are used rather than simply assuming that we know what their effects will be. This will entail an up-close examination. Law schools offer a useful vantage point, a good place to begin.

OVERVIEW OF THE BOOK

In chapter 2 we discuss in detail the context of our arguments and the theoretical contributions of the book. In particular, we lay out the history of accountability measures and the particular form of accountability that numbers provide. We then offer an explanation for why numerical accountability as embodied in rankings can produce such powerful effects and unintended consequences. In a nutshell, we argue that rankings and other measures are "reactive": instead of simply providing a neutral measure of social phenomena—as a thermometer provides a neutral appraisal of temperature—these measures change how people conceptualize the social world. In other words, measures change what they are designed to reflect and in doing so transform how actors see themselves and make decisions. We elaborate on the reactivity of social measures by outlining five key ways in which this reactivity drives change.

We organize the remaining chapters by constituency, loosely conforming to the academic cycle. We begin in chapter 3 with prospective law students, whose use of rankings illuminates the demand for rankings and their populist appeal. Rankings simplify difficult decisions about where to apply to and attend law school. We show how, why, and when rankings are used by students, how they use them to evaluate the competence of administrators, and how they become internalized as symbols of professional status.

We next examine how rankings affect the work of admissions officers who must juggle commitments to admitting accomplished and diverse classes with protecting their schools' selectivity as measured by *USN*. In chapter 4 we show how rankings affect who is admitted to which programs in law schools, the content of admissions work, and the moral and professional identities of administrators.

From admissions, we move to the deans' offices. Deans are responsible for defining and implementing the mission of law schools, overseeing the hiring and firing of faculty and staff, presenting the public face of law schools to external groups, and raising funds for their schools. In chapter 5 we describe how rankings have decreased the discretion of deans, changed the terms under which they are held accountable, and shaped how they relate to peers, alumni, and employers.

In chapter 6 we describe how rankings affect administrators in career services departments in their efforts to help students secure good jobs. We explain how rankings exacerbate pressures to improve placement statistics and how this has encouraged schools to shift resources toward tracking students for the purpose of *USN* reporting and away from the counseling and network building that have been their traditional purpose. In particular, we examine how employers use rankings to decide whom to hire and interview and how anxiety about this use drives reactivity in career services.

In chapter 7 we summarize the effects of rankings on legal education and describe how rankings have changed in reaction to law schools' responses to them. We also call for new and more sophisticated empirical studies of the effects of performance measures such as rankings and for research that evaluates alternative forms of evaluation to complement quantitative measures. We discuss how our findings can be applied to other types of rankings, emphasizing that while some effects are unique to law schools, the reactivity of public measures is a central feature of all modern institutions and modern identities. We conclude by highlighting the often-overlooked moral dimensions of performance measures.

Chapter 2 | Accountability by the Numbers

ONE OF THE most perplexing aspects of educational rankings is how a set of numbers produced by people with no expertise in education and using a methodology that has been consistently criticized by educational experts and insiders could generate such far-reaching changes and influence. In this chapter we try to explain the power of rankings by showing why numbers—both in general and in the specific case of law school rankings—are so effective at producing accountability. We first provide a brief history of accountability, focusing on the role that quantification has played in the evolution of this idea. This leads us into a discussion of how the useful simplifications provided by numbers, as well as the scientific and mathematical legitimacy that they imply, makes them especially valuable tools for manufacturing accountability.

We then turn to the specific ways in which numbers have generated such powerful consequences in the field of legal education. We show how the reactivity of social measures—the fact that people respond to being measured, often in unanticipated ways—changes how others make sense of the people or things being measured. In the case of law schools, for example, the rankings have altered people's orientation to particular schools and schools in general; the rankings have caused people to draw new cognitive maps that change how they conceptualize the identity of schools and understand how schools stand relative to one another. We conclude by distinguishing four influential mechanisms—commensuration, self-fulfilling prophecies, reverse engineering, and narrative—through which rankings have changed how we make sense of law schools and the field in which they act.

THE QUANTIFICATION OF ACCOUNTABILITY

Pick up a newspaper and you are likely to see calls for some leader or organization to be held more accountable. From the neighborhood school to the Red Cross, from Congress to Chrysler, lack of accountability is seen as the genesis of many failings. That officials should be held accountable is an old idea. According to Deirdre von Dornum, the ancient Greeks were "obsessed with keeping their officials legally accountable for their actions in office."[1] As early as the fifth century BCE, long before the emergence of classical democracy in Athens, official conduct was governed by an ideology of accountability that mandated visibility, rectitude, and the participation of citizens.[2] According to the *Oxford English Dictionary*, the first recorded use of "accountability" is in Samuel Williams's 1794 treatise, *The Natural and Civil History of Vermont*, in which he describes "Indian government" as "the most simple that can be contrived."[3] "A Modern statesman," he writes, "would smile at this idea of Indian government: And because he could find no written constitution, or bill of rights, no natural checks, and balances, accountability and responsibility, pronounce it weak, foolish and contemptible."[4] Nowadays the link between accountability and good governance is so established that we assume that one of the central accomplishments of law is to secure and protect accountability through elections, the distribution of powers, and control over the terms by which citizens participate in government.[5] But accountability also promises much more.

Whether in business or philanthropy, the army, or the local PTA, there is broad agreement that good management and good governance requires accountability. Evidence of accountability is central to the ideologies of most modern institutions, even if the vision of what accountability means varies. Accountability is often represented by elections, checks and balances, briefings, public meetings, audits, displays of rectitude or accessibility. "Accountability" derives from "accounts," which usually refers to methods for making policies and outcomes visible and reviewable to outside parties. Accountability is a means for institutionalizing responsibility and responsiveness.

The meaning and use of the term changes over time and with circumstance. For Samuel Williams, accountability signaled sophisticated governance that distinguished colonists from natives. Founding fathers believed that accountability required an informed citizenry and a free press. We now expect media to alert us to unsafe products, poorly managed companies, or badly waged wars. During the past twenty years or so, there have been other important shifts in the meaning of accountability. Like a sponge in water, the term has swelled to soak up any number of woes. Accountability and its handmaidens, transparency and audits, have become all-purpose solutions to a wide array of problems. An online search for "lack of account-ability" will result in hits for Christian homilies, management consultants, antiwar bloggers, policy wonks, marital counseling, and even advice for wayward celebrities.[6] Greater accountability, it seems, can improve almost any endeavor.

One significant trend in how we think about accountability is that it has become closely associated with measuring performance.[7] Being account-able is often bound up with being "transparent" and "auditable," achieve-ments typically derived from metrics. Max Weber, Georg Simmel, and other prominent social theorists have contended that a central feature of our modern self-image is that we know ourselves and evaluate our actions through numbers. We use polls, prices, surveys, bookkeeping, and censuses to tell us who we are, what we think, and what we should do.[8] Measures also offer a way to know others. Double-entry bookkeep-ing permitted wary sixteenth-century Florentine merchants to scrutinize the dealings of distant trading partners through an examination of their account books.[9] For European colonizers, numbers were fundamental to ruling, mediating relations between ruler and ruled, and making possible taxation, conscription, and production quotas.[10] Since at least the nine-teenth century, published statistics have become linked to enlightened policymaking, democratic governance, and reconstruction.[11] Drew Gilpin Faust has shown that, after the carnage of the American Civil War, one way we honored the dead was by meticulously counting them, even if it required inventing new forms of state intervention and new agencies to carry them out.[12]

We also devise numbers to indicate our evaluation of an individu-al's potential, to assess their performance, and to control their behavior. Standardized assessments such as tests, ranks, and other measures of improvement moved from schools and barracks to factories and corpora-tions, and back to schools again.[13] Quantification allows us to check on those we do not trust, those who are different or distant, or those who act as our agents. The discipline compelled by quantification, we suppose, makes visible and available the consequences of policies and decisions and curtails the biases, politics, self-interest, and discretion of those who work on our behalf. Theodore Porter has observed that we replace trust in persons with trust in numbers.[14] Numbers make a messy and danger-ous world seem easier to manage.

Quantification also offers a peculiar form of populism, bridging knowl-edge gaps between insiders and outsiders, the proximal and the distant, the expert producers and the users who know less but nevertheless must consume, invest, and decide. Quantification can reduce what we think is important to know to its bare bones. If the mass and complexity of information threatens to overwhelm us, numbers offer a reassuring strategy for abstracting away excess, providing a glimpse of the crucial weight-bearing structure. And, like radiologists reading X-rays, it doesn't matter if we never lay eyes on the patient. We can diagnose from a distance. We know what to do. Numbers bolster our courage to act.

The allure of quantification is clear. Its potential to direct attention and produce disinterested knowledge makes it a natural vehicle for oversight. It simplifies and organizes information. It creates robust rules for including and excluding. The rigors of quantification should improve our decisions, making us more rational, trustworthy, and disciplined. That this concise knowledge is easy to circulate and is expressed in a language that we imagine is universal, one that transcends culture, place, and time, makes quantification an especially authoritative accomplishment, one ripe with potential.

But the virtues of numbers are complicated by our uses of them and by what their particular cultural authority sets in motion. Numbers are restless cultural and material accomplishments that are hard to make but easy to recycle. Making credible numbers is an expensive investment. The money, time, staff, training, and coordination required to make new numbers helps explain why they are so often produced by large organizations for relatively stable populations. Making numbers requires categories with strong boundaries—a clear sense of what is or is not an instance of something. It requires numerate audiences that accept the purpose and legitimacy of measures, a form of deference that cedes the advantages of status and often hard-won local and experiential knowledge. These conditions for quantification are often dynamic and contested. But once numbers have been created, other groups can find new uses for them, partly because being removed from the particularities of context makes them amenable to other uses. Abstract knowledge seems portable and easy to transmit, whereas local knowledge seems cumbersome and contingent.

Because social scientists have generally been most concerned with devising credible and accurate ways to measure social life, they have paid less attention to the power of numbers to create new objects and new kinds of people, or to restructure the social spaces they depict.[15] Because we see measures as useful, authoritative cultural objects, we tend to change our behavior as we are measured. Measures simplify, creating relations as well as representing them. They hide as well as highlight. As tools for apprehending the world, measures can produce routines for seeing and knowing. Because we invest heavily in the potential of numbers, and because numbers can be transforming, it is important that we consider their influence. How do numbers accomplish the transparency, accountability, and rationality that we desire from them? Why do they inevitably introduce changes we never intended? Can we control them?

To answer such questions it is not enough to speculate. Our complex and varied reactions to public measures require that we investigate these new forms of accountability and visibility in the contexts in which they are produced and used by different groups. We need to map their journeys as they are inserted in organizations, accumulate users, mediate power, and come to appear to us as natural. We need to identify the unique effects of particular numbers and the patterns they share with other public measures. And we need to unpack their accountability to better understand what it is made of and how it works. To accomplish this requires a perspective that is close to the ground, attentive to meaning and human agency. And that is what we attempt here, with one controversial and visible set of numbers: rankings of U.S. law schools.

Rankings are one instance of widespread efforts to make public institutions more accessible to outsiders. If we take *USN*'s explanation for creating rankings at face value, their initial goal was not to transform law schools or even to hold them accountable. Rather, they simply wished to provide information to education consumers in a form that was convenient and easy to use.[16] But even if *USN* editors did not at first envision their rankings as instruments of accountability, that is what they became. And educators reacted accordingly. Editors, perhaps naively (although some critics would say disingenuously), report being astonished by all the fuss generated by their rankings and puzzled by what their rankings set in motion. Wasn't the publicity good for education? Why did administrators *feel* so threatened? Didn't rankings incorporate measures schools have long collected and cared about? Didn't educators, like students, find these numbers helpful? We must scrutinize these reactions carefully if we are to understand the important institutional changes that these performance measures launched.

Why Numbers Are Good at Producing Accountability

Numbers grant insight into complex entities such as organizations by translating, reducing, and integrating complicated information in ways that makes these entities easier to understand and compare. Evaluating an organization is as easy as noting if a number goes up or down or comparing the number five to the number fifteen. Because organizations embody highly specialized expertise and resources, are good at shielding themselves from scrutiny, and are often remote from the people who want to know about them, a numerical summary makes even the most ignorant person feel competent to assess them. Numbers allow people a new kind of access into complex social bodies.

A key factor contributing to the effectiveness of numbers in establishing accountability is the pragmatic uses to which they can be put. They can be useful as handy and straightforward remedies to informational problems. Their ability to fill these needs contributes to their proliferation and, eventually, their legitimacy. Rankings exemplify this usefulness, a feature that *USN* and its proponents highlight whenever possible. For instance, rankings offer heuristics for quickly sorting people and schools into categories for those who must make judgments about them. They simplify tough decisions for prospective students by making comparisons easy: higher is better. This clarity is reassuring and offers a way through an often-paralyzing volume of information, especially for those without in-depth, direct knowledge of the field.

The usefulness of numbers to outsiders is one important piece of their influence, but there is a broader, more inchoate cultural authority that envelops quantification. The integration and abstraction that numbers offer, the logic of their production, and the methods that inform their use resemble those used to produce scientific knowledge. This form of knowledge often seems inaccessible and unassailable to laypersons, and it is much easier to leave calculation and interpretation to experts than to do the hard work of deconstructing numbers. Numbers are simple representations, and their apparent straightforwardness signals objectivity and mathematical justification.

Another key aspect of quantitative authority arises from cultural assumptions about what it means to be rational. The idea that numbers can offer a strategy for countering uncertainty and risk or a technique for being virtuous is such an appealing idea that it has occurred repeatedly to thinkers over the millennia. Reconciling the incongruent features of decisions or forms of value can make our actions more potent and defensible. It offers protection against fate. And quantification does indeed deliver on some of this promise under certain conditions. Quantification requires that we consider the connections between the abstract and the concrete. It demands and promotes discipline in our thinking and often encourages us to be disinterested or even-handed in weighing advantage and disadvantage, costs and benefits.

It is partly this power that makes quantification so seductive, that encourages us to ask more of quantification than it can deliver, and that tempts us to overgeneralize its applications. A long line of organizational research on the decoupling of practices from rules has demonstrated that looking rational can be as potent as actually being rational.[17] Once quantification is associated with the virtue of disciplined thinking and of being free of biasing emotion, its symbolic value overwrites and sometimes supersedes its technical efficacy. Numbers confer legitimacy that becomes more robust as it becomes increasingly taken for granted, regardless of its appropriateness.

Another reason that numbers are a powerful tool in the development of accountability is that the simplifications they create allow them to be inserted into virtually all of the relationships among actors in the field. These numbers, because they are accessible and their use is intuitive, change how administrators relate to prospective students, employers, and trustees, how schools relate to one another, and how current students relate to faculty and staff. The thoroughness of the institutionalization of the rankings is striking. They are now an influential independent actor in this field, and it is almost unanimously accepted that rankings will endure. Now there is a growing consensus that schools need "to do something to address their rankings," and faculty, administrators, and deans alike often use this to justify various courses of action. Rankings, much like government regulations, employment markets, and demographic trends, are now an entrenched feature of the organizational environment in which schools operate, to the extent that their existence as well as their need to be managed now goes mostly unremarked and unquestioned.

Finally, we live in a period where many in the United States and other countries distrust government to offer the services that it has traditionally provided, a deep distrust that is the culmination of decades of conservative attacks on state policies. Porter has argued that one response to distrust is to substitute numbers and mechanical objectivity for discretion.[18] Traditional sources of knowledge and authority—say, expert authority or the discretion of elites—are constrained; reliance on the expertise of officials concerning municipal government, hospitals, and other public services is replaced by strict numerical guidelines. The decisions of judges, for instance, are constrained by sentencing guidelines that quantify the seriousness of the crime and criminal history and mandate specific sentences; likewise, police are themselves policed by quantified indicators such as CompStat. It is not surprising that performance measures have thrived in this context of distrust. These stringent modes of promoting efficiency and public accountability have a powerful affinity with neoliberal modes of governing: the numbers facilitate governing from a distance, deregulation, the proliferation of market logic, and the use of auditing techniques to classify populations in economically consequential ways.[19]

All of these characteristics and conditions make it easier to make decisions and evaluate performances. In the face of overwhelming amounts and kinds of information, this is no small service. But while it is the ability of performance measures to fill this need that makes them so useful for accountability efforts, the case of rankings underscores that it is crucial to remember that the accountability that numbers grant is always *selective accountability*. It obscures as it highlights, making certain characteristics invisible in the process of making others more apparent. The usefulness of quantitative accountability depends on how the measures are produced, for what audience, and in whose interest. Often, what gets included in efforts at transparency is numbers that are already available or features that are easy to measure, and these become the focus of attention and action.

This problem is amplified when the measure is taken to be the phenomenon it represents. For example, school administrators consistently complain that constituents "treat the numbers as gospel," "never look behind the numbers," and "don't question how *USN* comes up with these things." They express bemusement about how literally constituents regard the school's rank and how much small differences matter. Because the numbers look rigorous and objective, they are treated as such; this is especially true for more distant audiences who have less direct knowledge about schools and higher education. In this way, a school's quality is turned into a simple score, and the moral dimensions of decisions or their historical underpinnings end up conspicuously missing in quantitative accounts. At the same time, qualities that are expensive or elusive to measure get left out; and as numbers become more institutionalized, it becomes harder to see the biases behind them. We take them at face value rather than doing the hard work of deconstructing them, work that is necessary to expose their selectivity and prejudices. Over time, the things we care about that cannot be easily translated into numbers become increasingly irrelevant; they do not "count" in either sense of the word.

HOW RANKINGS GENERATE CHANGE: REACTIVITY AND COGNITIVE MAPS

Because people continually monitor, interpret, and act on their worlds, social measures are reactive: they change what they set out to measure.[20] Objects of measurement emerge and are reconstructed through measurement. Standardized tests create "gifted" and "underachieving" students, the census produces "Hispanics," instruments designed to measure precise levels of blood pressure generate categories of disease such as "borderline hypertension," and tests such as the SAT or LSAT come to define merit. This capacity to evoke objects and conditions can be unsettling for some uses of measures. Measures, as scientific depictions of some part of the world, should be objective, accurate, and inert. Their validity is compromised when the world changes in response to measuring. That is why reactivity is often depicted as a methodological problem in social science.[21]

The shift from description to control is a small but important one in measurement: in fact, we often design measures with an eye toward changing behavior. The purpose of such measures is intentionally to cultivate reactivity that will advance a goal such as improving worker productivity or student performance. Used in this way, measures shape aspirations by offering crucial feedback that makes visible the people and processes involved in the work.

In cases of rankings, however, where our intention is to transform behavior through the use of metrics, we want the world to stand still for measurement and, only after, change in relation to it. We prefer measures to resemble a series of snapshots to which people respond; it is less acceptable when they act as video cameras that encourage mugging. Alain Desrosières, one of the pioneering figures in the study of quantification, describes this feature as the tension between numbers used for descriptive and proscriptive purposes and identifies it as one of the most important features of quantification.[22] In Marilyn Strathern's apt formulation, "When a measure becomes a target, it ceases to be a good measure."[23] In many public measures, especially those calculated regularly, the tension between containing reactivity and harnessing it is hard to reconcile.

Most fundamentally, rankings are reactive because they change how people make sense of situations. Rankings have become the backdrop against which members of a community understand themselves and others. They help to organize the "stock of knowledge" that participants routinely use to understand what is going on.[24] They shape the premises that frame decisions and how attention is allocated.[25] One way to conceptualize this change in sense making is to say that rankings have transformed the cognitive map of legal education.[26] In the absence of other unambiguous representations of the hierarchy of schools, rankings construct a precise, hierarchical, and relative relationship among law schools. In doing so, they offer an accessible and easy way to chart where schools are located and how they stand in relation to one another.

This new cognitive map produces powerful effects as audiences begin to behave in accordance to schools' rank, and this process further reinforces habitual ways of seeing. It offers a generalized account for interpreting behavior, making claims on people and resources, and framing decisions and the judgment of peers. Administrators consider rankings when they define goals, assess progress, admit students, recruit faculty, distribute scholarships, help students find jobs, adopt new programs, and create budgets. This new way of thinking about the field of legal education permeates how people think about their schools and decide what strategies to adopt. Several law professors told us that rankings came up at nearly every faculty meeting.

Rankings also change how other constituencies understand law schools and their relation to them. Prospective students use them to decide where to apply and attend law school. Current students use them to assess their status in relation to students at other schools. Student law review editors use them to vet manuscripts. Faculty use them when considering changing jobs. Alumni use them to track how well their school is doing or in bragging contests with colleagues. Employers use them to evaluate candidates for jobs in law firms or clerkships. As rankings accumulate constituencies and come to mediate more and different practices, their influence spreads and their meanings change. Routines are built around them, including temporal ones. It becomes harder to evaluate quality without reference to rankings. By reordering the status system of law schools and by changing the terms by which schools are held accountable, rankings have produced broad, consequential, and unevenly distributed effects on these schools. They have created a relatively stable system of stratification but one with unstable positions, and this system has become a powerful lens through which the legal profession and law schools evaluate themselves and others. Rankings are now so tightly bound up with decisions of all sorts that it is hard to erect firm boundaries around their domain of influence.

For consequences as complex as those produced by rankings, it is not enough to simply identify patterns in the effects of rankings. A detailed qualitative examination helps us understand how these patterns are produced and how rankings generate the effects that they do. Social scientists describe this as depicting the mechanisms that generate consequences. Analyses of mechanisms produce deeper causal knowledge of social relationships and their dynamism. A mechanism is the event or process that describes the causal patterns that generate particular effects.[27] Explaining how rankings have changed the ways in which people think about legal education—*how* they produce the changes that they produce—helps us better understand why these measures create such powerful effects. We identify four mechanisms whereby rankings have changed how participants and outsiders make sense of legal education: commensuration, self-fulfilling prophecies, reverse engineering, and the introduction of new narratives. These are not the only drivers of change produced by the rankings, but they are the most common and illustrate how effectively rankings redraw cognitive maps.

Commensuration

Commensuration is the process of turning qualities into quantities on a shared metric. One important way that rankings change how people make sense of legal education is by making law schools commensurate. Prices, cost-benefit ratios, survey responses, and standardized tests, like rankings, are all forms of commensuration. Rankings are the end product of many processes of commensuration that transform GPAs, reputation surveys, test scores, placement statistics, number of library books, and budgets into a single number. Commensuration is fundamental to measurement and is so widespread and naturalized that we rarely notice how much work and discipline is required to do it, or how deeply it shapes our attention and changes how we think about difference and sameness.[28]

Commensuration changes sense making in several key ways. First, it imposes on knowledge a specific form that reduces and simplifies information. This is characteristic of all cultural forms, including art and language, but commensuration is distinctive for how radically and precisely it edits and integrates knowledge. One way in which commensuration shapes our attention is by drastically reducing the magnitude of information that we have to pay attention to and imposing on the remaining information a shared form: a metric. By subsuming or making irrelevant so much information, the numbers that commensuration produces take on added significance and become more visible, as in a spotlight on a stage. Information that is not assimilated to this form—things that are hard to quantify or qualities that are excluded from the algorithms—is easier to ignore. So, in the *USN* rankings, the quality of a law library is measured by the number of volumes in its collection. The more we focus on the number of books, the less we consider the quality of the books, the librarian's expertise in helping students access the books, or the building's comfort or beauty. Such is the power of formalization that, over time, qualities that forms exclude can become increasingly "unreal" no matter how fundamental.[29]

Like all processes of formalization, commensuration organizes the information it culls. It changes how we make sense of situations by creating an especially rigorous and transgressive form of integration. Commensuration is designed to subvert all former modes of classification that mark and distinguish objects and people. The objects it encompasses are structured like an analogy, where the relationship between two things is expressed in terms of a third dimension. In this case, the third thing is a metric, which we use to unite even the most disparate experiences: children's ability, satisfaction with government, the experience of pain, the efficiency of new environmental policy. Commensuration renders all forms of difference as a matter of more or less rather than of kind.

The sameness and difference that commensuration constructs derive from objects' relations to their shared metric. The power to reduce and reconcile the pace and volume of information we confront, the capacity to make precise comparisons across time and contexts, makes commensuration an almost irresistible strategy for managing the overwhelming flows of information and decisions we confront. But the abstract precision that commensuration confers comes at a price: a harsh editing of the social worlds it expresses. Intelligence or ability rendered as test scores must willfully bracket distinctive biographies, deep knowledge of context and circumstances, creativity, and intractable inequalities in order for these measures to be constructed. The sharp constraints that commensuration creates render most nuanced knowledge irrelevant. The practice of squeezing complex social conditions or practices into sturdy predesigned boxes is seldom easy, so we develop complex rules for doing so.

Another reason commensuration is so alluring is that it produces information that circulates easily. As business and political relations become more expansive, this ease of transmission becomes increasingly valuable. As concise summaries of highly complex conditions, the parsimony that commensuration constructs allows us to replace long written texts with short tables and graphs. It makes possible the "bottom line."[30] Furthermore, there is the tendency to suppose that numbers, like music, are a universal language. Once basic numeracy is achieved, numbers can encourage political participation by expanding the number of people who can respond to them. We may recognize the widow's mites as a nobler sacrifice than the rich man's expensive gifts, but we nevertheless trust numbers more than words to speak a common tongue, to overcome the disharmonies of contexts. Even if commensuration sometimes threatens social boundaries or if magnitude is too crude a marker of value, we find in it an indispensable strategy for creating the simplicity and comparability that orders our worlds.

Numbers offer opportunities and challenges in their interpretation because the meaning of numbers is less inert than we sometimes imagine. Even if we admire their cosmopolitanism, their capacity to strip away context and evoke a shared language, numbers are restless signifiers. Like all symbols, their meaning is reconstructed through use. The superficial consensus that we attach to the meaning of many symbols, a consensus that glosses over differences in interpretation and use, is not enough for numbers. We hold them to a higher standard of consensus and are more reluctant to acknowledge particularity in their meaning. Because the deep usefulness of quantification appeals to so many, and because numbers' very abstractness makes it easy to insert them in new places for new uses, numbers often go places and acquire users that their creators never imagined. As new groups begin to use numbers in new ways, they mediate cognition in new ways, too. Numbers can solve many problems for far-flung groups: they summarize, synthesize, connect, deflect, display, defend, and define. To understand how they shape our cognition and perception, the context of their use must be closely scrutinized.

Self-Fulfilling Prophecies

One of the most important ways in which rankings reshape sense making is by triggering self-fulfilling prophecies.[31] A self-fulfilling prophecy occurs when an expectation, once defined as real, amplifies or confirms the prophecy's effect. In the case of public measures such as rankings, self-fulfilling prophecies realize the expectations or predictions that are embedded in measures or otherwise improve a measure's validity by encouraging behavior that conforms to it.[32] For instance, even though early polls in political races are known to be very unreliable, poor results in these polls can cause donors to curtail support for viable candidates—a response that can lead to the poor outcome predicted by the flawed polls.[33] Rankings create expectations about law schools, and people change their behavior accordingly. These changes in behavior can lead to real changes in school quality that affirm the manufactured expectations. Our research suggests four ways that self-fulfilling prophecies shape the reactivity of rankings: external audiences' use of rankings to make decisions, the influence of prior rankings on reputational surveys that affect subsequent rankings, the influence of rankings on funding decisions within universities, and the ways school activities begin to conform to rankings criteria.[34]

One form of self-fulfilling prophecy generated by the rankings is tied to the precise distinctions that they produce. Although the raw scores *USN* uses to create rankings are tightly bunched, sometimes separated only by tenths of percentage points, listing schools by rank magnifies these statistically insignificant differences in ways that produce real consequences for schools as external audiences treat these distinctions as if they were meaningful. These distinctions become increasingly important and taken for granted, along with the advantages and disadvantages associated with the numbers. As a faculty member at a top law school told us, "[Rankings] create inequality among schools that are rather hard to distinguish. They create artificial lines that then have the danger of becoming real."

This form of self-fulfilling prophecy is particularly harmful to lower-tier schools. Schools must respond not only to the reactions of prospective students, but to other constituents such as trustees, boards of visitors, and alumni, all of whom provide financial and administrative support to the schools. These reactions are most pronounced when a school's rank drops—whether this reflects changes in school quality as measured by *USN* criteria, the improved ranking of a close competitor, or fluctuations in how rankings are calculated.

A second type of self-fulfilling prophecy occurs when old rankings influence new ones. *USN* uses two surveys to measure the reputation of some 190 accredited U.S. law schools, one sent to academics and one to practitioners. Even the most experienced deans, including those who have participated in accreditation reviews at numerous schools, admit that they know little about most of the law schools they are asked to evaluate. Practitioners, whose ties to legal education are often remote, will know even less than deans and faculty. For many, the one feature they may know about other schools is their ranking. So past judgments about a school's reputation, as embodied in rank, may influence current evaluations, which reproduce and strengthen these judgments.[35] As two administrators put it:

> Well, hell, I get the rankings [forms] and I get 184 schools to rank. I know about [this school], something about [that school], I know about [my school] obviously, and I've got some buddies here and there so I feel like I know something more about some of those schools. But beyond that, guess what, I'm basing these decisions on the rankings; it's a self-fulfilling prophecy.

> If partners [at a law firm] do anything to prepare themselves for this [reputational survey], they probably go out and get a copy of past *USN* reports and fill it out from that.

Research by Jeffrey Stake on the effects of school rankings on reputation scores demonstrates that these scores have slowly converged with overall rank over time, leading him to conclude that past rankings are the strongest predictor of current reputation score.[36]

A third type of self-fulfilling prophecy occurs when budgets are linked to rankings. Schools affiliated with universities must often compete for funds with other programs. Lacking other benchmarks, some administrators use rankings as a heuristic to help allocate resources. A university president informed members of the university planning committee, which included the law professor we interviewed, that "new money" would be allocated partly on the basis of the quality of the program as defined by its *USN* rank. An important criterion for receiving funds was whether a claim for resources was likely to move a program into a top-ten *USN* rank. Budgets that are allocated according to the ranking or potential ranking of units reproduces and intensifies the stratification they are designed to measure, resulting in a "winner take all" strategy.[37] We don't know how widespread this strategy is, but we do know that in many academic programs, requests for new faculty lines, new programs, or even new buildings often invoke improved rankings as their rationale. Most deans worry about how rankings shape impressions and the implications of this for their budgets.[38]

A final way that self-fulfilling prophecies propel inequality is the way law schools respond to the conception of legal education that is embedded in rankings factors. Rankings encourage schools to become more like what rankings measure, which reinforces the validity of the measure. Rankings impose a standardized, universal definition of "high quality" that creates incentives for schools and students to conform to that definition. So applications of nontraditional students are scrutinized more closely, missions are revised, and pre-law students who invest in test-prep classes instead of community service, or replace challenging classes with easy ones, are rewarded by law schools. These kinds of strategies all reinforce *USN*'s definition of merit.

An even more self-conscious form of this self-fulfilling prophecy occurs when administrators adopt improved rankings as an explicit goal.[39] In framing aspirations using *USN* criteria, members work to produce an organization that conforms to and makes tangible the terms of the measures, a process that renders the measures increasingly valid. Another version of conforming to the assumptions of measurements is when members use rankings to define or market their school to external audiences. When law schools (or central administrations) tout their rankings on their websites, brochures, or press releases, they are complicit in producing and disseminating identities that align with rankings, which, conversely, shapes internal processes of identification. The imposed organizational identity that is embedded in rankings and members' sense of individual identity can interact in complex ways that sometimes reinforce the meaning and legitimacy of rankings.

Reverse Engineering

A third way in which rankings drive changes in sense making, especially for those in charge of managing the numbers, is through pressures to reverse-engineer the rankings formula. Administrators learn to think about the rankings not only in terms of their overall rank, but the individual factors that constitute the composite score. In so doing they begin to conceive of the law school itself in terms of these discrete, measurable units.

Reverse engineering is generally understood as the process of working backward through the construction of a completed object or artifact to gain knowledge about how it works.[40] In much the same way as experienced cooks have traditionally reconstructed recipes from careful tastings or good tailors have replicated articles of clothing after thorough examination of a finished product, scholars in fields as diverse as genetics, network analysis, property law, and computer programming decompose genes, network structures, the history of intellectual property, and code to develop a deeper understanding of phenomena and improve on existing approaches.

For our purposes, reverse engineering describes a tactic that almost all law schools use to improve their rankings. By deconstructing their rank into its component parts, schools decide which factors they believe are most amenable to their control. Once they figure this out, they can make decisions about the types of changes to adopt and how resources might be most effectively deployed to optimize their rank. One administrator at a school making concerted efforts to improve its ranking said, "We've done a lot of careful studying of the *USN* methodology to figure out what counts the most and what is perhaps the most manipulable."

One very common example of reverse engineering concerns how schools deconstruct the selectivity measure used by *USN*. Most schools now carefully examine the components of this measure—LSAT scores and GPAs—and then estimate how their standing on each of these measures compares with those of their peers and competitors. These estimations allow them to create target numbers. Then they devise an admission formula that will optimize these selectivity factors and give them an edge over schools ranked near them. These calculations can also provide valuable information about whether more can be gained by distributing scholarship money to students (a practice that is commonly referred to as "buying students" by administrators and faculty) with high LSAT scores or high GPAs.

More generally, by comparing themselves to peers in terms of each factor, law schools can assess exactly where they lag relative to others or, especially, why they fell in the rankings in a particular year. One dean at a school that had dropped precipitously in the rankings explained, "Basically we did an analysis of why we fell, you know, and as best that we could tell when we took our major dive it had to do with two things. One had to do with financial resources and the other had to do with placement."

Being able to make these calculations depends on keeping careful track of every element of the statistics used by *USN* to construct their ranking system. Schools now consistently invest in elaborate record keeping and statistical analysis of their data to see where they stand and to project where they might stand in the future. Nearly every administrator we spoke with described, ruefully in many cases, how such demands have increased as a result of rankings; many schools now even have institutional research departments whose job it is to create and sometimes massage the requisite statistics.

All of these efforts contribute to a school's ability to reverse-engineer the ranking algorithm used by *USN* as accurately as possible. This may sound like a straightforward process—one need only scrutinize the methodological appendix published by *USN* along with the rankings—but many precise details are difficult to discern. Initially, *USN* did not provide much detailed information about its methods, only reporting the categories and their respective weights. This left many unknowns and was the subject of a great deal of criticism as schools tried to figure out how they were being evaluated and how they might improve. Reputational surveys, the single most heavily weighted factor, serve as an enlightening example. For years *USN* did not disclose how its reputational surveys were conducted, despite the fact that this factor determined 40 percent of a school's overall rank. Only later did schools learn that a consulting company was hired to write and administer the surveys of both practicing lawyers and law school staff, that the response rate was very low (especially for the practicing lawyers), and what the positions were of those who were typically surveyed within law schools—all information that is valuable if you are trying to develop strategies to improve your reputational score. Schools still do not know how *USN*'s sample is constructed and what the biases of this likely non-random sample are; one of the questions that many of our interviewees put to us concerned whether we had learned how practicing lawyers were selected as survey respondents.

Given these unknowns, reverse engineering the rankings becomes a challenging and ongoing process. Administrators try to gather information by monitoring stories about rankings in a wide array of media, including the many blogs on rankings written by law professors, journalists, and others. Colleagues exploit formal and informal professional networks for information and gossip. Tips for manipulating rankings are often carefully guarded secrets passed on only to trustworthy friends. On multiple occasions we were asked not to reveal what many considered trade secrets for managing the numbers, and nearly as often we were asked what we knew about *USN* methodologies. Schools also learn from past experience, accumulating techniques for manipulating rankings, not all of which are demonstrably effective. In short, a great deal of institutional effort is dedicated to figuring out how scores are constructed so that these scores can be manipulated more efficiently.

Reverse engineering is a fruitful way to conceptualize the motives for manipulation of rankings because it is such a common strategy, one that members often use to name a bundle of practices used to make sense of and manage rankings. The people we interviewed routinely described what they did in terms of "engineering" or "reverse engineering" the numbers, and some reported that it is a helpful tool in explaining their rankings to various audiences or overseers. Reverse engineering is simultaneously a way to know something (how rankings work), a way to do something (influence the numbers), and a way of checking something (are our plans working? are people doing their jobs properly?). More generally, this concept highlights the connections between the management of rankings and other related strategic social processes such as creating "audit trails," which make it possible to trace backwards the calculations performed to ensure transparency, accountability, or reproducibility. Similar processes have been documented in research on auditing, risk assessment, performance evaluation, and governmentality.[41]

This concept also focuses our attention on unpacking how this form of thinking and action shapes organizational members' understanding of rankings. Deconstruction, the primary cognitive practice associated with reverse engineering, is based on the assumption that something can be known if it is taken apart and reduced to its core components. This is a sensible approach to understanding end products, but it is one that depends on other largely implicit assumptions. In many cases it is extremely difficult to reverse-engineer something, especially if—as in the case of rankings—crucial information is missing. Although calculation is considered one of the most transparent and therefore reproducible forms of knowledge, divining proprietary algorithms is hardly easy. The classifications that create the definitions that are used to construct measures create a complex cognitive infrastructure for rankings that is often obscure.

Narrative

A final mechanism that shapes the consequences of rankings is that of narrative. One of the oldest cultural forms, narrative organizes people, events, and places into stories that make sense of the world. "Narrative" comes from the Latin narrare, which means "to recount." The kinds of narratives that are salient for rankings often have to do with recounting, in both senses of the term: telling a story and re-counting the calculations that make up rankings.

There are many definitions and genres of narrative, but typically a narrative is a story, told from the point of view of one or more narrators, that features characters, a sequence of events, a scene, and a plot involving some conflict or problem.[42] Narratives usually start with a catalyst that stimulates events and often end with some sort of resolution or a renewed ambiguity. Narratives have many purposes: they entertain, inform, persuade, or make sense of an experience, which is why, to paraphrase the literary scholar Kenneth Burke, narratives are "equipment for living."[43]

Rankings evoke narratives about the ranked institutions. These narratives can be celebratory or defensive. They often include causal explanations of recent events in relation to rankings, and the narrators may make ethical charges about the rankers or about participants whose failings have contributed to poor rankings or whose hard work has improved rankings. One important feature of narratives is that, because they offer context and interpretation, they are more memorable than a series of numbers. An impressive single number may be relatively easy to remember, but a story, by organizing time, place, and details, helps us retain more information, for longer.

It is useful to compare narrative and commensuration as cultural forms. Both organize, edit, and simplify ideas or information in order to produce order and meaning. Both are treated as authoritative but are often directed toward different audiences in different contexts. Narratives are usually more effective for invoking empathy or conveying compassion, but numbers are seen as better for producing rigorous, objective, impersonal knowledge. The forms of simplification that narratives and numbers produce are very different, and so are their effects. Where numbers are abstract, impersonal, and understood as reproducible and transparent, narratives are specific and concrete and showcase both human agency and fate. Narratives provide context whereas numbers remove it. Narratives integrate a variety of forms of information, making use of devices other than metrics, such as space, time, human qualities, and sequence.

Given these differences, it is not surprising that quantification is often understood as the opposite of narrative. This makes intuitive sense. People do not like to be "reduced" to numbers. However, they also worry that stories are highly selective and exaggerate. Quantification makes comparisons easy and permits us to understand how widespread or generalizable something is. Stories "flesh out" numbers and produce feelings such as identification, empathy, and guilt. Quantification can be understood as a systematic stripping away of author, protagonist, scene, and other core components of narrative, leaving information that is objective, defensible, and potentially reproducible to others. Yet this binary division of numbers and stories does not capture their complex interplay, the way numbers sometimes evoke a narrative, and vice versa. People find it difficult to let the numbers speak for themselves, and almost invariably create narratives to explain or explain away the numbers.

Ranking narratives fall into several genres: they can be heroic accounts of how schools accomplish a goal, persevere despite being unfairly evaluated, or hold fast to values even if rankings punish them for doing so. Faculty at one fourth-tier law school relayed to us a memorable faculty meeting where the dean "put on the table" the sacrifices they would be making by holding fast to the school's mission of providing opportunities to students who would not be accepted at more conventional schools. The dean told them they needed to understand that in affirming their mission they would be relegating their school and themselves to permanent fourth-tier status. The faculty reported that they unanimously declared their support for this mission and their sacrifice. This type of story, we suspect, is one that has been told many times at communal occasions, to colleagues at other schools and to each other.

More commonly, the stories evoked by rankings revolve around the crisis of a drop in rank. The narrative is usually provided in response to demands by students and faculty for explanations. These responses are remarkably consistent and generally involve a quick dissection of why the rank changed, sent in an email to the entire school community, at a "town meeting" with students, or as part of a long discussion at a faculty meeting. The narratives to address a drop in rank usually include the following points: do not overreact, the change only represents a statistical anomaly; rankings are poor measures that do not capture what is best or most important about this school; nothing significant has changed about the school in the last year; we understand the problem and how to deal with it; we are working hard to fix the problem. Occasionally, an administrator—most often a director of admissions or career services, but sometimes a dean—is made a scapegoat and a resignation is announced. The important rationale of these stories is to reassure, and they must be delivered by the dean in a public and sincere way. Narrative, like numbers, offers a form of selective accountability.

We can think of narratives as a means of talking back to what might be termed the "disciplinary power" of rankings, the way rankings govern law schools indirectly through bureaucratic practices and internalized notions of self and subject.[44] Stories about rankings are good for sense making and for channeling emotions, but as forms of resistance they are weapons of the weak—not a characteristic that would typically have been applied to American law schools before rankings came along. Deans, faculty members, and students now understand rankings as an indicator of status that they cannot escape. We often personalize the organizations we belong to, often by participating in the construction of organizational identities, identities that become part of how we as its members understand ourselves. Talking back to rankings is a means of talking back to ourselves.

How did numbers published in a popular magazine, numbers that many considered illegitimate, come to have such an extensive impact on legal education? Our research indicates that they were able to do so because they changed how both insiders and outsiders made sense of the field of legal education. Rankings created new conceptualizations of how schools compared to one another, what it meant to be successful, and how identity is constructed and maintained. We have identified four key mechanisms through which rankings have changed this sense-making process. The mechanisms that we describe are not, of course, the only ones that mediate how people react to rankings, nor are they as distinct as we present them here—they often overlap and interact. We believe that understanding these processes is crucial for understanding the impact of rankings, and so it is useful to distinguish these processes for analytic and heuristic purposes. In the remaining chapters of the book, we show the consequences, both intended and unintended, that these reactive processes have produced.

Chapter 3 | 0L: How Prospective Law Students Use Rankings

It is nearly midnight on a Sunday night in late June. The "cycle" of the law school application process is over for most applicants, or 0Ls, as they call themselves in the blogosphere, and the cloud of anxiety that has enveloped them for the past eighteen months or so is gradually replaced by the more agreeable stress of preparing for law school.[1]

But not everyone is lucky enough to be on the far side of these matriculation decisions. Some have been relegated to the purgatory of the waitlist. If more fortunate peers are taking preemptive vacations or skimming law school memoirs, for the waitlisted the immediate future remains agonizingly uncertain. "I feel like I have a scarlet W on my chest," posts one. Some hope to hear from their "reach" schools. Others hope to hear from anyone. For some, the waitlist generates hard choices. They turn to the solace of the Internet.

"Player 30," a regular on the popular message board *Top Law Schools*, conveys his dilemma succinctly in his subject line: "Waitlist craziness: BLS vs. Pace($) vs. PSU vs. Rutgers-C." Translated from the dialect of this community, this means: "I'm waitlisted at Brooklyn Law School, have a 'merit' scholarship from Pace Law School, and have been admitted to Penn State Law School and Rutgers Camden Law School." Player 30 (we're guessing he's a Jersey boy) writes:

> I prefer the NYC area to the Philly area, in which case it is probably BLS vs. Pace. Pace gave me 18K and I have an interest in environmental law, although I would rather limit myself as little as possible. Rutgers is a good deal in-state but I'm not crazy about the area, and Temple and Nova might be a little better for Philly jobs. PSU just offered me a spot off the waitlist at either Carlisle or UP—I would only consider UP. For PSU, I keep hearing it's rising, but I worry about being stuck in central PA. And then there's BLS (offered PT off the

waitlist), which I like but is obviously expensive with no guarantees unless you are very high in the class. The Pace scholarship is at least doable to keep. I could save over 60K in 3 years between that and BLS; I could graduate from Pace or Rutgers with very little debt. I actually like many aspects of Pace—the area, the people, the curriculum, but there is a reputation gap between that and other schools. I think I might regret taking a T3 when I got offered spots at 7 T2 schools. So TLSers, tell me what to do here.[2]

Player 30's decision amounts to this: accept a spot at a third-tier law school with a good scholarship in New York, or attend a second-tier school in a less interesting place with a more restrictive labor market and take on debt. The contours of the decision are familiar to applicants: the trade-off between status and debt. How to reconcile this is not obvious, especially to young applicants who are unsure about how to calculate the long-term advantages of a "better" if more obscure school versus the burdens of the potentially staggering debt that they may face after graduation. The decision is made harder by the dismal job market accompanying the recession.[3] Questions beget questions. Where do I want to live for three years? How tied will I be to local labor markets? Which type of law do I want to practice? Is worrying about money now professionally shortsighted? How much and for how long will the relative status of my law school matter? These are questions that applicants routinely ask each spring in the esoteric world of pre-law Internet sites, and the recession has made them even more pressing.

As waitlisters (yes, it's become a noun) go, Player 30 has it good. He has choices, some with scholarship money, and his options are not restricted to attending an "inferior" fourth-tier school or waiting a year to begin the whole agonizing cycle over again. Notice how deeply rankings frame his questions. The distinctions Player 30 makes between T2 and T3 refer to the tiers of law schools, tiers that rankings created. Before *USN* there were status differences among schools, but no rankings, no clearly delineated positions, no precisely defined tiers. In describing PSU as a "rising" school, Player 30 means "rising in the rankings," and "better" is tantamount to higher in the rankings. The "reputation gap" among schools that Player 30 alludes to is the precise interval between their rankings. So, in soliciting the opinions of his online interlocutors and expressing preferences about location and cost, Player 30 demonstrates that rankings are not *purely* determinative in his thinking; but the parameters of his decision, how he thinks about excellence and the value of his degree, are largely defined by *USN* and its rankings.

Pre-law websites are saturated with what we call "tier talk." Applicants constantly invoke tiers and the language of rankings to describe aspirations and options, make decisions, or depict schools, students, and, sometimes poignantly, themselves.[4] In chat rooms, interviews, and observations made at admission events, we see students obsess over rankings and their proper influence in calculations about applications, scholarships, matriculation, and job opportunities. Casual conversations evoke many versions of tier talk: "I'm not applying out of the top tier," "Is it even worth it to go to a fourth-tier school?" or "I'd like to hear from those admitted to a T-fourteen [top-fourteen] school." A common epithet is to refer to a school or a person as "TTT," the acronym for "third-tier toilet."[5] Some students internalize rankings as expressions of their own abilities and constraints. One disappointed applicant whose options were limited to third-tier schools posted at the pre-law website called *The Princeton Review*, "I guess I'm just a TTT kind of guy." And it is not only the low-tier students who are shamed in this way. When Clarence Thomas was criticized for choosing clerks from less prestigious law schools than is usual for Supreme Court justices, he defended them in a speech as "not TTT." Reactions to his speech on a popular gossip site were often damning, none more so than one comment: "TTThomas."[6]

Concerns about these distinctions extend to the top of the spectrum as well. Some successful applicants bragged online and in interviews of "having numerous first-tier options." Others told us that if they didn't get into a top-tier (or top-twenty-five, or top-fourteen) law school, they would reconsider law as a profession because, according to a young African American woman who serves as an assistant dean at a law school struggling to reach the second tier, "What's the point of joining a profession where your options are already so limited? Maybe that test [the LSAT] is telling you something."

And it is not only 0Ls who see the world of law schools through the lens of tiers and rankings. Current students also think in these terms. The expression "TTT" has now become generalized beyond law schools to become an expression of general mediocrity. Disappointing lectures, movies, or even jobs are TTT. The media now routinely depict schools in terms of tiers or rankings. A headline in the *Buffalo News* on April 18, 2010, read "UB Law School Slips out of Top Tier"; the previous day, the *Mormon Times* had run the headline "BYU and Utah Tie in U.S. News Law School Rankings" (they were both ranked in the same tier).[7] In his memoir, *Barman: Ping-Pong, Pathos, and Passing the Bar*, Alex Wellen describes a celebratory dinner with an indiscreet senior associate from a well-heeled Philadelphia law firm after Wellen had secured a much-coveted spot as a summer intern. It was rare, the associate explained, for them to hire someone from Temple Law School. "For whatever reason, they haven't made any other Temple Law offers this year. I hope you decide this is the right place for you. If

you don't, I'm not sure whether they'll make any more offers to Temple."
Wellen, stunned, explained,

> It was all *U.S. News and World Report*'s fault. . . . Temple Law was *not* among
> the top fifty accredited schools. It was one of the top schools in the next best
> fifty, tier two (read: second rate). It didn't matter that Temple's trial advo-
> cacy program was ranked above that of Yale, Harvard, Cornell, and every
> other tier-one law school in the country. Who cared if Temple offered its
> students riveting lectures from accomplished professors, a diverse curricu-
> lum, and hundreds of international programs, legal clinics and internships?
> None of this improved the *U.S. News* ranking. Year after year, Temple bore
> the same brand: tier two.[8]

Rankings now subtly, powerfully, and enduringly shape perceptions of
ability, achievement, and desirability and influence what people attend to
in their decisions.

Before *USN* began publishing its annual rankings of graduate schools
in 1990, there were guidebooks for prospective law students, the most
popular of which was *Barron's Guide to Law Schools*.[9] *Barron's* does not
rank schools; instead, each accredited law school is described in a page
or so of prose that is organized according to general categories such as
a school's history, academic atmosphere, library, faculty, and application procedures. Entries also include some basic statistics about gender
ratios, average test scores, GPAs, and number of applicants and admissions, but the bulk of information is presented in highly standardized
narrative form.

Contrast this with *USN* rankings, in which law schools are divided into
tiers with entries restricted to a school's ordinal rank and a line of statistics
including its reputation scores, the 25th and 75th percentiles of GPAs and
LSAT scores, admission rate, and placement percentages. With no supporting narrative, the overwhelming "fact" about a school is its rank: its tier,
whether it is high or low, and the "nearby" schools. There is little to notice
but this ordinal hierarchy.

Barron's provides listings by state, emphasizing geographical locations.
USN rankings, in simplifying differences among schools, construct a social
location. Both guides offer statistics that allow students to gauge their
chances for admission. But *Barron's* contains more and different kinds of
information about schools than does *USN* and highlights different aspects
of law schools. Most important, because it depicts schools in terms of variable qualities rather than quantities, it requires more of the reader. Instead
of presenting a single, definitive number that integrates and obscures other
forms of difference, readers must assimilate and integrate information in

ways that make sense to them. The form and variety of information provided by *Barron's* challenges the notion that there is a "best" law school or that law schools only vary by degrees of shared qualities. Nor does *Barron's* suggest trajectories for schools, clear improvements or slippage from year to year. Absent rankings, apprehending change in a school is a more challenging cognitive task.

UNPACKING THE "DEMAND" FOR RANKINGS

One way in which proponents of rankings justify them is by citing the public's demand for them. "Demand" is conceptual shorthand for messy social processes. As with a lot of core social science mechanisms, it is usually far easier to project demand backward than to predict its emergence or explain its effects. Marketing proves that demand can be created and manipulated; organizational scholars warn of projecting too much rationality onto groups or individuals; and historians show how difficult it often is to apprehend change in real time. Understanding rankings simply as a strategic response to demand misses most of what's interesting about the creation and growth of rankings. Cohen, March, and Olsen have suggested that the process of defining something as a solution to a problem is rarely as linear or rational as retrospective accounts suggest: the processes of discovering or creating problems and linking them to solutions can be haphazard, dispersed, and disjointed.[10] Status, organizational culture, visibility, and time all shape who has the power to define something as a problem, or a solution to a problem, and get that decision to stick.

Hindsight reveals that Mort Zuckerman's decision to create annual rankings of colleges and graduate programs was a brilliant strategic response to a changing educational and business landscape. But exactly which conditions or concerns was Zuckerman reacting to? Why did rankings emerge as the right "solution" at that particular time? And why did students respond to rankings as they did? These are the questions we take up next.

Let's begin with the political landscape. Economists and sociologists often view education as an investment with returns—in income, health, status, standard of living, or even happiness—that accumulate over a lifetime and are passed on to children and grandchildren. This sense of education has become increasingly dominant in recent decades. In colonial North America, most colleges were religious colleges and were places to cultivate faith. In the late nineteenth and early twentieth centuries, principally elites attended college, where they studied Greek, Latin, and mathematics. A college education was less important for one's career trajectory than as a means of maintaining a family tradition, becoming a cultivated young gentleman, or meeting the right sort of people. Later, college became the path for upward mobility for a wider swath of people.[11] Beginning in the late 1970s and early 1980s, politics in the United Kingdom and the United States (later elsewhere) shifted in ways that broadened and deepened our understanding of education as an investment with what seemed like clear analogies to business. One's education increasingly was seen as a valuable commodity that signaled something about the person who obtained it, and the value of the commodity increasingly was understood as reflecting the value and selectivity of the school that had produced it.

This change corresponded to the growth of a market logic in the field of higher education. According to this logic, the variable return on one's education depends largely on a particular school's reputation or "brand"; applicants are "customers" choosing among products with an eye toward maximizing their returns; universities are competitors in the market for the best students, faculty, researchers, and donors; current students are clients wishing to appeal to future employers, who compete for the best employees; and colleges and universities are like businesses that can be improved by hiring administrators who adopt business practices and act like CEOs.

The reforms enacted by Margaret Thatcher in the United Kingdom and Ronald Reagan in the United States were among the earliest in stimulating and coalescing the broad global political movement known as neoliberalism. Reforms included sweeping efforts to privatize government services and extend market logic to government by encouraging competition and new forms of accountability. Neoliberal policies were expressed variably and disjointedly in different parts of the world. Very often, however, higher education was a prime target of movements to shrink government, lower taxes, and empower consumers by making public more and more "transparent" information, permitting "consumers" to choose their child's school on the basis of that information, and exposing universities to the rigors of market discipline.[12] Universities' status as unique institutions and repositories of nonmarket values was challenged, and they became subject to many of the same criticisms directed at other government institutions: they were inefficient, self-interested, unaccountable, and inattentive to the concerns of ordinary people. Added to these were familiar charges of elitism and irrelevance that now seemed to carry more weight than in previous decades.[13]

Neoliberal reforms in education were expressed earliest and most dramatically in Great Britain as part of Thatcher's vision for shrinking government and harnessing market forces. An extensive and intrusive audit system linked to institutional budgets and designed to measure teaching and research quality of all departments and universities prompted a radical reordering (and shrinking) of budgets, changes in hiring practices and research focus, and the closing of some departments.[14] The results of these audits were published by leading newspapers as rankings—or "league tables," as they are called in the U.K.—which increased their impact.

In the United States, neoliberal reforms took a different tack. Since the budgets of colleges and universities are less directly supplied by the federal government with grants and student loan programs, the systemwide audits adopted by the U.K. weren't an option. Instead, Reagan's administration focused on school choice, an attempt to abort the Department of Education (it failed), and forge closer links between higher education and the needs of business. Many districts pressured local schools to become more competitive by expanding choice through the creation of charter schools or vouchers that subsidized private school tuition, or by dropping requirements that children attend neighborhood schools.[15]

In 1981, alarmed by Japan's economic success, especially in the automobile industry, a burgeoning trade deficit, and concern that the United States was losing its prominence in science and commerce, Secretary of Education Terrell Howard Bell created a blue-ribbon commission to examine America's economic competitiveness. The National Commission on Excellence in Education concluded in its report, "A Nation at Risk," published in 1983, that poor training in math and science was damaging U.S. firms' chances to compete in an increasingly global marketplace. These conclusions fueled pressures for educational reform, which included a "back to basics" approach to curriculum, calls for greater accountability, and questions about the power of teachers' unions to protect incompetent teachers. Standardized testing, already widely used in the United States, was the favored tool for implementing reforms. The best-known reform was the legislation passed by the George W. Bush administration called No Child Left Behind in 2001.[16]

Ideas about education were changing. But it was not only governments that changed Americans' understanding of education. The landscape of higher education had shifted profoundly after World War II. One reason was an extraordinary broadening of access to college as the GI Bill flooded universities with young veterans. This wave of new students was followed by subsequent waves as women, African Americans, and other underrepresented groups claimed their right to college and as postwar prosperity made college seem within reach of lower-middle-class and working-class families. This influx of students was accompanied by enormous expansion in the size and number of colleges and universities. To take one example, Arizona State University went from a small teaching college with 553 students in 1945 to a university of some 45,000 students in the 1970s to enrolling over 83,000 students over five campuses in 2014.

For elites, this broadened access to education was unthreatening as long as the newcomers didn't aspire to attend the same schools. But the rules were changing. As merit gradually replaced race, class, and religion in admission decisions (and moderated the effects of family connections) among the Ivy League institutions, the competition for spots at elite universities escalated.[17] Competition for admission to the "best" schools has morphed into an admissions arms race that now begins, for some wealthy parents, with consultants hired to prep three-year-olds for interviews at the "right" preschools. The bedrock American principle of education as the entry ticket to the middle class has morphed into a billion-dollar industry of getting kids into the "best" schools in order to maintain upper-middle-class status. Barbara Ehrenreich, Patricia McDonough, and others have argued that the anxiety parents feel about their chances of passing on their status is palpable in most affluent suburbs. These parents know that competition for elite schools is becoming fiercer and that the schools to which they were admitted twenty-five years ago would likely reject someone with the same credentials today. On the April day that Ivy schools collectively announce their admission decisions, results spread at the speed of scandal.

The market for selective colleges is extremely competitive, even though only about 6 percent of high school students meet the criteria for admission.[18] One indication of this emphasis on selectivity is that applicants now apply more broadly and more intensively than did their parents.[19] Admissions officers at selective schools can tell remarkable stories of the lengths parents will go to improve their child's odds, ranging from prophylactic donations to elaborately arranged internships to charitable projects funded primarily by relatives. Predictably, cracks that threaten the structure of privilege are quickly repaired with new practices that reproduce and reinforce it. Mitchell Stevens shows that producing the biographies, transcripts, confidence, and test scores that appeal to colleges requires a long and extensive cultivation that favors the affluent and the informed.[20] The soccer games, piano lessons, travel, "service," test preparation, counselors and transcripts, and, above all, the aspirations and sense of entitlement that middle-class children take for granted are fantasies for many families who dream of sending their children to college. Despite the growth in the admissions "business," admissions at selective institutions are still far more defined by "merit"—even in its narrow test- and GPA-driven form—than at any earlier time in the history of education.

The growing number of colleges, increasing numbers and dispersion of applications sent by applicants, and the growing impression that elite credentials matter more than ever—all have increased the anxiety surrounding college application. Moreover, parents know that the increased selectivity of elite colleges has rendered their experiences less useful in guiding their children, and the informal networks that worked so well when they chose among a small number of regional schools are no longer adequate for assessing colleges nationally. Rankings—by providing simple, comparative information about all schools—offered a strategy to address these concerns.

Rankings are appealing for other reasons as well. The decision to go to college is usually the first major decision that young people make, and for many the stakes weigh heavily on them. They, too, know that competition is fierce, that their families are counting on them, and that their schools and their friends are keeping score. College choice is typically a one-shot decision, and it feels fateful. Young people, even more than their parents, may think that their school will define their lives in irrevocable ways. In addition, applicants must confront the avalanche of marketing that is designed to sway their choices. Many organizations profit from culling and selling names of desirable applicants, none more than the Educational Testing Service, which publishes and administers the SAT. Ask anyone whose child did well on the PSAT or attended a "gifted" program.

Too much information has become as big a problem as too little. Given the resources now devoted to marketing and the challenge of sifting through the huge volume of information available on the Internet, it's easy to understand why the simplicity and clarity of the rankings, the sense that there is a definitive, objective expert opinion to guide one's choice, is so comforting to applicants. Too many choices can feel as oppressive as too few.

Another big factor in the rush to rankings is the rising cost of college tuition. Between the 2000–2001 and 2010–2011 school years, tuition, room, and board at public institutions rose 42 percent; for private (not-for-profit) schools, it rose 32 percent. Average tuition, room, and board at public and private schools for 2010–2011 was $13,000 and $36,000, respectively.[21] The prospect of spending $50,000 to $300,000 on college, a decision that in many places is comparable to buying a house, may squeeze even well-off families. Again, clear, comparative information about quality seems paramount.

The trends that redefined universities and colleges in postwar America played out on a smaller but equally crucial scale among law schools. The number of accredited law schools rose in response to increasing demand driven by the expansion and accessibility of higher education. Universities noted that law schools are good at generating revenue and donors. Elite schools became even more selective as the sense grew that the reputation of one's law school mattered. At law schools, too, tuition increased at an alarming rate: according to the American Bar Association, between 1985 and 2012 the average tuition at private law schools increased from $7,500 to $40,500; the average public law school tuition increased more than tenfold during this same period.[22]

Prospective law students have always had to weigh the potential benefits of a legal education with the debt that they will incur during their three
years of legal training, and the rankings—because they provided information about how graduates of schools stood relative to one another—quickly
became a proxy for predicting job outcomes. Since the Great Recession, a
very tight labor market has led to acute concerns about the value of a law
degree and available employment opportunities. In this environment,
rankings become even more important to students looking for guidance as
to which schools will and will not be worth their investment.[23]

MARKETING RANKINGS

The analogy of education as an investment is the centerpiece of *USN*'s
marketing of rankings. Over and over, readers are told that rankings are
a quick, objective, and easy-to-use means for evaluating colleges and professional schools and that the monumental decision of choosing a school
demands systematic comparison among schools. As we noted previously, early editions of the rankings described the folly of neglecting to
make careful comparisons among law schools. Later, Robert Morse, the
man who oversees the production of all rankings at *USN*, would reiterate
this theme:

> The main purpose of the rankings is to provide prospective law school stu-
> dents with much-needed—and clearly desired—comparative information
> to help them make decisions on where to apply and enroll. In today's legal
> job market a student's choice of law school plays a considerable role in
> getting that all-important first legal job. That job is particularly important
> since some new law school graduates have accumulated over $150,000 in
> debt just to get their J.D. degree and many need to start paying off their
> student loans.[24]

The words "fit" and "value" feature prominently in *USN* promotions. In
response to critics, *USN* became careful over time to instruct applicants
that they should not rely *solely* on rankings to inform their decisions, that
advisers and professional experts were important, too. As the rankings
gained popularity and new groups discovered uses for them, *USN*'s framing of rankings adapted as well.

How and When People Use Rankings

Many college students consider law school at some point. "Going to law
school" offers a response to troublesome questions about what to do with

one's life or a degree in English. And law school does not require job experience as do many MBA programs. While law is certainly a calling for some, many applicants see it as a more practical or appealing option than one's current job or entering other graduate programs. Plus, it's over in three years.[25]

When considering where to apply to law school, applicants face what economists might term "asymmetric information." Insiders know important information about schools that applicants do not have access to, especially information that might harm a school's reputation. For example, insiders might know that a prominent faculty member wants to leave, or that the dean is incompetent, or that entrenched conflict among faculty may spill over onto students, but applicants are unlikely to have access to this information. Knowledge of a school's reputation is unevenly distributed because the networks through which such information is passed around vary dramatically. Applicants from less wealthy or nonacademic backgrounds and international applicants are at a disadvantage when it comes to getting informal information about reputations and recent changes. Rankings seem to level the playing field, offering what seem like objective and timely evaluations to everyone.

Sam Weissman was an articulate, successful law student at a top-twenty law school in California when we interviewed him. He had just completed his second year of law school and was about to start an internship at a prestigious firm in Los Angeles. After finishing his undergraduate degree at a good public university in California, Sam moved to New York City to do a master's degree in Middle East studies. Having completed that, he was torn between working toward a Ph.D. in the same field, or a J.D. Sam opted for law school in what he describes as a "career choice." Law school, he says, was "palatable" to him academically, and he seems pleased with his decision, even if there is a hint of wistfulness about the path not taken. Location was an important factor in Sam's thinking about where to apply to law school: most of his applications were sent to New York and California.

Sam also applied to one midwestern and one southern school, but only because he received waivers for application fees. Fees are another part of the application puzzle. Most law schools charge an application fee to defray the expenses of processing applications. City University of New York Law School charges $60; Harvard charges $85. One way that schools signal their interest in students and broaden their application pool is to waive their fee. Reasons vary, but schools are more likely to waive fees if a student has a strong record relative to other applicants, is a member of an under-represented group or is from an under-represented region, has a compelling background, or has interests that mesh well with a school's mission or specialization.

Fee waivers serve many goals, one of which is to boost rankings. A higher ratio of applicants to admissions improves the selectivity factor, and waiving fees encourages applications from students with good grades or test scores who might otherwise not apply. Because most students apply to multiple law schools, fees can add up to a hefty bill and prevent some students from applying to schools that they know less about or that they consider long shots.[26]

For Sam, the fee waivers did encourage him to apply more broadly. He applied to several schools he wasn't especially interested in because, aside from the extra work of sending his materials, he didn't need to write any checks. He was accepted at these schools. Sam says he wouldn't have considered going to either the midwestern or the southern school unless he got a "really good deal, lots of scholarship money." He described these schools as "not all that prestigious and not in desirable locations." And prestige is important to Sam because it is important to the profession. He explains: "The prestige of your law school really does give you some capital later in your career. At every stage of your career, where you went to law school might help you in some way." When asked how he defined prestigious, Sam quickly replied, "*U.S. News and World Report.* It's the only way to go." Sam believes that most prestigious law schools are on the coasts, where he'd like to settle one day. He described how "I got into and seriously considered" attending a good law school in California, but "it was second tier." The school had many desirable qualities—"I got a good scholarship and it was in a good location, a wonderful location"—but Sam turned it down. The school he opted for "is a higher-ranked school and in [a] bigger city. It really does come down to prestige." It's clear that Sam has thought long and hard about these sorts of calculations.

Because admission to elite law schools is so competitive, prospective law students, even ones as accomplished as Sam, are an anxious bunch.[27] Many find reassurance in talking to like-minded strangers, which is why pre-law blogs and discussion boards are so popular. Sam now says, "I'm embarrassed to say I was very involved in the discussion boards. I wasted a lot of time on them. A lot of time." Topics on popular discussion boards like *top-law-schools.com* or the earlier pre-law forum *The Princeton Review* reflect the anxieties of the admissions cycle. Talk in the late spring and summer centers on the LSAT, and in the fall questions about applications dominate: "What's realistic given 'my #s'—LSAT scores and GPA?" "How do I explain my lackluster grades?" "What makes for a compelling essay?" These topic threads are followed by months of anxious waiting and considerations about where else to apply, since most schools have a rolling-admissions policy whereby they evaluate applications as soon as they begin to accumulate. Finally, talk turns to decisions about where you got in, where you should go, and what is known about various law schools or cities. Rankings are either an explicit or implicit feature of many posts. In March, when rankings are released, there is a flurry of talk about which schools moved up or down.

Martha Mulindwa took a different path to law school.[28] Martha's family emigrated to the United States from East Africa when she was a child. Her parents struggled financially and culturally, so Martha played a role common to children of immigrants: her family's mediator between languages and cultures. A serious student, Martha attended a prestigious university on a generous scholarship and graduated with honors. Unlike most students at her school, she usually worked two or three jobs to help pay her way. Martha maintained her connections to her natal community at college through her volunteer work tutoring the children of new immigrants and helping them with college applications. Martha loved her volunteer work and decided to go to law school after working several years after graduation. She wanted, she said simply, "to help children." She hoped to focus on issues related to immigrant rights, especially as they affected children. Martha had terrific grades, an impressive résumé, decent if not stellar LSAT scores (she didn't have the money for a test prep course and had to organize her studies around her demanding schedule), and glowing letters of recommendation from professors she had inspired. She applied to schools with strong programs in human rights, public interest law, and good clinics. She wanted to work in a big city with large immigrant populations. With no family financial support, the prospect of huge debt frightened her, so she considered working as a paralegal while attending an evening program. Martha was admitted to a top-ten school's part-time program and to several top-thirty schools' full-time programs. She was also admitted to a fourth-tier school with strong clinical programs in immigration and human rights law, from which she received a hefty scholarship. She chose the last.

Six years out of law school, Martha is part of a small and bustling, if not lucrative, practice that centers on immigration and family law. She declares her decision to attend her school "one of my best decisions," saying that unlike many law students, she left law school "knowing how to practice law" because of the depth and variety of her clinical experience. She is grateful for a loan forgiveness program for public interest lawyers because it made her debt "manageable." It's clear that Martha is a happy lawyer. "I practice law that makes a difference to families and their kids," she says. "At the end of most days, I feel pretty good about that."

Sam and Martha illustrate the diversity of the legal profession as well as the diversity of those who practice law. Sam is white, Martha black. Sam went to a top-twenty law school; Martha attended a fourth-tier program.

Sam is hoping to clerk for a federal judge and then practice corporate law at a large law firm, while Martha serves a poor community of mostly recent arrivals. But the experience of these accomplished people also illustrates some important constraints that rankings impose on law schools.

Sam's interest in rankings is hardly unique. The sheer amount of information about law schools and how to apply to them is overwhelming, and it's growing. In considering law school, there are many options, especially for undergraduates or recent graduates. Most colleges have pre-law advisers, pre-law clubs, and plenty of faculty who are willing to talk to students about law school. Many middle-class kids know lawyers they can consult. And of course the Internet is now the first source for those even mildly curious about law school.

When asked why they used rankings, students talked about feeling overwhelmed by the daunting task that applying to law school has become. Anne, a first-year student, reported, "There are so many schools, and you're so unsure of how you measure up, and there's so much stuff going on, it just seems impossible. So you just use what's easy." Duncan, another first-year student, said, "Where else are we supposed to get this information? I don't have time to go digging through all the sources. I was busy with my classes, with LSAT prep, and my extracurriculars. And it sure doesn't take long before all the material that law schools send you starts to look alike." Almost everyone we interviewed was convinced that it was harder than ever to get into a "good law school," that you need to apply to more schools than people did in the past, and that rankings helped you make sense of it all, mostly by narrowing the range of schools you needed to worry about. Amanda, a second-year student, said, "Once you know your numbers [LSAT scores, GPA] you can look at the rankings to eliminate a bunch of schools, either as impossible long shots or as not selective."

Rankings are, as one law professor described them, "omnipresent," but how, why, and how much people consult them varies according to their circumstances. Some people view rankings as a modern oracle, revealing what is to be done. For others, rankings are merely a heuristic for winnowing down broad choices. Nate described his decision process this way:

> From the very beginning, rankings had a lot to do with my decision where to go to law school. I don't know what got me to look at the rankings, but I know that's where to look—the *USN* guidebook. As soon as I got my LSAT scores back, I used *USN* to tell me where to apply. I didn't apply anywhere where I didn't fit between the 25th and 75th percentile. Location was also important to me—I wanted to be on a coast. Location was an important factor but after that it was the rank. I went to the highest ranked school

I got in. Students who use *USN* aren't necessarily concerned about measurement error in the rankings. The ranking is important in itself. I wasn't concerned with methods. I just figured they know what they were talking about and I didn't know any way to compare these schools and so I wasn't concerned about measuring errors or how accurate the rankings were. I knew that this is what everybody is looking at and what everybody else is using, so I was willing to take their [*USN*'s] word for it.

Students were sometimes a little sheepish when they described how important rankings were in their decisions. The first time Marisa applied to law school, she was right out of college and not sure which kind of lawyer she wanted to be. She "wasn't very realistic about law school" and "relied almost exclusively on rankings" in deciding where to apply. Marisa said she talked to a few friends about good law schools, but after she received her test scores she mapped out the top-ranked schools she thought she had a shot at: schools like Georgetown, New York University, Cornell, George Washington. Marisa decided to postpone law school after taking a job in New York City. Three years later, she was more focused. She had become interested in international human rights and wanted to attend a school with a strong program in that. She wound up going to a top-tier law school in the Midwest. The second time around, she was more critical of rankings, but she realized, like all the administrators we interviewed, that rankings have to matter because employers take them seriously.

It is not only prospective law students who take rankings seriously. One dean recounts his experience as associate dean at another law school:

The second year of the rankings, I would get all the phone calls that [staff] wouldn't know what to do with. The phone rings and the woman on the phone was an undergraduate alum and she felt comfortable calling the law school to ask questions. Her son had gotten into Emory that was ranked twenty-third and another school that was ranked twenty-sixth, and he really wanted to go to number twenty-six. And she wanted to know if he was destroying his life by going the lower-ranked law school. And I told her that it depends where he wanted to practice law and, more importantly, it's how he does at law school that will determine the options he has.

The importance of rankings in decisions about where to apply and attend law school is corroborated by a variety of evidence. Michael Sauder and Ryon Lancaster analyzed the effects of rankings on student decisions, relying on fifteen years of statistics compiled by schools and reported in public sources. They found that a school's rank has statistically significant effects on the number of students who apply to the school, the number of top students who apply, and the number of students who matriculate at the school.[29] The effects of changing rankings are not limited to the immediate changes in the applicant pool or class composition. Where top students apply not only is powerfully influenced by *USN* rank but also is a strong predictor of the future rank of a particular school. If a school's ranking changes, something that often happens owing to the tiny differences that separate schools, this change affects where top students apply, which affects a school's future rank. Actual school quality is affected by the *USN* definition of school quality because rankings magnify statistically insignificant differences rather than just reflecting differences among law schools.

Debra Schleef conducted interviews with a representative sample of students at an elite law school from 1992 to 1994.[30] Although *USN* had been publishing annual law school rankings for only two years, she found that over 75 percent of the students consulted some rankings data when deciding where to go to law school. Even students who did little research on the schools they applied to consulted rankings. Over 70 percent of these students listed their school's rank as one of the top three reasons that they chose to attend this school. One of the main reasons given for doing so is that students believed that school rankings affected their employment opportunities (discussed further in chapter 5).

A survey published in 2006 by the LSAC reports that 58 percent of students excluded schools because of their rankings and 76 percent applied to a school for the same reason. Moreover, 84 percent of admitted applicants said they consulted rankings when making a decision about where to attend.[31] Our less formal, unrepresentative survey, conducted during the Chicago Law School Forum in 2003, affirmed the importance of rankings in students' decisions about law schools.[32]

Some applicants are reminded of the importance of rankings in other ways. John Mitchell, a second-year student at an elite West Coast school, recalls receiving a surprising email from the dean of one of the law schools to which he had been admitted. It was April, the new rankings were out, and this school had dropped significantly. The dean explained to all admitted students in what must have been carefully crafted language that this sudden drop did not reflect any real changes at the law school but that their career services director had calculated their placement statistics in a more restrictive sense than did other schools. The dean went on to reassure students that their employment figures were strong and mostly unchanged and that the person who had been responsible for those figures was being replaced.

But, as Martha's case illustrates, there are clear exceptions to these patterns in the importance of rankings for decisions about law school. Rankings matter less for older applicants; those who wish to practice solo or in small firms; those who wish to practice in a particular region, especially if it has few law schools; those invested in particular legal specialties such as family, immigration, or real estate law; and those who can't afford high tuition. Mark Andrews worked a few years after college before deciding to apply to law school. He grew up in a midwestern state and attended college there, and he knew he wanted to stay in state. Location mattered more to him than rankings, so he only applied to law schools in his state. Older students are more likely to emphasize location than newly minted college graduates, because they are more likely to have property or relationships that tie them to a place.

Conversely, rankings matter most for those who aspire to careers with large, prominent firms (often called Big Law), those deciding among schools close to tier cut-off points, and those in competitive law school markets, such as New York, Chicago, or Los Angeles.

Despite this variation in rankings' importance to different groups, the evidence shows that rankings, as clear, precise indicators of relative status, *have* changed how students assess the quality of law schools, and this is reflected in their decisions about where to go to law school.

Rankings and Current Students

Applicants and their families are not the only ones who care about rankings. Riley is a second-year law student at a top-twenty private law school. Last year her school dropped two notches in the *USN* ranking. Riley reports that this small shift had big effects on student morale, causing "lots of students to second-guess their choices" of where to go to law school. They are worried that maybe they made the wrong decision. She said:

> Everyone is rethinking their initial offer. I turned down an 85 percent scholarship from an eastern school which is ranked in the top twenty-five because it was ranked below [my school]. I'm paying full tuition out of pocket. Now I'm wondering if that was a big mistake. There's lots of gossip going around about company offers. People are worried. People are especially upset about [a rival public school, now tied with her school]. And [it] is a public school and people are now saying even [this school] is tied with us.

According to Riley, "The entire culture of law school is rankings." She describes how students attending top law schools are continually reminded of how elite they are. Professors often say things like "The hardest part is over. You have already been admitted to a top-twenty law school." In the first workshop she went to, on financial planning, the speaker told them, "You will be among the top one percent earners in the country. All you have to do is graduate."

RANKINGS AND SELF-FULFILLING PROPHECIES

Rankings are important sources of information in most people's decisions about where to apply to and attend law school. This is just one of many examples of how rankings become self-fulfilling prophecies. Rankings create precise distinctions among schools whose relative status might once have been considered ambiguous or even equal. The distinctions produced by rankings are increasingly important and taken for granted, along with the advantages and disadvantages associated with them. As Sauder and Lancaster's work shows, even small differences in rank affect the number and quality of applications a school receives and its yield (the proportion of accepted students who attend the school).[33] Shifts in applications and yield change the selectivity score used by *USN* to compute its ranking and in this way reinforce the original differences, which were often largely a product of measurement noise.[34] These results confirm the claims of administrators who carefully analyze cross-application data on where students matriculate when they have been accepted by multiple schools. Nearly every admissions director interviewed reported that students' decisions correlate with rankings: if a school's rank declines, they lose students to schools to which they had not lost them in the past, and vice versa. Such differences can harden over time.

The experience of two elite schools, Harvard and Yale, illustrates this point. Henry Hansmann, a professor at Yale Law School, reports that Yale has enjoyed an increasing advantage in competition with Harvard.[35] Before rankings, Harvard often enjoyed a slight advantage in head-to-head competition with Yale. No longer. Now, roughly 80 percent of students who apply to Yale and are accepted choose to go there, and the majority of those who decline Yale decide not to attend law school at all. In head-to-head competition with Harvard, roughly two out of three students now choose Yale over Harvard.

Interviews also confirm the importance of rankings in matriculation. Nearly all of the law students we interviewed described rankings as playing a significant role in many aspects of their decision-making. Most used rankings to establish some threshold such as only applying to schools in the top ten, or twenty-five, or just first or second tier. Students with lower test scores and grades used rankings, too, sometimes as a way to judge their suitability for law. For example, one student told us that if he only got into third- or fourth-tier law schools, he would seriously consider alternative careers.

RANKINGS AND IDENTITY

Rankings are critical resources in the decision-making of prospective law students, but that is not the only important role they play. Rankings have become the foundation of the status system of legal education and now directly shape the aspirations and identities of prospective and current students. One current student at a top-twenty-five law school said:

> My understanding of how good a school was, was based on rankings. That's where I started off. That's where I got my idea of the hierarchy from. Where the school fit in was tied to rankings. I had friends going to schools, somebody got in here or there, well the book would come out and I would check where that school [where they got in] was ranked. Something about it is appealing. It's fun to pull out a list and see where we fit, who's going to a better or worse school. That's enjoyable information.

An assistant dean at a third-tier law school also reported a connection.

> I think about [rankings] a lot when I hear students use it as an excuse. We were talking about our problems and what other schools are trying to do to improve their rankings and it shocked me when I came here and the students said, "Well, they're just smarter than us anyway." And they said that because that is what the rankings told them. That's problematic—I don't know that they are smarter. I think they might be willing to work harder. But I think they are convinced that the things that the rankings tell them about themselves are true.

When Riley was asked whether rankings mattered for her own professional identity she said:

> I'll give a recent example. Yesterday the woman I met from the EPA, I asked her where she went to law school. She said, "Brooklyn Law School" and I thought, "OK, I can get a job here." So, it does make you elitist. But lots of places only hire by pedigree: Harvard, Yale, and so on. And pedigree is defined by rankings. I think it probably matters less for the lower top twenty. But between [two top-twenty local law schools] there is a big rivalry and rankings is part of that.

Rankings solve practical problems for applicants. They allow applicants to quickly compare the approximately two hundred American law schools while helping them to tame the seemingly limitless information that is now available about the schools. Rankings create a clear status system, and they help students learn how they might fit into it. The fact that students *use* rankings is the crucial first step in understanding why rankings have become so important in education today. Because students pay attention to them, others have to. In subsequent chapters we discuss how they do so.

Chapter 4 | Rankings and Admissions

If law schools are gatekeepers to the legal professions, admissions officers are the porters with the keys. In managing the crucial decisions of whom to admit and reject, admissions staff control the professional fate of tens of thousands of applicants each year. Because their staff solicit, vet, and recruit applicants, admissions offices are also one of the locations inside law schools that experience ranking pressures most acutely.

PROFESSIONAL CONTEXT

One reason why admissions personnel are so sensitive to rankings is that they oversee the production of the three important numbers—the median GPAs, median LSAT scores, and the acceptance rates or yields of entering students—that *USN* uses to create the "selectivity" factor, which determines 25 percent of a school's ranking. These are numbers that everyone around law schools knows and monitors closely, especially deans and the provosts, presidents, and trustees who oversee them. One dean of admissions described how parking lot encounters with the university president always begin with "Hello, Mark! How are our LSATs going?"—a query that sounds much different when sympathetic colleagues on coffee breaks at recruitment fairs gently inquire, "So, how *are* your numbers this year?"

Rankings penetrate admissions work in other ways, too. Admissions staff help broker relations between what the sociologist Erving Goffman would call the "front stage" and "back stage" of law schools: the front stage is the public parts of schools that are carefully orchestrated for outsiders, whereas the back stage is the vast, mostly invisible bureaucratic apparatus that supports these performances.[1] Admissions staffs are prominent players in producing the public face of law schools. If first impressions of law schools are now formed by websites, their content and follow-up discussions reflect the intensive monitoring of admissions staff who target potential applicants, answer emails and phones, write admissions blogs, update files, monitor chat rooms, organize visits, mail follow-up postcards, and generally manage the communications between schools and applicants. These are carefully orchestrated exchanges between schools and the prospective students who, if things go well, become law students, alumni, and donors.

But audiences for admissions officers also include colleagues at other schools, anxious parents, and even the curious neighbors who wonder over cocktails how these decisions really get made. Increasingly for admissions staff, the work of representing their school and cultivating its reputation involves regularly confronting and managing the fallout of rankings. In their contacts with potential applicants or admitted students, in their travels to meet and greet pre-law students and their advisers, or in the tours they organize, admissions officers help shape and defend the reputation of their law schools. This now entails crafting strategies for responding to rankings.

As informants go, admissions officers are an energetic and congenial lot. Their job demands it. Articulate, well-groomed, and more prepossessing than your average faculty member, their gifts for putting people at ease are so pronounced they hardly seem practiced. Along with their expertise at working a crowd, admissions people are also proficient presenters to groups that range from obstreperous faculty to earnest pre-law clubs, deft handlers of anxious applicants, and people who can patiently answer the same questions over and over again each year without looking grumpy. Stamina is important, too, especially during the fall "travel season" when admissions staff crisscross the country recruiting applicants and wonder if they will return home to any living plants. Admissions staff must be organized people capable of juggling complex recruiting schedules, managing huge databases, and remembering the visiting student who needs a 5:00 A.M. taxi. Staff must promptly respond to email and rarely hit "send" when they shouldn't. And they must be good at tracking the numbers.

Admissions offices are usually led by an associate or assistant dean. A few with long service are deans. A newer term used at some schools is "enrollment manager," a usage that reflects the growing salience of business models in higher education. Most deans of admissions have a J.D. and several years of practicing law, as well as extensive administrative experience, often at several law schools. They usually report directly to the dean of the law school, and their responsibilities may include budgeting, financial aid, and recruitment. The staffs they supervise vary depending on the size and wealth of the law school, but generally include several officers, many with J.D.s (sometimes from the school they work for) who have titles such as director or assistant director of admissions, director of financial aid, director of recruitment, or director of operations, as well as other admissions and administrative assistants.

Admissions staff cultivate and enjoy close ties with colleagues at other schools, even if these are, broadly construed, "competitors." This is most apparent with the veterans who have worked at multiple schools, are more active in professional associations, and hold the senior positions of director or assistant dean of admissions. Perhaps because their jobs demand so much diplomacy, they can be a raucous group. They savor moments and colleagues that permit frank talk. They seem like good company, asking about a sick partner, scrutinizing baby pictures, noticing neckties. When someone's wallet was stolen at a recruitment event, there were quick offers of cash or an extra bed in a hotel room. Gossip about who has been hired or fired, is retiring, or has an incompetent dean spreads quickly, if discreetly. At a dinner party, you'd hope to sit by one of them.

Friendships are fostered by the huge regional recruitment fairs they attend each fall, where they spend long days in ballrooms crammed with tables and students. Unless you are a Harvard, Yale, or a local school swarmed by students, there are usually plenty of occasions to chat with neighbors at adjoining booths. They watch each other's booths during breaks, stay at the same hotels, and share dinners. Admissions people also become friends during joint visits to college campuses, where they host smaller admissions fairs and appear on panels designed to demystify the admissions process for pre-law students. They keep company in more luxurious circumstances at annual conferences hosted by the LSAC at good hotels in interesting places where their annual talent show plays to enthusiastic audiences. But most central for their close professional community is the empathy that grows from sharing the same peculiarly difficult and satisfying job.

Annual pressure to improve the numbers of incoming classes has intensified the stress of admissions work at most schools. Fluctuations in the flow of applicants are one source of stress, especially for less selective schools with tight budgets and tiny endowments—schools where tuition pays the bills. A few admissions people still mention the "*L.A. Law* effect" of the mid-eighties: the alluring glamour of TV lawyers had spurred a large jump in applicants. Conversely, the lure of the dot-com bubble of the mid-nineties and, a decade later, the booming financial markets trumped law school as a goal for many graduates. More recently, applications to law school have dropped precipitously as students worry about debt burdens and the job market for lawyers. A college admissions director told us, "My career depends on what millions of clueless, anxious eighteen-year-olds with surging hormones decide to do. Now that's scary." Prospective law students are older and more sophisticated than their high school counterparts, yet for admissions staff it is still challenging to try to anticipate admission trends. Educators say that law school is too often the default career path for those who don't quite know what to do with their liberal arts degrees or their lives. Rankings amplify the uncertainty surrounding admissions because they fluctuate. And admissions officers know that prospective students pay attention to changes in rank when they decide where to apply and attend law school. If representing and recruiting are the main tasks of front-stage admissions work, deciding who gets in is decidedly backstage work. Although the process varies somewhat from school to school, the core technology is bureaucratic in classical Weberian terms.[2] Before any decisions are made, applicants are methodically transformed into files by test results, rules, and procedures that make them amenable to bureaucratic scrutiny. This transformation is carried out by armies of workers who coordinate across hundreds of institutions. Along with the applicants who have worked assiduously to appear to be the kinds of people law schools admit, the process of rendering applicants as files relies on the professors and registrars who generate, regulate, and verify grades from undergraduate institutions; the LSAC, which writes, administers, and scales the LSAT and which collects and disseminates students' applications through its Law School Data Assembly Service; and the law schools, which must organize all this information into files, about which decisions can be made.

The LSAC prepares a report for each applicant that is sent to each school to which an applicant applies—currently $30 for each school, paid by the applicant. This report contains biographical information and an "academic summary," which includes a student's undergraduate GPA (standardized across institutions), LSAT results (including average scores if taken more than once, records of canceled scores, missed test dates, and writing samples), complete transcripts for all institutions attended, letters of recommendation, and personal statements. For law schools who request it, the LSAC also calculates an "admission index" for each student that combines a weighted GPA and LSAT score into one number. In order to help law schools evaluate the quality of an applicant's undergraduate institution and her or his relative performance, the report includes statistics about the average test scores and GPAs from applicants from that school. And, of course, this transformation of applicants into bureaucratic units depends on admissions workers who track, print, copy, compile, and distribute the documents that constitute "the file."

Most law schools create their own admissions index, the so-called "magic number" they use to screen applications. This figure is a weighted combination of test scores and GPA, with schools usually weighing LSAT scores much more heavily than GPAs. The index provides an expedient way to sort some files quickly. It is the culmination of extensive deliberation, experience buttressed by statistical analysis, hope, and sometimes pressure from the dean. And the index exemplifies the competing concerns that confront most law schools of securing the tuition revenue that funds the school and selecting the "best" students. If the index is too high, schools risk empty seats and fewer dollars. Set too low, their selectivity statistics drop and they may get a bigger class than they wanted. This is why the index is often a subtly shifting target.

Although some schools are reluctant to admit it, having an index makes it possible for schools to conduct "rolling admissions": Students whose numbers are well above a school's index are admitted early. Those with numbers well below are rejected. Students with numbers near a school's index, usually the bulk of applicants, are subject to further review, often by committees that include faculty as well as admissions staff, although this, too, varies across schools. As the admissions process unfolds and the strength and size of the applicant pool becomes more apparent, this "magic number" may shift. Conventional wisdom holds that a school's index is lower early in the admissions cycle out of concern for filling seats. But once schools see that they have ample applicants with the right credentials, they may increase the number. This circumstance prompts pre-law web sites to urge applicants to get their applications in early.

Not all schools use an admissions index. And they may use the magic numbers differently. One associate dean who had chaired many admissions committees described the process this way—his top-thirty law school had a new dean for whom improving the school's rank was an administrative priority:

> Well, we certainly know what the numbers were the previous year and we start there. In fact, if you are looking at three places both with LSAT and GPA [the 25th, 50th, 75th percentiles] that gives you a pretty good standard against which to measure your class. So what we sort of say to ourselves at the beginning of this cycle is, "We know how we did last year, and our first goal is not to do any worse than last year. And if we can do better, that's fine." And we particularly watch the bottom quarter of the class because frankly I think that is where, admissions-wise and quality of the class-wise, that is where you have to work.

Top law schools such as Yale and Stanford needn't worry about "filling seats" with stellar applicants and don't bother with rolling admissions. The luxury of having more accomplished applicants than they have places for allows top law schools to focus more closely on the so-called "soft" factors in an applicant's file: evidence of character, a commitment to public service, an interesting job or hobby, qualities that enhance the diversity of a class such as race, age, economic status, gender, work experience, military service, geographic location, or undergraduate major.[3] For example, many law schools want to be seen as "national" or even "international" rather than "regional" or "local" schools. Geographical diversity is an important attribute, one that signals an appealing cosmopolitanism that schools tout with statistics about out-of-state students or countries represented. If there is a pool of students with similar numbers, a school with national aspirations may favor the distant applicant over someone local. Similarly, to achieve diversity schools may select members of under-represented minorities, older students changing careers, mothers returning to school, or veterans over more "traditional" applicants.

Rankings have shaped the use of indexes, as they have affected so many admissions practices. Instead of focusing on the composite index, some schools factor the impact of students' test scores and grades on their admissions statistics separately, keeping a running tally of their medians for both numbers. Less selective schools must usually be more attentive to an applicant's numbers and often feel most acutely the tension between filling seats and improving selectivity statistics. This tension has only increased with the precipitous post-recession decline in numbers of law school applicants: some schools must now decide between smaller cohorts and significantly worse selectivity scores, while others must do anything they can to fill seats regardless of scores.[4] One exception to this is schools with distinctive missions such as a commitment to community service or providing opportunities to students who otherwise would not get into law school, and schools founded by religious communities. But these schools are penalized for missions not endorsed by the rankings—for selecting students for reasons other than by their numbers.

Reconciling the tension between the "hard" facts of numbers and the "soft" attributes of people is a perennial one in large organizations. Numbers such as test scores and grade averages are part of the infrastructure of calculation that makes possible the scale, pace, and comforts of modern life. How else could timely decisions about so many different kinds of people get made? The point of numbers is to reduce the individual to a comparable, impersonal entity, to exclude from decisions the irrelevant noisiness of biography and bias—things that make people hard to compare. As Weber suggested, and as scholarship on the history of testing has shown, numbers can be a vehicle for circumventing ugly barriers of exclusion.[5]

But the facility of numbers comes at a price. However much we need them, we know numbers exclude much that matters about people, things that will affect their performance and comportment inside organizations. Numbers can erect new barriers to inclusion. And being "reduced to numbers" can feel demeaning even to applicants whose "good numbers" spare them the shame and disappointments of low scores and middling grades. Judgments that define one as a dot on a distribution are hard to square with full lives, evolving selves, and enduring inequalities. Admissions people know this, and that is one reason why the maxim "We evaluate applications, not applicants" is so reassuring.[6]

We have different ways of describing and framing what is at stake in this tension between "hard" and "soft" criteria and our ambivalent reactions to them.[7] We may ground judgments in either "universalistic" or "particularistic" criteria, evaluate "whole persons" or rely on "objective indicators," or use experience or algorithms to predict performance.[8] All of these emphases generate highly stylized objects of assessment. People become applicants by following rules, filling out forms, and mobilizing authoritative testimonials. During review they are turned into informal categories of persons: presumptive admits, stars, close calls, slackers, one-day wonders, over-achievers, under-represented minorities, reaches, at-risk candidates, or those worthy of "taking a chance on." People use guidelines or rules of thumb to construct applicants categorically, as "cases" that create or reinforce a precedent.[9] The "whole persons" that emerge from applications, like test scores, are highly standardized objects. "The applicant" is the culmination of carefully edited information that is dispensed in forms, essays, and recommendations that conform to the conventions of established genres. From the anecdotal lead in personal essays to the obligatory, "feel free to contact me if you have further questions about Nicole," in letters of recommendation, the rendering of the personal is as stylized as the numbers, if less reductive.

As Mitchell Stevens notes, Americans have contradictory impulses when it comes to access to higher education.[10] Our nation invests heavily in education. We don't see this as social welfare—we relish the fairness of treating everyone the same. But at the same time, we celebrate the uniqueness and power of the individual. In admissions we want it both ways. This balancing act can be hard to negotiate—a school's capacity to do it is constrained by status, resources, and law.[11] All schools pay attention to numbers and personal or demographic characteristics, and most admissions officers are adamant, at least in public, that numbers are only a "starting place." But the degree to which numbers dominate decision-making, and how much discretion they absorb, is itself mediated by the status system of legal education. In general, higher-status schools are wealthier and enjoy more discretion than lower-status ones.

Decisions made in admissions offices shape every aspect of a law school. First and foremost, admissions committees create that most fundamental unit: the class. Part of the balancing act that admissions officers routinely perform is to simultaneously focus on two units of analysis: the individuals whose applications they scrutinize and their relation to the emergent thing they are making, the class. Admissions people often describe their job as "crafting" a class, as an artful synthesis that is more than the sum of its parts. Edward Tom, dean of admissions at the University of California, Berkeley's Boalt Hall, said of the process, "Putting together an entering class is like organizing a choir; we want two hundred seventy distinct voices."[12]

Each class develops a shared history. Each has its share of law review editors and failing students, moot court champions and meek 1Ls (first-year law students) just trying to get by. Admissions officers are charged with trying to anticipate the performance and character of persons whom their decisions turn into classmates, from the middle-class twenty-somethings who have been honing their resumes since grade school to the "nontraditional" students who have not, from the long shots who paid off to the slackers who didn't. Over the course of three years, a class reveals itself to every part of a law school. Secretaries chat with students. Librarians teach them Westlaw. Faculty members teach them torts. Janitors clean up after them. Deans brag about them. Alumni hire them. And it all begins in the admissions office.

An important way that classes become defined is by their admissions statistics. Admissions statistics can be viewed not simply as "proxies of status" but as "status itself."[13] And the implications of this status-by-statistics are amplified by rankings. Rankings provide a powerful and public indication that things are going well or badly. Admissions statistics seem easier to control than more amorphous ideas such as "reputation," and they seem less ambiguous than budgets. After all, people come or they don't and test scores and GPAs are fixed. Those in admissions share the glory (and, sometimes, bonuses) when rankings improve and make easy scapegoats when they slide.

PROFESSIONAL NORMS ABOUT RANKINGS

Like most workers, admissions personnel have informal rules for how to do their jobs and manage collegial relations. One important rule involves not badmouthing other schools, despite—or perhaps because of—their competition over attractive applicants and tuition dollars. Instead, in conversations with students, admissions staff highlight the virtues of their school, educate applicants about important qualities to consider, and almost to a person emphasize "fit," the importance of picking the law school that's "right for *you*." Students are repeatedly told that no law school, no matter how illustrious, is best for everyone. The art of applying requires a careful matchmaking that entails knowing who you are, want you want, and what's realistic. A dean at one elite law school told us:

> I travel to visit with students after we've admitted them. And then we have three big events here. And the theme of those events is that even though we've admitted all of you, not all of you should choose [our school] as your

law school. And I'm very, very adamant about this theme; that as educators we ought to be involved in helping students sort themselves to the right school, not treating them as if they were basketball recruits or something like that, to be drawn to our school under any flag possible. . . . I usually give six or seven or eight reasons why they might, why [our school] might be wrong for them, and then we open it for questions.

Along with not publicly badmouthing other schools, another professional norm of comportment involves trying to deflect or minimize "rankings talk" with prospective students. In public forums or when counseling potential applicants, to tout one's ranking is "unprofessional," an indication that one is poorly socialized. Rankings talk is seen as unseemly, a norm that applies to staff at all schools, regardless of their rankings.

Trying to deflect ranking talk can be tricky. Rankings have become part of the core infrastructure of law school status. Like Dad's ugly recliner, they are totemic objects stuffed with meanings and hard to dislodge. How do you not acknowledge something that everyone knows and seems to care about, even if you resent the imposition? In conversations with admissions staff, prospective students in public forums sometimes invoke rankings in ways that can be awkward, and it can be hard not to react defensively. One admissions director said, "I get asked all the time on the road, 'Where are you ranked?' We're not ranked [ordinally]. 'So why aren't you ranked?'" According to another:

The ones who are more informed ask, "Why aren't you in the top tier?" The less informed want you to tell them where you are ranked, which is a game I don't play with people. People will come to my table and ask where we are ranked, and I will explain that we're a regional school. But it always seems to come from a student who is from a modest school, in other words a school that I am not familiar with. So I always feel prompted to ask them about the ranking of their own school.

Another director commented, "I spend an inordinate amount of time educating people who do not know how to use the ranks effectively. And I would say that's the most distressing part. The fact that, again anecdotally, you have someone calling up and saying, '[A local school] is ranked higher than you are,' and I'll have to say, 'Well, not really, because in the third tier, they're listed alphabetically.'" Such interactions with prospective students show how difficult it is for admissions personnel to avoid talking about rankings and the invidious comparisons that they promote, despite their best intentions and efforts.[14]

REACTIONS TO RANKINGS

Most admissions administrators dislike *USN* rankings. While some concede that rankings have forced schools to provide more information to prospective students or have encouraged accountability, few think their benefits outweigh their liabilities. Others are emphatic. One director of admissions at a top-tier school described *USN* as "a half-assed, shitty magazine." Others called the rankings "evil" or said they "hate them."

Hostility Toward Rankings

It's not hard to see why people might resent interactions that one professor characterized as "some kid insinuating not too subtly that your school stinks," especially when such conclusions seem so ill-informed. One head of admissions at a top-tier law school described how "students will email you and they will say, 'This school is ranked one place ahead of you. Why should we go to a lower-ranked school?' We've gotten emails about schools who, literally, one year will be above and the next year below us, and they will say, 'This past year, this school was ranked above you — why should we go to your school?' "

Certainly such experiences can seem professionally demeaning. But it would be a mistake to ascribe the widespread disapproval of rankings that most people in admissions express to sour grapes, because it is shared by people attached to institutions up and down the ranking hierarchy. Admissions directors from even the most elite schools disapprove when applicants cite rankings as their reason for wanting to attend that school, a response they see as not properly appreciative of their school's distinctiveness. Elite schools want students to aspire to them for the right reasons, not because of a number they saw in some magazine.

Two common complaints we heard from admissions staff were that rankings do not capture what is distinctive about schools and that prospective applicants rely on rankings too heavily and uncritically. One assistant dean described students as "obsessed with rankings." One professor at a top-ten school said, "I think it dumbs down students in making selections because they just look at those numbers that reflect so little, and they give them more weight than they deserve." A young law professor echoed this point: "There is a lot of misuse of that information, and the consumers are not very sophisticated about how to evaluate the source and the reliability and validity of that information. So, are there people who are misled? Yes, there are people who are misled."[15]

By not questioning the validity of rankings, students limit their searches and treat trivial differences as if they were meaningful. They also ignore important characteristics of law schools: the quality of teaching, accessibility of faculty, class size, "fit." The following complaint was typical: "Most [students] don't know anything about each school they apply to. Their decision is driven by what's the highest-ranked law school they can get into. And ranking here is largely a *USN* ranking based on, as we know, lots of crazy and fairly irrational things."

Despite administrators' belief that rankings are poor measures and that they are used uncritically, they are obliged to attend to rankings, because they *are* used. One dean explained, "I mean, I care about rankings because they hurt us if we don't get good rankings. I want to have a better ranking because it means that we'll have better students and they'll have more opportunity."

The administrators we spoke with resented what they saw as the unwelcome and ill-informed intrusion of outsiders. For them, rankings are coercive. Schools that ignore them are punished, so managing them becomes part of almost everyone's job, especially in the admissions office. "[I]t would be stupid in a competitive environment not to do the things that are better for the *USN*, if it could ultimately lead you to getting worse students overall. So the cost-benefits of making decisions cannot be done without considering what the external effect may be." And if the dean at your law school makes rising in the rankings a priority, the pressure can be intense.

Support of Rankings

Not everyone shares this dim view of rankings. A small proportion of administrators and faculty think rankings provide accessible, useful information to students. They see the denouncement of rankings as self-serving. Efforts to improve a school's ranking, they contend, are not misguided compromises or capitulation to unprofessional pressures. Rather, rankings are reasonable proxies for important features of legal education that prospective students have a right to know: status, student quality, employment opportunities, and administrative competence. Moreover, these proxies are not so different from those schools use to assess students— and themselves: test scores, grade averages, yields, graduation rates, and placement figures. And law schools need to be held accountable for their performance, not only to the American Bar Association, but also to their students.

Some characterize the many warnings that educators issue to students about the use of rankings as patronizing and self-serving. There is more than a whiff of hypocrisy in the profession's public damnation of rankings. As students point out, sometimes in stinging editorials, the same administrators that berate rankings have been ranking students each semester for generations. And grading that is based on a strict curve is not so different from ranking, is it? Supporters of rankings contend that even if rankings aren't perfect measures, they provide good enough information to students and employers, for whom they serve as inexpensive "signals" of quality that improve the efficiency of the labor market.[16]

Furthermore, rankings can be useful to schools. Schools with numbers that seem better than their reputations may benefit from the visibility that rankings provide. Also, rankings can sometimes provide useful explanations for admissions decisions. For example, it can be hard to say no when powerful alumni try to influence admissions decisions. One experienced professor who had chaired admissions committees multiple times reported:

> Every school gets involved in legacies, special admits, university president's scholars—whatever you want to call them—they are all the same thing. And one of the things that the *USN* survey has been really helpful on is that it gives us a rationale to say no. At least with respect to that, I think it has been helpful. And there are a lot more people who see that. . . . It becomes a justification for saying no or a lot of times when we should say no. . . . If you go back and look at [our] admissions fifteen years ago, we had a lot more of those special admits than we do today. And at some point we just made a decision to cut that down. [I]t had gotten out of hand. But I do think that the *USN* survey made that quite easier. These would be people who on their merits would not get in . . . students who we wouldn't accept except for the fact that someone says, "This is really important to me and I want this person admitted." Now, we are not going to admit anybody too low down, but there is a very wide range between that standard and what might otherwise be the bottom of your class. And those are the people I am talking about and we have cut down on them substantially.

A Russian law professor told us she wished they had something like law school rankings in Russia. After the dissolution of the Soviet state, proprietary law schools that are, she said, "terrible" sprang up like mushrooms. Rankings would help applicants know which schools are a waste of their time and money.

Those who are sympathetic to rankings point out the disadvantages that students face in evaluating law schools.[17] Law schools are complex and powerful organizations that skillfully market themselves to students. As is true of all organizations, insiders know far more about many aspects of the organizational field than outsiders—recent turnover, resources, future plans, conflict, and other things that reflect poorly on a school.

The boundary between what insiders know and what would-be insiders wish to know is frustrating for students who assume that more information would improve their decision. Rankings seem to shrink this gap. In reflecting the collective opinion of the profession, and in incorporating organizational statistics, rankings appear to offer students a form of inside information. Taking this seriously is not simply a way to make better decisions. It is also a way to *become* more of an insider before one gains access to the profession.

David Van Zandt, former dean of Northwestern University's School of Law, is a vocal supporter of rankings. In a published interview he said:

> I feel strongly that rankings are an important form of consumer information about a significant investment of time and money—the biggest investment of many law students' lives. My position, which is not universally shared among my peers, has always been that *U.S. News* rankings offer invaluable comparative data to anyone trying to make an informed choice. Many law school applicants take on substantial debt to pay for a legal education (often over $150,000) and devote three years of their lives to pursuing a law degree. No ranking is perfect, and reasonable people can disagree about how data is put together; if I was putting together the information to create a ranking, I would do it differently than *U.S. News* has done. Still, the *U.S. News* rankings do provide valuable information for consumers of what we law schools do. I think it is hypocritical and patronizing for us in legal education to assume that our future students lack sufficient judgment and thinking ability to be able to give such rankings the appropriate weight in their decision about which law school to attend. *U.S. News,* along with other media, has capitalized on the need to provide the information that applicants deserve to make a law school choice.

Elsewhere, Van Zandt has pointed out the irony of law schools having such low regard for students' decision-making, given that their mission is to attract people to a profession in which good judgment is a crucial capability.[18]

Van Zandt makes a good point. In response, we draw on the science studies literature that analyzes how forms of knowledge spread and become authoritative. In many ways, students' use and interpretation of rankings is unexceptional. That is, they are usually no more or less statistical dupes than most of the rest of us when it comes to using numbers. Their use of rankings reflects broad patterns in how numbers and other forms of knowledge are diffused and become legitimate.[19] As forms of knowledge, rankings have circulated broadly and enlisted many different constituents who use them for new purposes and, in so doing, recreate and embellish their meanings in ways that make it less necessary for some groups to take them apart and examine their contents. This is another way of saying that rankings have become institutionalized in different contexts such that they now appear to many to be "natural" forms of evaluation that solve many types of practical problems. Prospective students treat rankings as forms of unproblematic knowledge that solve pressing informational problems. This reinforces the authority of rankings by requiring others to attend to them, which affects the networks that link rankings to other constituencies, the infrastructure of law schools and magazines, and organizational practices. When students use rankings to help them pick a school without reflecting too closely on the ranking's methodology, they are simply doing what most people do in confronting forms of knowledge that seem secure: they take them at face value. Admissions offices are just one location inside law schools where the uses made of rankings by outside groups have led to new policies.

HOW RANKINGS CHANGE ADMISSIONS DECISIONS

So what has changed in admission policies because of this pressure to attend to rankings? A lot, it turns out. One director of admissions states, "Rankings have completely changed the application and admissions process." Even if others might consider this an exaggeration, there is no one who argues that rankings have *not* changed admissions practices. The most important effects include changes in the criteria used to evaluate applications, the allocation of scholarship money, recruitment, the use of transfers, and the structuring of part-time and probationary programs, as well as the criteria used to hire and fire admissions staff.

Managing the Numbers

There is a strong consensus among our respondents and in the law school community more broadly that the growing influence of rankings has led schools to place greater weight on "the numbers" — test scores and GPAs that rankings emphasize in the admissions process. The LSAT is intended to help predict academic success. Repeated studies have found that the median correlation between LSAT scores and first-year grades is about 40 percent, with a range from .01 to .62; for GPA, the median is .25 with ranges from .02 to .49. Combining the two raises median correlations to about .49. These measures have always mattered in admissions decisions, and most admissions staff see them as helpful indicators of future success in law school. Early pre-law guidebooks such as *Barron's Guide to Law Schools* often published tables based on GPA and LSAT scores that indicated the odds of getting into a particular school.

Since the advent of rankings, however, students' GPAs and especially their test scores have come to dominate admissions decisions in ways they never did before. One dean of admissions said, "You never take your eye off the numbers." Another director of admissions observed, "We're basically talking about LSAT and GPA scores. We'll still say all the right things, how we read applications for every factor under the sun. And in some cases people still do stand out above their credentials. But the vast majority of admissions decisions—the vast majority at every school I know—are really driven by the numbers now. So that's a big impact of *USN*."

The numbers become the default method for creating classes and making comparisons with peers. A faculty member who chaired her admissions committee explained, "I've got the list always on my bulletin board now because it tells me exactly what the twenty-five- to seventy-five-percent range is on the LSAT and GPA of all of the people that, I guess, we are competing with."

The numbers that matter most for admissions are LSAT scores. Although they account for only 12.5 percent of overall rank in the *USN* formula, their influence is disproportionate to that of GPAs because they are weighted more than grades, the latter being worth 10 percent of overall rank. Schools can manipulate LSATs more directly and quickly than measures for reputation and placement because high LSAT scores are rarer than good grades. Another point is that LSAT scores are weighted nationally, whereas high GPAs may reflect an easy course load, a less demanding institution, or grade inflation. A faculty member at a first-tier school explained:

> You're not going to be able to push your GPA up very much, and the GPA doesn't count as much as [the] LSAT anyway. And what [my school] has done is basically focus its entire decision making on [the] LSAT score. It hasn't done this formally, but the dean basically controls who is on the admissions committee and makes sure the people on the admissions committee will admit people primarily on the basis of [the] LSAT.

If one of the biggest changes initiated by rankings is greater attention to test scores, how is this attention manifested in admission offices? Mainly, law schools work extremely hard to make small improvements in applicants' test scores. Small improvements matter because rankings are so tightly bunched that even a small shift in a factor can produce a big shift in rank. Usually the pressure to improve median test scores comes from the dean. One administrator recounted, "I know some schools focus heavily on what that LSAT is. The dean will say to the admissions director, 'I want a 160.' And I've had admissions directors tell me that. 'I have been instructed to produce X if at all possible.' Well, that tells you what their admissions process is going to be like."

Another admissions director who was pressured by the dean to raise the school's median LSAT scores related:

> The University of Toledo does a symposium every year where they have deans come in and they give the status of the academy, and I have lots of quotes of people saying that they had to choose between a person with a 160 and a 3.5 and a person with a 170 and a 2.2. Well, the 160 won't help you in the *USN* but the 170 will. But realistically you think that the person with the 160 and 3.5 is more likely to succeed, but they are gaming the rankings so the 170 person gets in. It happens all the time. It happens in conversations between admissions directors and deans.

Most schools include faculty on their admissions committee; one professor recalls:

> I served on the admissions committee last year. One of the things our dean of admissions said was that "I don't care what the [faculty] committee says, I'm not sending a rejection letter to anybody with an LSAT score above 151 or 152 because I need to keep them in case I need to keep the numbers up." . . . He gets paid a large bonus for keeping the numbers up. . . . It's just an unusual thing to hear at a faculty committee, [say] "I don't care what the committee says." . . . And even if you did this, the fact that you would say it suggests to me how much the culture of numbers and rankings have spread. I'm not sure ten years ago you could have said that, to this faculty anyway.

The frustration goes both ways. Admissions personnel tend to sigh when they talk about collaborating with faculty members, some of whom they see as naïve about the impact of rankings and others who seem "obsessed" with them. One dean of admissions described how educating faculty about the costs of admitting that student with mediocre test scores "that they fell in love with" was a key part of his job. Many schools keep running tallies of the median scores of the students they admit. And as the professor just quoted suggests, directors of admission are given target median GPA and LSAT scores each year, and some receive bonuses for meeting these targets.

Some schools' response to a small shift in *USN* methods illustrates how carefully schools scrutinize their median scores.[20] For sixteen years *USN* used a school's median test score and GPA to calculate its selectivity factor. The median, a measure of central tendency, is the number that appears in the middle of scores if they are organized from lowest to highest. It is the 50th percentile: half of all scores fall below it and half above that number. Each year law schools must fill out a survey for the American Bar Association (ABA). Instead of requiring schools to record three statistics—their median, 25th- and 75th-percentile LSAT scores and GPAs—in 1996, the ABA dropped the median requirement because it was "redundant," and space in their guidebook was limited. Instead, it asked only for the 25th and 75th percentiles. This meant that there was no longer a way independently to verify the accuracy of a school's reported median, and *USN* became suspicious of how schools were calculating their medians. In 2005 *USN* devised a new selectivity statistic by averaging the 25th- and 75th-percentile numbers. The ranking of four schools dropped more than two positions as a result of this unannounced change, and Southern Methodist Law School's rank plummeted ten places, knocking them out of the top tier. The reason for such a drop was that before the change, if schools "protected their median," they could admit any student with scores below the median that they liked—say, students with interesting backgrounds, members of under-represented groups, or students with impressive accomplishments other than test scores. *USN*'s new and unannounced "hybrid statistic" subverted this policy of using broader criteria for admitting students below the median. For SMU, the difference between the new statistic, 160, and their median, 163, was the difference between being ranked forty-one and fifty-two.

Effect on Merit Scholarships

The greater emphasis on raising median LSAT scores prompted a cascade of other changes in admissions practices. One of the biggest shifts involved offering "merit" scholarships to students with high test scores. One dean of admissions said, "The biggest things that you can have an impact on [that affect your school's ranking] are the LSATs and GPA scores of the incoming students. And the main way to impact that is money. The more you spend on scholarships, the better the credentials of the class that you're going to have. And this is where I find dealing with *USN* extremely unpleasant like everybody else."

This has prompted big changes in budgets. A faculty member at a first-tier school recalled how his school tried to raise its LSAT score: "We were scrapping faculty salaries—not filling [faculty] lines, raising money out of graduate students through our LL.M. program—and all of that money was going into funding three or four hundred thousand dollars in scholarships for purely number-driven reasons. And we got the LSAT up a point or two points, and we got a dean of admissions who was, in fact, paid in part based on the numbers he brought in."

This redistribution of scholarship funds is not limited to highly ranked law schools. An admissions director described the same pattern at a fourth-tier school: "We didn't have merit scholarship awards when I left in 1996. When I came back in 2000, not only were there merit scholarships to attract students with better LSATs, but the budget for [merit scholarships] exceeded the entire financial aid budget . . . for the three years that I was there before. And that was just for one year. . . . It was phenomenally more, it was more than double."

Because budgets are complex, it is often hard to know exactly how cuts are distributed; nonetheless, many administrators in admissions explained that this increase in money spent on merit scholarships has corresponded to sharp decreases in need-based scholarships. As one admissions director commented wryly, "I have had to shift dollars away from need-based to the merit-based. The purpose of that is to pump the numbers up to get LSAT scores up. Again, this is not nuclear physics to understand." Another described the process at his school: "So we focus on how much money can we squeeze out of the budget and raise for scholarships. . . . We still have need-based scholarships, but that has shrunk significantly because we can't afford it anymore. If you don't care about your ranking, that's one thing. But law school faculties are pretty competitive minded and they want to do well and be seen as doing well. So there's not near as much money around for need-based scholarships."

Another director said that currently 25 percent of the scholarships given at his school were need-based. But he wasn't sure how long he could sustain that level: "Yes, I am getting tremendous pressure, but so far I am fighting it." A group of four admissions deans at the Law School Forum agreed that merit scholarships have all but replaced schol-arships based on need, prompting one member of the group to state somewhat defensively, "But I still give out a few need-based scholarships each year."

The emphasis on the median statistic encourages some schools to allocate scholarships according to which students' scores will improve the school's median and guesses about different students' recruitment potential. If a school's median LSAT score is, say, 155, it will do more to raise its score to offer partial scholars to three students who test 156 or 157 than to offer a full scholarship to someone with a much higher score. Moreover, students with higher test scores are harder to recruit because they will have more options. And being turned down by them hurts a school's yield statistics and delays negotiations with other, more attainable prospects.

Several deans have described the careful formulas they use to parse out their scholarship budgets. One director explained:

> I am aware of explicit discussions about not wasting scholarship offers on students you are not going to get anyway.... I would rather have three 163s than one 178 because the three 163s have a bigger impact on my median. And, yes, it's absolutely true, the 163 might have a crappy GPA, and might have a track record where they haven't done any kind of volunteer work or social commitment or [anything] like that. [But] that student in this market is very likely to get a free ride somewhere. And it won't matter what their GPA is or the rest of their record or recommendations are, as long as they didn't commit a crime, or their track record did not contain affirmative evidence that you were going to flunk out of law school.... A high LSAT score is going to get you a full ride, probably from multiple schools.

Another dean described her reaction when she first realized that the students with the top test scores weren't the ones getting the scholarships; it was those in the middle of the distribution.

> Every year at the time we make offers, I will get emails from the admissions people saying this student just got offered $15,000 at X, are we going to do anything? And I think, "Why?... It just seems odd to me because I'm used to the very best students in the pool getting offers from other places, but somebody that's got a 153 LSAT, that's not where we're aiming, but I guess it's where other people are aiming. And so I guess for a fourth-tier school, if they can get more of those students, I guess it has a little extra bump.

The increasing importance of LSAT scores because of rankings has been confirmed and elaborated by quantitative analyses conducted by law professors William Henderson and Andrew Morriss.[21] They find that the competition for high test scores has created a robust, segmented market among law schools in which students are willing to pay higher tuition to go to an elite school but are still sensitive to scholarship offers among non-elite schools. They argue that an equilibrium is emerging in which non-elite schools are adopting expensive strategies to boost their reputations while elite schools reinforce their higher status. They also find that a school's initial position in the rankings affects whether a school's median LSAT score increases or decreases over time. The medians of higher-ranked schools have risen over time and the scores of schools in the third and fourth tiers have declined.

The proliferation of merit scholarships has complicated the admissions process. Students with high LSAT scores now expect scholarship offers, especially from lower-ranked schools. Students now also use scholarships as a bargaining tool among schools, something that rarely happened before rankings. One admissions dean said: "[Some prospective students] will say, 'I have a scholarship offer from a higher-ranked school. I'll consider coming to your school but you'll have to pay more.' *USN* has turned this business into a marketplace with all the good and bad things that go along with marketplaces."

This change has clearly benefited students with good test scores while complicating the jobs of administrators who must secure and manage funds for scholarships and engage in more protracted negotiations with a few students. A longtime head of admissions at a top-tier public law school described an angry phone call he received from a student who was not offered a scholarship despite having a master's degree, a high GPA, and a 159 LSAT. It turned out that her roommate—with a 3.1 GPA, no master's degree, and a 164 LSAT—had been offered a $10,000 scholarship. This administrator said he told the unhappy student, "That LSAT score made all the difference. The roommate's LSAT score raised [the school's] median while the former was below their median, and that was what the scholarship was based on. This is completely driven by *USN*." When the prospective student responded that this was a terrible way to make such decisions, he replied, "You're right. It's bullshit. But it's not my fault." He asked her where she applied and she listed all schools in the top tier. When asked why she hadn't applied to any schools in the lower tiers, she responded that they weren't ranked well. He tried to point out the irony in all this but said it was "lost on her."

Cutting Positions and Redistributing Students

Another tactic for boosting LSAT scores and GPAs is to cut the first-year class size with the aim of eliminating the bottom scores. The dean of a top-tier school said, "So basically we got approval [from the president of the university] to keep our [budget] allocation the same and lose thirty students a year over three years. That's ninety students. What this allows us to do is to become more selective, and, indeed, it worked, and our LSAT and GPA numbers will be higher than they were last year. Not tremendously so, but noticeably so, and the chances are that it will kick us up several places in the rankings." Another dean reported that his alma mater also cut thirty students one year "in order to maintain a 160 LSAT."

Tuition revenue represents a large proportion of most law schools' budgets, so few schools can afford to cut the number of students without replacing lost revenue. Highly selective schools, often among the most wealthy, attract so many applicants with strong credentials they generally don't need to cut class size to maintain their statistics. But even some selective schools cut the first-year class size to improve their rankings. Because *USN* did not include part-time students in their selectivity statistics until 2009 (their 2010 rankings released in 2009 using 2008 data), another strategy many law schools adopted to raise their ranking and protect tuition revenue was to redistribute admitted students rather than eliminate positions. They did this in several ways.

Some schools reclassified a portion of admitted students as "probationary" and excluded their scores from the calculation of median LSAT and GPA scores. Students who were "special admits" would typically take a summer class or one less class their first year with the option of transferring into the full-time program for their second year if they did well. An associate dean at a third-tier school reported:

> I know for a fact that [school X] and [school Y] have created these artificial probation programs where students with low scores come in and they don't have to count them as part of their LSAT. That's complete nonsense. . . . They have huge numbers of people on probation and it's only in the first year, and it all disappears in the second year. And [these students] do it by taking one fewer course in the first year and then they take a makeup course in the summer. That's the rankings. We suffer because they do that and we don't.

Some schools simply admit fewer students into the full-time, day program and more students into the part-time day or evening programs. This tactic improves the median LSAT and GPA scores of the full-time students (and the student-faculty ratio, since these are also counted only for full-time students). If enough students were admitted into part-time programs, schools would not lose tuition revenue. A faculty member who chaired admissions at a top-tier school explained: "It's in the nature of any well-structured game that it's subject to strategic choice and strategic influence. So, one thing that we did was to shift students from our full-time into our part-time program, and I'm aware of other schools doing that." According to another professor, "We went from a day class of about 350 and an evening class of 120 to an evening class of 160 and day class of 320. It was not solely because we only report the day numbers, but that was certainly a factor. And I have been involved in discussions in which we have considered making efforts to cut the day class further."

Some schools were unapologetic about this tactic. Phillip Closius, dean of the University of Toledo College of Law from 1999 to 2005, helped to engineer a notable and rare ascent in the rankings, moving the school from the fourth to the second tier. Since 2007, when Closius became dean at the University of Baltimore School of Law, the school has risen from 170 to 125.[22] In both places, a key ingredient of this remarkable rise was cutting full-time and adding part-time students. Closius defends the practice, noting that some students are more likely to succeed if they start law school with fewer classes. Furthermore, *"U.S. News* is not a moral code; it's a set of seriously flawed rules of a magazine, and I follow the rules . . . without hiding anything."[23]

Schools without part-time programs see it otherwise. Some characterize the practice as "lying" and "cheating." Others complain about their relative disadvantage. Some worry that the practice creates a two-tiered system of admission that may stigmatize part-time students as less able. A faculty member from a second-tier school stated that the use of part-time students to manage numbers is "one thing that has happened that I'm very upset about."

> We used to have a unitary admissions system around here. We would admit students and then ask them if they were going to come full-time or part-time. We're not doing that anymore because part-time students don't count in the rankings. So we have situations where we'll tell students that we'll admit them, but they will have to come part-time the first semester. They have lower test scores. The evening program gives us a unique tool to recruit people, but I don't think it's a good way to do business. To me, the danger of having a part-time program is that it gets labeled as second-class. . . . This is one of the most dangerous aspects of the rankings—that we have to play games with our students.

But this professor also pointed out one of the advantages of part-time or probationary programs: they allow schools more discretion to admit promising students who "don't fit the *USN* profile but who you want" to be able to accept, but without being penalized by the rankings. The dean at this law school defended the practice as providing opportunities for students who might otherwise not be admitted. He says, "We're more willing to actually encourage some people who we might think are marginal to go part-time at first—ours is a school where you can switch from part-time to full-time."

In addition to its part-time evening classes, this school also offers summer courses so students can take one first-year course during the summer. Although the dean concedes that this program helps protect his selectivity statistics, this is not the only reason for keeping this program. The revenue generated during the summer goes directly into his discretionary account rather than to the university's budget, "so even if *USN* went away tomorrow I would keep [the program] going." The summer program actually also helps them recruit a few strong students, those who have high LSAT scores but who believe that a slower summer start and fewer fall classes will improve their grades.

Others reiterated the importance of the discretion that part-time programs provided. A dean at a second-tier school said, "We now have a larger part-time class and that is rankings-driven. And we realize that that is also an area where we have more discretion. So, just as we can admit anyone we want in the bottom 25 percent of our full-time class, our part-time class is where we can admit students who we think deserve admission but whose numbers don't show it. And we can even decide that we can't admit this person in the full-time class, so we admit them in the part-time class." Some schools report a greater proportion of minority students in their part-time programs, so there is a serious risk of a stigma being attached to students in those programs.

Quantitative analyses offer strong corroborating evidence of the spread of these tactics to manage the numbers by reducing the size of first-year cohorts. Henderson and Morriss show that between 1992 and 2004, sixty-four law schools reduced the size of their full-time entering classes, twenty-four doing so by more than 10 percent. During the same period, part-time enrollment rose dramatically.[24] Among tier-three and tier-four schools ten new part-time programs were added. And this tactic works. Median LSATs for schools in the top sixteen increased an average of 1.69 points from 1992 to 2004; for schools in the third-tier scores declined by 1.56 points, and in the fourth tier, by 1.34 points. Controlling for a school's location and starting position, Henderson and Morriss found that a shift in 10 percent of an entering class from full-time to part-time resulted in a .54 gain in a school's median LSAT.

When *USN* in 2008 first floated its proposal to include the GPAs and LSATs of part-time students in the rankings, the reactions of some schools were swift and fearful, as committees were formed and possible responses were debated.[25] They had to consider whether to shrink their part-time programs or cut them completely, whether they should admit only students with statistics similar to full-time students', and how much revenue they could afford to lose. Ellen Rutt, associate dean at the University of Connecticut Law School, predicted that the change would "catch the outliers but punish part-time programs that have existed forever and aren't doing it to game the system."[26] In 2010, the first year that this change was implemented, a number of schools with part-time programs saw significant shifts in their rankings, probably the result of the new policy. For example, Chicago-Kent College of Law dropped eleven positions in the rankings, from sixty-six to seventy-seven; the University of Connecticut School of Law fell from forty-six to a three-way tie for fifty-two, which also moved it from the top to the second tier; and the University of Toledo Law School, where Closius had so successfully improved the ranking, dropped from the second to the third tier.

It is clear that an apparently minor "tweak" in the methodology of rankings, such as including part-time students in the calculations of GPA and LSAT averages, can have big effects on a school's rank, effects that neutralize earlier tactics used to manage rankings. *USN*'s consistent efforts to improve its methodology may be commendable, but each change represents a new set of rules in this status game and leads many schools to recalibrate responses to the rankings. Obviously this can be a frustrating process. For example, the decision to include part-time programs in the rankings might have encouraged schools to scale back or cut their part-time programs (that some of them had only recently scaled up), only to find that a few years later, in 2013, *USN* began to publish a separate ranking of schools with part-time programs.

A different strategy for boosting test scores and cutting class size involves admitting transfer students after their first year. Again, because *USN* calculates median LSAT scores and GPAs on the basis of entering students, this practice allows schools to admit students as 2Ls without affecting their admissions statistics. The transfer school gets two years of tuition revenue from the student, and so with enough students transferring in, a school can make up the revenue lost from cutting 1L slots.[27] Meanwhile, the lower-ranked schools from which students transfer lose some of their best students.

Transfers are nothing new. There have always been students who switched law schools because of family circumstances, dissatisfaction, or to trade up in institutional prestige, and schools have long used transfers to compensate for attrition. But our respondents report a big increase in transfers since the advent of rankings.[28] One dean of admissions explained:

> We need a student population of three hundred students to support our unit, but if we admit one hundred students every year, then we have a tough time getting the median and the 25th- and 75th-[percentile] credentials we want in order to look good for *USN*—if we have to enroll one hundred for the entering class. So we'll only enroll eighty in the fall, we'll enroll ten over the summer, we'll enroll ten as transfer students, and then with eighty we can get to the median that put us where we want to be but we'll still have a hundred students.

Morriss and Henderson report that from 1992 to 2004 there was a 41 percent increase in the academic attrition of first-year students. In 2007 tier-one schools had 694 net transfers and tier-two schools, 223, while tier-three and tier-four schools lost a total of 114 and 739 net students, respectively. The tier-one schools who admitted the most net transfer students were Georgetown (+14 percent) and Washington University (+18 percent); from tier-two they were Florida State (+20 percent) and Rutgers-Camden (+16 percent). The biggest net losers were Thomas Cooley (–28 percent) and Valparaiso University (–18 percent). In earlier work Henderson and Morriss show that, like the increase in part-time students, the transfer strategy does improve median LSAT scores.[29] A 10 percent drop in the size of the 1L class corresponded to a .37 gain to the median.[30]

The growing significance of transfer students is reflected in the institutionalization of practices that cater to them. Law schools' transfer policies have become more routine and extensive. Some schools now regularly send letters to students who were close calls in admissions, encouraging them to reapply next year if they do well their first year at another school. We suspect that students of color are more likely to receive such letters. A law professor told us: "I had fifteen students in my first-year class who got letters in January from [one top-ten ranked school]: 'We were sorry we weren't able to accommodate you, we know you were on the waitlist last year and expressed interest in enrolling. If you've enrolled in law school, please consider us as a transfer. Enclosed is our transfer application, we've waived your fee, we have your LSDAS report on file.' "

Indeed, this professor said that the school in question, a top-fifteen law school, was quite open about this practice. Most schools now include policies and advice for transfer students on their websites. Many have student organizations and mentors devoted to helping transfer students integrate into their community. Some reserve editorial spots on law reviews and journals for them. They provide them with supportive letters for recruiters. There are now many blogs and bulletin boards devoted to discussing transfers, and, perhaps most telling, law school admissions consultants now advertise their expertise in helping students transfer.

Schools who admit transfer students defend the practice as providing opportunities for deserving students. First-year grades, the most important consideration for admitting transferring students, are a better predictor of passing the bar than the LSAT or GPA.[31] Advocates argue that students who perform well should be allowed to transfer to a better school if they wish because their careers will benefit from the broader range of career opportunities, better access to employers, better students, and the status of their new school. And, like part-time admissions earlier, admitting transfer students offers schools the luxury of focusing on other qualities in composing their classes.

Critics, however, see these transfer policies as yet another cynical attempt to game rankings. One administrator told us, "It is not a terribly well-kept secret that many upper-tier schools or aspiring upper-tier schools will take no chances at all on their entering classes and then will raid places like here for students of color who have done well and give them lots of money and take them in. Then they can report that their overall student population has diversity, even though their first-year class looks very white."

Schools who lose their top students—students they worked to recruit, those most likely to become law review editors, get the best jobs, pass the bar on their first try, and offer diverse backgrounds or perspectives—resent this "poaching." Is it good for students and for legal education, they ask, to prolong admissions so that it lasts two years? To encourage students to become less invested in their first year? To endure the disruption that transferring inevitably brings? Students with an eye toward trading up will no doubt work hard to achieve good grades, but they also may invest less heavily in their first school and its community. Those who switch will have missed opportunities to forge durable friendships, create stable study groups, and get to know faculty. Other critics suggest that schools who admit students with lesser credentials as transfer students risk "diluting their brand" with potential employers.[32]

Transfer students offer mixed reviews of their experiences.[33] A blogger who reported transferring from a part-time program at a "low top tier" school to a "top-ten school" to improve her chances of getting a job at a "big elite firm" encouraged others contemplating transferring to "dream big." "It is possible," she writes almost breathlessly, "to climb the *USNWR* by leaps and bounds—I am proof." She concludes her advice to potential transfer students by recounting all the privileges that come with more prestigious schools, privileges that had been unavailable to her at her former school. But, she says, "I will be the first to say that the law school hierarchy imposed by both the profession and the *USNWR* sucks, but part of being in the legal profession is learning how to play the game and use things to your advantage."[34]

Rankings have also changed how admissions staff manage their waitlists.[35] In the past, students who accepted waitlist offers would typically opt for the better law school. What "better" means is now precisely defined by *USN*. An experienced admissions director at a top-ten law school reported that she has never lost a student to a lower-ranked school as a result of a waitlisted offer and has only lost students to higher-ranked schools.

We were told that when rankings were new, some schools would submit their numbers to *USN* before admitting students from the waitlist. This improved median scores but left students dangling, forcing some to make last-minute cross-country moves and to search frantically for an apartment. After *USN* cracked down on this practice by publishing lists of schools who reported different statistics to the ABA than to *USN*, schools responded by meticulously tracking the median numbers of their admitted and waitlisted students, which changed which criteria were emphasized. One administrator explained:

> I think schools are much more concerned about median LSAT and GPA averages than they were before, especially when it comes to the waitlist. . . . Usually with the waitlist you are dealing with candidates who are not as good as the students that you admitted in the first instance, that's almost inevitable. But what you're trying to do, I think, is—let's say that your median as you approach the last ten admissions decisions that you make, suppose you have a 165 LSAT and a 3.50 GPA. The logical people to admit, and you probably have some on your waiting list, are people who have 164s and 3.45s, but if you admit ten or twelve or fifteen of those you may pull your medians down to those numbers. If instead you find people who had a 166 LSAT and a 2.7 GPA, you can stabilize your medians, but you're admitting a handful of high-risk students who are not as good as the ones that you are not admitting off of the waitlist and you are doing it simply to exploit the statistical anomaly that they [*USN*] use medians instead of means.

The rankings statistic on yield is the difference between offers and what one director called "butts in the seats." One tactic for protecting yields is to screen for the level of interest in actually attending the school. Schools also use waitlists to help with this. One head of admissions at a third-tier school reported:

> What you do now is if you have a student who you think is good but you don't know if you are going to take them or they are on a waitlist and we want to take them at the end, we don't send them a letter saying, "Now you're admitted," we call them and ask, "Are you still interested in [our school]?" Because we don't want our selectivity numbers to go down. So you spend man-hours doing this stuff. It consumes people's minds when we could be thinking about other things than how these issues will affect *USN*.

A dean of admissions at a second-tier public law school reported that although they still "sometimes" admit students who obviously consider them a "safety school," they are wary of stellar applicants:

> If [an in-state resident] expressed interest in us, what will happen is if they apply to us and we are clearly their safety school, then we will follow up

and try to call them or send them an email and tell them we are very interested in them and ask them if they are seriously interested in us. If they don't respond to us, we don't admit them. If they respond, then we admit. Because even if we're their safety school, if they are interested enough that they respond then we go ahead. We do at least one or two outreach things to those people. But if they don't respond, then we know that we were one of a hundred applications that they sent out and they aren't really interested. And then some people are so fabulous that it would be wrong not to admit them—they paid their fifty dollars, their application was fabulous, they wrote a great essay, you can't in good conscience not admit that person.

An experienced dean of admissions reported that at his former school, his dean pressured him to reject strong applicants who seemed unlikely to accept. Offended by this technique for "protecting the yield," this man threatened to quit, and his dean backed down.

Heike Spahn, an admissions consultant and former admissions officer at the University of Chicago Law School, describes how volume affects waitlists. Applications to law schools have declined in recent years. Spahn suggests that "schools might make fewer outright admissions offers and then use their waitlist to round out their classes." He says,

> It's a question of admissions statistics. Schools don't want to see an increase in their acceptance rates. So if there are fewer applicants this year, I think most schools will initially focus on admitting about the same percentage of students that they have in past years and then fill out enrollment with the waitlist, which generally provides a better yield. For example, say there's a school that received five thousand applications last year and admitted five hundred people. That's a 10 percent acceptance rate. If the same school only gets forty-five hundred applications this year, it would still hope to maintain its 10 percent acceptance rate. That would mean initially admitting only four hundred fifty people.

Being placed on a waitlist can be a nail-biting experience for students. A former student's experience illustrates the trauma. After enrolling at a West Coast school and signing a lease on an apartment, she received a last-minute offer from a higher-ranked school in the Midwest. With just days to decide, she opted for a cross-country move the week before law school began, which involved losing her security deposit, having just two days to find a new apartment, and starting law school in a daze. Overall, rankings have resulted in considerable churning among cohorts.

Cultivating Rejection

Because 2.5 percent of a school's rank is determined by its acceptance rate — the ratio of applicants to admitted students — schools have also devised strategies for lowering this ratio. One obvious tactic involves increasing the number of applicants by, for example, making it easier or cheaper to apply, developing more accessible electronic admissions, and waiving application fees. An admissions dean told us: "One of the things we tried to do was we tried to be more aggressive in increasing our applicant pool. We made a major effort [with] the website and we made a major effort [with] electronics. We got the university to commit to letting us have applying free online. So that helped. We made the website a lot more informational, a lot more functional, a lot more attractive, all those kinds of things; we started mass emailings."

Schools also market heavily to prospective students who have taken the LSAT. A few schools have adopted the dubious practice of soliciting applications from prospective students whose scores make them extremely unlikely to be admitted just to improve the selectivity statistic. One professor reported that a friend's son's undistinguished test scores and grades fell well below the typical range of one law school. Nevertheless, this young man received a letter from the admissions department strongly urging him to apply. The father contacted the admissions director who "more or less admitted what was going on," that the school was courting applications to reject in order to improve its acceptance rate. The law professor and sociologist Richard Lempert notes that schools that actively discourage unqualified applicants in an effort to make the process more humane and efficient are penalized for doing so.[36]

Variations in Strategies Among Schools

It is unremarkable for organizations to adapt old practices for new aims. The use of class size, part-time programs, transfers, waitlists, and scholarships to manipulate admissions statistics represents a broadening of uses rather than a more fundamental innovation (although the algorithms some schools use in admissions decision are relatively new tools in the admissions office toolkit). It is, however, much more rare to find so much effort expended on adapting practice for what most see as a dubious goal. The LSAT, first administered in 1948, was initially conceived of as a "law capacity test," a tool to shrink attrition by screening applicants unlikely to complete law school. William P. LaPiana has suggested that its creators would likely be appalled at its recent use to attack affirmative action. They would likely also be baffled that the test has become tantamount to a measure of "merit" and the basis of a vast change in the way scholarship money is distributed.[37]

Admissions officers have an array of strategies for improving the statistics that the *USN* uses to create its rankings. But all of these strategies are not all available to all parties. Some schools can cut class size without compensatory revenue, but how they make up for this lost revenue varies. Most elite schools don't have part-time programs, so it is the lesser-ranked schools that have shunted students into part-time programs. But because students virtually always transfer up, students at lower-tier schools transfer into higher-tier ones. As students become more sophisticated about the privileges of rank, they are more likely to consider transferring up the rankings food chain for smaller improvements. Highly ranked schools in cities with multiple law schools enjoy advantages because students can avoid the trauma of moving long distances. The lower tuition of highly ranked public schools for in-state residents is appealing to students from lower-ranked private schools in the same state. Moving its median can give an edge to Yale in its competition with Harvard, or to smaller schools over bigger public ones, but it is much harder for schools with big classes to move the median.

THE PRICE OF HIGHER TEST SCORES: DIVERSITY CONCERNS

These efforts to improve LSAT scores come at a price, of course. Our respondents worried about how these changes affected who gets into law school. In nearly every interview, admissions staff talked about their concern that strategies for improving their statistical profile affected the diversity of law students at their schools and access to the legal profession by all social groups.[38] Views like the following were common:

> The most pernicious change is that I know a lot of schools who have become so driven by their LSAT profile that they've reduced the access of people who are nontraditional students. I think that more than anything else has been a pernicious effect.... Particularly, the higher [the] echelon [where] you are, the more worried you are that if you let your student numbers slide to reflect your commitment to diversity, you're going to be punished in the polls for that.

It is well established that some groups perform less well on some standardized tests than others.[39] In discussing this fact it is crucial to emphasize that these patterns are measures of central tendency that necessarily obscure variation. Generally on standardized tests, men score better than women; whites and Asian Americans do better than African Americans, Mexican Americans, Native Americans, and Puerto Ricans; and people living in the Northeast do better than those from the Southeast. One study found that the LSAT mean scores for men were consistently about 1.47 points higher than for women. For 2003–2004, the mean for Caucasians was 155.37, for Asian Americans 152, for Mexican Americans 147.4, for Native Americans 148.49, for African Americans 142.43, and for Puerto Ricans 138.44. Minorities who were not Asian Americans scored roughly between one and one and one-half standard deviations (10 points) or more below white students. Average regional scores were 153.52 in New England and 147.23 in the Southeast.[40]

The legal profession has been grappling with how to encourage greater numbers of minority applicants for decades. In light of the profession's shameful record of minority representation and pressure from faculty, students, and civil rights groups, in 1981 the ABA adopted Standard 212 that made minority admissions and retention an accreditation standard.[41] This standard helped to expand minority recruitment and the adoption of affirmative action policies that produced slow but gradual improvement in the number of applications to law school by members of minorities through the 1980s and mid-1990s.[42] But the early 1990s saw drops in the enrollment of some groups, notably African Americans and Mexican Americans. Despite improving grades and test scores and an additional four thousand seats in law schools, enrollment of African Americans and Mexican Americans combined decreased by about 8.6 percent from 1992 to 2005. Conrad Johnson, a professor at Columbia University Law School, has helped publicize these declines on the website *Disturbing Trends in Law School Diversity*.[43] Ronald Roach charges that rankings have contributed to this decline:

> Law schools are paying a lot of attention to the *U.S. News & World Report* rankings, and, as a result, they are over-relying on the LSAT. . . . This over-reliance and trend has played out in a number of ways. One is the decrease of inclusivity of African Americans and Mexican Americans and that's reflected in their numbers and percentages within entering classes but also in the shut-out rates as you compare different ethnic groups.[44]

Partly in response to these declines, the ABA and the LSAC jointly launched a broad array of initiatives to "expand the pipeline" of minority recruitment and to increase efforts to educate schools about the danger of too narrowly focusing on LSAT scores.[45]

The importance of considering race in admissions in order to maintain minority enrollments is well established. Studies repeatedly show that sustained minority enrollment depends on schools using factors other than GPA and LSAT scores in admission decisions. Furthermore, the LSAT is a poor predictor of becoming a successful lawyer. Linda Wightman found that the graduation rates of black students who would not have been admitted to law school had the decision been restricted to these two quantitative indicators was 78 percent.[46] Lempert concludes from his study of University of Michigan Law School graduates that although the LSAT and GPA are for many schools "the most prominent admissions screens [they] have almost nothing to do with measures of achievement after law school."[47]

Studies also reveal persistent class effects.[48] Students from wealthy or middle-class families do better on the LSAT than those from working-class or poor families, and younger applicants score higher than older students returning to law school after working or starting families. Race is correlated with class because minority students disproportionately come from poorer families. Explaining these persistent "test gaps" has proved challenging, partly because different reasons pertain to different groups. Returning students may find it hard to carve out the time and energy to study, and their test-taking skills may be rusty. Wealthier applicants have accumulated years of privileges that may include better schools and counseling, the time and money for test-prep classes or private tutoring, high expectations, and the confidence that these can be met. A law professor at a prominent school told us that it was not unusual for students at her school to have taken an entire year off after college to study for the LSAT. Some of these students were supported for the entire year by their parents, so they wouldn't have to be distracted by holding even a part-time job.

Furthermore, test anxiety is not distributed evenly. Racial, gender and class gaps in LSAT scores also reflect debilitating expectations about what testing will reveal about you. The social psychologist Claude Steele and his colleagues have found that people experience what he calls "stereotype threat" when their identities are linked to negative stereotypes associated with their group.[49] The anxiety this generates affects their performance in ways that are consistent with that stereotype, which results in a pernicious self-fulfilling prophecy. This pattern pertains to many groups in many circumstances. For members of racial minorities, women, and working-class people, the anxiety arising from stereotype threat can lead to poor performance on standardized tests.[50] By creating strong incentives for law schools to focus more narrowly on test scores, rankings make it seem more risky to admit diverse students when those students tend to have lower test scores.

Rankings also ratchet up the already intensive competition among schools for poorer students and students of color who do have high scores. An administrator and law professor observed, "The thing [the ranking] does is that it induces some constituencies—particularly the faculty—to be very anxious, to focus admissions on students with high LSAT scores. That's probably the single most pernicious consequence of the *USN* survey. It puts enormous pressure on law schools to become homogeneous and to all compete for the same students."

Administrators say they often feel forced to choose between a higher median LSAT score and a more diverse student body, a decision that the rankings have made much more acute than in the past: "What I would say is that how much people are willing to take a risk in the admissions process, or how diverse they will become, or whether a school is willing to take one more student who if you take that one student puts you at a tipping point where it changes what your bottom quarter or your top quarter looks like, I think it does have that effect, absolutely. Yeah, I think it has [a homogenizing] effect."

Administrators describe performing "balancing acts" between goals that are often conflicting. A faculty member at a first-tier school explained:

> We're making it much more difficult for those who aren't upper-middle-class kids to get into law school. Because there is clearly a correlation between family income and how you do on that test—whether you can afford preparation on that test. I teach half the students in a tax class every year and I've always done a poll, which I use for pedagogic reasons, where I'm correlating family income to attitudes toward valuated tax issues like progressive rate structure. And I don't do it anymore because last year in my class there was only one person who indicated that their family income was less than $40,000. The school has always been somewhat that way, but it has been much more extreme in the last few years.

An assistant dean of student affairs at a second-tier school said, "My perspective is that LSAT scores are very closely tied to socioeconomic factors. I know that I spent a lot of money and time preparing for the LSATs. I took the Kaplan course twice before I took the exam. But I was fortunate because my parents could afford to pay for the course. So as much as there is a correlation between racial, ethnic, and socioeconomic identity, there is going to be a clear fallout there."

One faculty member told us, "We have set up a system where we can develop a balance in our class where a quarter of the class is high GPA and low LSAT, a quarter of the class has high LSATs and low GPA, a quarter has both, and a quarter is students who we want." A law professor noted that rankings do not reward schools that do a good job with diversity, saying:

> I think the rankings miss something. I think that one thing that I always thought was terrible [is that] there are some pretty good schools that really outdistance everyone in terms of the diversity of their student body ... and that's not factored into the rankings as a meaningful part of it, and I think that *should* be a criteri[on] of excellence of law schools. And I think it's shameful that USN doesn't value it high[ly] enough to include the diversity of the student body as one aspect of whether it is an academically excellent student body. When you see schools [that] year after year after year are pushing thirty percent entering class student diversity and [you] know that a large component of that is black and Hispanic, as well as Asian, you see schools that are doing something right. And I think they illustrate that high academic standing and good, strong diversity dovetail and support one another. And I think USN is out to lunch in not insisting on that as a criteri[on] because they could have a huge socially beneficial impact if they would [add to] their criteria some of those important factors.

The balancing acts that admissions offices perform include juggling multiple and sometimes competing goals and values, and the concept of diversity has come to encompass many different attributes: race, class, family background, legacy, geography, sexual orientation, undergraduate major, interest in a legal specialty, special accomplishments (in art, athletics, public service, business, etc.), and being the pet candidate of a powerful person. We can't say precisely how rankings have affected admissions for different groups because we don't have the quantitative data that would allow us to isolate the independent effects of rankings. Nevertheless we can be certain that USN rankings have become a powerful new force in legal education that shapes how schools balance these factors, and this in turn affects how opportunities to attend law school are distributed.

Some suggest that all this concern over diversity is misplaced because of the "magic of the median." USN uses the median, the number that cuts the distribution of LSAT scores and grades in half, rather than the mean in its admissions statistics. The median is more forgiving of outliers in a distribution than the mean and is more useful to law schools. They are not worried about outliers, since outliers at the top are good and outliers at the bottom are almost never admitted to most schools. More important, the median permits much more latitude, since schools can admit students below the median without affecting the number too much. Just how many students can be admitted below the median without causing the number to drop depends on the distribution of test scores. If the distribution is a bell curve, more students with lower test scores can be admitted below the median without moving the number much.[51] Some schools take advantage of this statistical bias to admit "whomever we want" below the median. Others are concerned that even though *USN* uses the median to calculate statistics, they also publish the 75th and 25th percentiles. So the fear is that students will infer that a lower 25th percentile will translate to a less selective and therefore less desirable school. These schools "protect the 25th." Some schools have developed sophisticated regression models to use in admissions while others simply adopt a policy of balancing below-the-median scores with above-the-median scores. The trick here, of course, is that admissions offers are more likely to be accepted by applicants whose scores are below the median than those with scores above it; consequently, either more applicants with above-median scores must be admitted or above-the-median students must be offered scholarship money. But regardless of the statistical implications, the fact that so many administrators believe that rankings hurt diversity and threaten an important professional ideal has significant consequences for admission practices.

In legal education today, students who test well are more likely to be admitted to more prestigious schools, offered scholarships, and recruited more vigorously than students who do not. Conversely, students who do not test well are less likely to be admitted to prestigious schools, are more likely to be admitted to part-time programs, and are less likely to receive scholarships, regardless of their impressive accomplishments. Schools that "take a hit" to their ranking because they accept applicants with lower grades and test scores are likely to lose some of their best students, especially their students of color and those from economically disadvantaged families, to higher-ranked schools because these students will tend to transfer. The practices used to boost admission statistics represent just one way in which status relations in legal education are reproduced and strengthened.

THE JOB OF ADMISSIONS

When we asked admissions officers what they find satisfying in their work, several themes emerged. They are proud of their school and its role in the legal profession. They take pleasure in watching the students they admitted thrive and enjoy successful careers. Many keep a mental list of students they admitted who made good: made partner in a big firm or became a respected judge, famous law professor, politician, or public advocate. They remember the risks that paid off and the students who succeeded despite long odds. They talk of providing opportunities to people without many. They speak of the creativity and satisfaction of assembling what they call "a balanced class." Just what balance means may differ among schools, but it always involves admitting students with a range of backgrounds and professional goals.

For many admissions professionals, these goals seem threatened by rankings. The pressure that rankings generate to boost selectivity scores and acceptance rates has, not surprisingly, changed the jobs of people who work in admissions offices. Time and attention are scarce resources in any organization. Since the advent of rankings, admissions staff have had to allocate these differently. Most obviously, they spend more time monitoring their own and their competitors' selectivity statistics and devising strategies to boost these. Rankings have also changed how staff understand the resources at their disposal. Now that financial aid is often seen as a device for boosting test scores, those who make aid decisions have become more intimately connected with schools' projects for their own upward mobility in the rankings. And greater emphasis is now placed on recruiting students who can "move the median"—students who might be persuaded to trade money for law school status. Financial aid is often accompanied by elaborate courting rituals, including phone calls from professors and staff, lots of email, and special websites. An experienced director told us that if admitting students has become more mechanical—so much so that he could "admit a class over the weekend"—recruiting them is now much more time consuming.

Many admissions people complained that the strategies used to improve rankings have made their jobs less appealing. They say the numbers dominate in ways they never did before rankings and that admission decisions now involve less discretion. Numbers often trump experience, judgment, or even professional principles. One hallmark of this profession has been autonomy and authority that is rooted in specialized expertise. But as numbers have come to matter more, the work of admissions has become more mechanical and less professional, and this can present uncomfortable ethical dilemmas.

A number of admissions people concede that they admit students that they believe are a bad fit for their school because their test scores are above the median. One dean said, "We are now torn between decisions that will bring a better class and a class that does better according to *USN*.... There was this student with a 162 LSAT score (high for this school) and a low GPA. I thought this guy was probably immature, a slacker ... but I couldn't pass on that score so I admitted him." Another dean of admissions reported, "So we're actually deliberately admitting a student who [our own] study predicts has a lesser chance of succeeding than the student [with lower test scores]. So I think it has been really horrible for the reasons that I've mentioned that we've rejiggered our admissions."

As admissions has become more oriented to numbers, experienced admissions personnel have been replaced by individuals who have stronger quantitative skills and, perhaps, fewer qualms about the implications of such an approach. We heard numerous accounts of long-serving admissions personnel being eased out of their positions or even fired for not producing the desired numbers. One former dean stated:

> We started this huge—by our standards—scholarship program to try to get higher-LSAT-number students. And this effectively drove out our dean of admissions . . . who did not believe that you admit on numbers alone, and we were convinced that that was how we would get our rankings up, even though the evidence shows that it wasn't exactly true and it wasn't that big of a factor. But, nevertheless, it was the one we felt we could change. . . . And we got the LSAT up a point or two points, and we got a dean of admissions who was in fact paid in part based on the numbers he brought in.

For many, it is not only the loss of discretion and the greater job pressures that are at stake in raising stats. Many feel they are being forced to compromise their professional values. One anxious respondent told us:

> I think for everybody—this is confidential, right?—I don't know how many people would say this, but I think there is this real schizophrenic atmosphere right now where there's huge humanitarian and selfless wishing the LSAT away because it seems to penalize certain groups of people. And I think that most admissions officers really care about the face of legal education. . . . There is tremendous pressure from faculty, from deans, from students themselves in that because it is the only quantitative measure that is across landscapes.

Clearly, the emphasis on rankings has ratcheted up pressure on admissions staff. To the extent that the quality of a class is judged primarily by numbers, it is easy for anyone to judge how well admissions staff have done their job. One administrator said, "You live and die by your numbers." And because admissions administrators have less status than faculty they often get blamed when rankings drop. One director of admissions told us, "We can easily be used as scapegoats when we drop in the rankings." Another said, "I think there's a morale problem that happens and I think the pressure on admissions people is really horrendous. As though an admissions person makes all the decisions and, secondly, that they can have that much influence on who comes or why they come or who hears about their school and why they do."

This pressure can be acute, even for those schools resolving to resist the dominance of "the numbers": "We still don't do it by the numbers," said an admissions director, "and there is a lot of tension among different members of the committee about how much numbers should matter, but I think everyone has more of a feeling of looking over your shoulder at what's happening to the numbers. And that just never used to happen."

Many in admissions also worried that the people who are now entering admissions positions are not professionalized to the same extent as in the past. "Just like for faculty, where it takes a long time to become a good and effective scholar, it is also true for admissions: it's hard to break in somebody," said one dean. "And there are a lot of deans who are looking to take the art out of admissions and create a science. That's what a lot of people are doing and a lot of long-time people are leaving."

One consequence of this lack of socialization of admissions personnel is that newcomers to admissions do not learn (or do not care about) the unwritten ethical codes that once characterized this field. They are much more likely, for example, to boast about their school's ranking or make direct comparisons between schools, practices that were shunned in the past.

Finally, we were told that the admissions profession has become more volatile since rankings. One of our interviewees reported, "I have colleagues who've been fired because of the rankings." A dean of admissions compared the job to that of an athletic coach who must produce results quickly or get fired:

> As far as incentives go, it was basically, "It's your model. We are giving you the money to do it. You do it. If you don't do it, you're fired." It's like you are a basketball coach. For admissions professionals, USN has made their jobs much more like [those of] athletic coaches—we could still have a winning season and be canned. I have colleagues right now—and I don't want to say at what school—but they brought this clown in, and I call him a clown because he violated our agreed-upon code of ethics and that is you don't make invidious comparisons to other schools.

It seems plausible that if people are fired for their failure to produce the desired numbers, then producing the desired numbers will be heavily emphasized when a school chooses that person's replacement. This further reinforces and institutionalizes these changes to admissions work. An administrator told us:

> I had a friend who I actually trained who left [admissions] to work for a law firm because the school she was at had a formula: for every two you admit

above the median you could only admit one below. They had figured out this mathematical formula and this was just last year. And a lot of people who are new to law school admissions are fairly recent graduates and they are being hired to bolster the hiring numbers. I told one of my deans that we needed to hire someone and I was very specific about the skill set I needed, and he asked me if I thought we could hire one of our graduates because it would help bolster our [placement] numbers.

Administrators with long experience feel the changes most acutely. They resent the more managerial approach and the loss of discretion in admissions. For some, the stress keeps them up nights. For others, the monotony of the more mechanistic admissions process is dispiriting. For many, the job has become less rewarding, and they worry about the long-term consequences of the dominance of rankings and the over-reliance on test scores.

Not all admissions people feel this way, of course. The lucky ones work at schools where deans are less concerned to improve rankings. These are often comfortably secure elites or schools who bravely reject status in favor of a populist or religious mission. But outside these exceptions, there is a growing contingent of admissions people who were hired to produce numbers and accept the numbers' dominance as the way things are done. For them, the hand-wringing of the old-timers sounds like nostalgia or even an admission of irrelevance. Like the young who are bemused by their technologically impaired superiors, they sense that time and their competence at managing the numbers are on their side.

THE CONSEQUENCES OF UNINTENDED CONSEQUENCES

These changes in admissions practices all devolved from *USN*'s effort to create a reasonable measure for the relative selectivity of law schools. The indicator that *USN* produced was made up of numbers that every law school routinely collects, numbers that have always mattered. Prospective law students used these statistics to decide where to go to law school. But the use of this new product brought about other changes that were mostly unintentional, changes that began in admissions offices and spread throughout law schools and across constituents. Rankings came to shape how prospective students think about the status of law schools and introduced powerful new incentives. It is important to consider how these shifts in organizational practices led to broader, often troubling, consequences.

In admissions, the most significant consequence of rankings is to amplify the importance of "the numbers." This shift in emphasis initiated a cascade of other effects. Rankings have changed what admissions officers pay attention to, how they allocate resources, which students are admitted to which kinds of law schools, how schools recruit and sort students into programs, and why students transfer. Rankings have led to refigured budgets as scholarship money has been reallocated. All lines in a budget must now must compete with lines that pay for activities that might raise rankings. In the language of organizational theory, one of the core decision premises in admissions offices is how proposals might intentionally or inadvertently affect a school's rank.

The precision of rankings makes it easier for outsiders to judge admissions staff. Rankings seem to offer a peek into the less public parts of a law school. For students this "back-stage" glimpse helps them predict their odds of admission—and so, their futures. For faculty, other administrators, and their bosses, admissions statistics are tantamount to performance measures, tangible goals, tools for manipulating rankings, or identifying someone to blame. Rankings may permit a limited access to the "back stage" of law schools, but staff have also learned to be guarded about the various strategies they have developed to manipulate rankings. There are more secrets since rankings emerged as a powerful force in legal education; there is also more suspicion, and a new sense of wariness and even embarrassment in acknowledging how much time the management of these measures consumes. Often only at the end of interviews did we learn the nitty-gritty of how some of this gets done. Most people were less reluctant to talk about their former employers than about their current one.

Commensuration makes obvious and reifies even tiny differences in admissions statistics. Statistically meaningless differences become real and powerful. The difference between 160 and 162 is useless for predicting success but pivotal for breaking a five-way tie in rank. And those two points never hint at what may be radically differently lives. Commensuration obscures important, relevant differences. Even if rankings have escalated the competition for students with the best statistics, the endpoint is mostly the same: the winners win more and the losers lose most.

Phillip Closius, the dean at the University of Baltimore Law School, insists that the *USN* rankings are not a "moral code." He's right. They are the product of an algorithm. But one does not need to spend much time in an admissions office to see that the algorithm makes ethical demands on those who cater to it.

Chapter 5 | Rankings at the Top: Inside the Dean's Office

ROBERT INVITED US into his office, interrupting his tightly scheduled day to answer our questions about rankings. The office had the usual displays of power—big windows, dark wood, a polite but firm assistant guarding his door. Robert's professional biography is the stellar record required of a dean: a J.D. from a top law school, clerk for a federal judge, an associate at a large law firm, followed by tenure at a first-tier law school. Robert has been associate dean or dean at a handful of schools scattered around the country, schools with rankings ranging from the top twenty-five to the fourth tier. His administrative history almost exactly spans that of rankings; he remembers when they were launched; since then he has watched them infiltrate law schools and has managed their growing influence for vastly different kinds of law schools. Like most deans, Robert now sees rankings as tangible, forceful, and nearly impossible to dislodge or unsettle.

Because of Robert's broad experience and the generous access he permitted, we interviewed him twice and spent several days at his law school interviewing staff and faculty. We have also listened to him speak on panels, at workshops, and during coffee breaks at professional meetings. Robert has thought about rankings a lot and summarizes his views: "The effects are horrendous. . . . What is the purpose of it? Every point in the measurement system has its arbitrariness, and if you add ten arbitrary variables and get a ranking from it, it still doesn't tell you anything that is valuable."

He is hardly alone in his views. In this chapter we closely examine how deans view and respond to the rankings. We show how rankings influence the deans' jobs; how deans view rankings in relation to their schools, colleagues, jobs, and themselves; and, on a more personal level, how rankings insidiously come to affect their own thinking and self-perception.

THE JOB: HOW DEANS TALK ABOUT
WHO THEY ARE AND WHAT THEY DO

No one feels the pressure of rankings more acutely than deans. Like CEOs of big companies, deans are the public face of law schools. In consultation with faculty and upper administration, they make key strategic decisions about what their school's future should look like and how to get there. And, receiving more advice than they would sometimes prefer—from groups ranging from trustees to blogging students—deans oversee and manage "the numbers" that *USN* turns into the rankings that are sent out into the world to be noticed and bought.

Rankings and the numbers used to calculate them create new kinds of decisions and trade-offs for deans who hope to boost or maintain their school's ranking. Should the school invest more in scholarships or marketing? Shrink the size of the entering class? Recalculate employment figures according to looser standards? Start an LL.M. program to raise discretionary funds? They must even decide whether they will misrepresent their numbers or encourage lower-level administrators to engage in "creative accounting" or even fraud. These are the kinds of decisions that land on a dean's desk, and nearly every dean finds them distressing, distasteful, and sometimes dispiriting.

When deans describe their job to strangers like us, it is in a rich language that sounds more pragmatic than lofty. They are managers, institution builders, caretakers, people who shake things up, build on traditions, make connections, answer email (endlessly, with lots of anonymous help), attend meetings, and sometimes make mistakes. Their job, as many see it, is to make it possible for students, scholars, and staff to thrive, to take their school to the "next level." They do so by recruiting and rewarding talent, and the opposite: denying tenure, firing, or selectively encouraging retirement. Deans work to build the school's reputation, raise money, raise standards, build "brands," sustain intellectual communities, and try to create good value for their students. They are problem solvers, morale builders, instigators, catalysts, and flak catchers. They are also teachers, scholars, and lawyers in addition to being administrators. And they are all extremely busy.

When talk shifts from their jobs to their institutions, their tone subtly changes as they adopt a more expressive vocabulary of legacies, communities, privileges of office, and pride. There is less about particular projects and plans, hoped-for or realized accomplishments, and more reflection on qualities that bind, what is shared or singular in their schools, what is durable or fragile. Talk is more deliberative, with more pauses in their speech, something noticeable only because they are enviably articulate people who tend to speak in paragraphs. Deans are often witty or sardonic when speaking of "the faculty" or "the central administration," but this tone changes when they describe their school as an institution or a community; they use language in which their agency is muted.

Talk of rankings evokes yet another vocabulary and emotional tenor, one that is vivid, specific, and feels personal. It seems less guarded. Maybe this is partly a response to being interviewed, with repeated reassurances of confidentiality, about a particular topic for our research project. We ask the questions, after all. But almost regardless of what questions we pose, rankings take on a specific role in our interviews. Agency is transposed by deans from themselves and their colleagues to "*the* rankings," never "*our* rankings." Rankings are imposed, agentive; rankings *act on* deans and schools. They pressure deans, alarm their students, produce effects. And rankings can compel deans—or, more often discussed in interviews, their colleagues—to make choices that would otherwise be unthinkable. Words not uttered in public come up often in our interviews, marking a clear verbal boundary between rankings and everything else we talk about—words like "evil," "sinful," "lying," "cheating," "abomination," or, Robert's word, "horrendous."

Deans like Robert resent the time and energy they spend thinking about rankings. They feel bound by them. Most wish they would just go away. And they recognize that as wishful thinking. As Robert said, "We can't make them go away. We don't control them. I would say that the bottom line on rankings is that they are here and you've got to deal with them." So, deans feel forced to manage these numbers as best they can. Boards of trustees, state legislators, university presidents, employers, alumni, and prospective students and their parents are all external groups with opinions about rankings, groups that possess the resources that make them matter. Deans worry about how these groups might respond to a decline in rankings, and this anxiety drives many of the changes that rankings have introduced into legal education. Robert adds a warning: "If you are consumed with trying to affect your outcome on these rankings, you are certain to do a bad job as a law school. The schools that are successful in the long run are those that care about the quality of what they are doing as opposed to manipulating the system." But the powerful incentives that rankings create make it difficult for deans to take the long view.

Deans also worry about the constituents they see regularly; students, faculty, and other administrators also scrutinize rankings, and they may demand, sometimes vociferously, that "something" be done about them. These groups may not command the same kinds of resources as university presidents or hiring partners at big law firms, but deans still cannot avoid them and their opinions.

Rankings force deans to become masters of impression management as they try to mediate the volatile reactions that rankings can inspire. A drop in ranking requires prompt and plausible explanations—of, say, "a statistical blip," nonresponding graduates, or *USN*'s having changed the definition of a measure. These explanations must always be accompanied by clear plans for redress. Responses to drops in ranking also prompt what have become standard narratives about how rankings misrepresent a school's unique community, why they are poor measures, or why it is imprudent to overreact. It is common for deans to schedule "town meetings" with students if the school's ranking drops, in order to listen to their concerns and demonstrate responsiveness. And rankings feature prominently in many faculty meetings.

Even good news must be managed. Along with the champagne and pats on the back, deans often offer mild cautions about methods or expectations. In 2009, when Dean Hiram Chodosh announced that the University of Utah's S. J. Quinney College of Law had climbed six places in the *U.S. News* rankings, from fifty-seventh to fifty-first place, he noted:

> We are well aware of the instrumental importance of rankings as a rough (albeit profoundly imperfect) proxy of value for applicants, peers, donors, employers, and others. As we celebrate this recognition and many other terrific achievements this year, let's continue to stay focused on what really matters in our pursuit to improve the world around us. If we take any pride and excitement from a boost in the rankings, let's be sure to channel it in service of our core objectives: the dedication to develop insightful research on the critical issues of our time, dynamic training of the next generation of leaders, and collaborative service contributions at the local, national, and global levels.[1]

Four years later, Chodosh announced that S. J. Quinney had again moved up six spots in the rankings and that the law school had climbed a remarkable sixteen spots since 2008. He cautioned, slightly more succinctly, that rankings are "an important, albeit imperfect, measure of value" and "that the *U.S. News* methodology does not consider the College's many extraordinary achievements," including, he added, its record-breaking 47,000 hours of formal public service in 2012.[2] One admissions director wryly recounted how, after being presented with coffee mugs commemorating their school's breakthrough ranking, their school dropped in rank the following year, after which they had to remind colleagues to hide their mugs when applicants visited the school.

Despite the use of words such as "flawed," "partial," and "influential" to temper over-enthusiasm, the general trend has been toward greater publicity and less hand-wringing when announcing improved rankings. If less than a decade ago it was considered distasteful to even mention rankings in speaking with potential applicants, now they are routine features of websites and marketing. Some schools even have links on their websites dedicated to rankings. Click on "About the School" at the University of California, Davis School of Law and you will be led to a section entitled "Rankings."[3]

Deans invest a lot of time and energy attending to rankings and people's reactions to rankings. Even skeptical deans are not necessarily immune to the influence and allure of these measures, especially since rankings have become a shorthand for their performance. Most deans are ambitious and care deeply about their schools, and it's easy to see the rankings as a public judgment of their performance and of them. Deans are wary of being defined by these measures, and this is harder to tolerate if you believe that rankings are lousy measures. Nonetheless, it is difficult not to be seduced into thinking that you can manage the numbers, a reaction that intensifies their effects.

FEAR AND LOATHING IN THE DEAN'S OFFICE: HOW DEANS VIEW RANKINGS

Deans use vivid language when they are discussing rankings. One said:

> I hate to say this, but when the USN comes out it reminds me of when I used to live at an apartment that had roaches. And I developed a protective instinct, which is that I would close my eyes before I turned on the light to give them time to run away so that I didn't really have to see them. The last time USN came out, I just closed my eyes and I looked in the fourth tier just to make sure that we weren't there, because I live in dread fear that we will fall to the fourth tier on my watch. That's ridiculous! We're a wonderful law school.

This type of negative reaction, often expressed in visceral terms, was common among the deans we interviewed. Conversely, our interviews suggest that very few deans think that rankings are good for legal education, a surprising consensus for those in a profession famous for finding three sides to every argument.

As a group, deans have been sharply and publicly critical of the USN rankings since their inception. After USN published its very first ranking issue in 1990, many deans were disparaging. Others were dismissive, refusing to believe that these numbers, produced by journalists and stat-isticians with no expertise in legal education, would be taken seriously. Robert described how he and his colleagues reacted to the first ranking survey: "The survey came and we sort of looked at it and said, 'Isn't this interesting, somebody's doing a survey.' And then we probably filled it out and that was about it. And then all of the sudden some rankings came out and we were in the top twenty-five, which was a good thing for [our school]. It looked so crazy and arbitrary that we started laughing."

Such dismissiveness seemed reasonable, given that the most promi-nent ranking before *USN*, *The Gourman Report*, was viewed as a curios-ity, not to be taken seriously.[4] However, it quickly became apparent that the public *was* paying attention to the *USN* rankings and making deci-sions based on their outcomes. As this happened, deans became more vociferous in their criticisms of the enterprise. In 1997, Judith Wegner, then dean of the University of North Carolina School of Law, said, "*U.S. News*' methodology is so seriously flawed that it makes any thinking per-son despair of journalistic ethics."[5] Carl Monk, executive director of the Association of American Law Schools, called the rankings "dangerous and misleading."[6] The general sentiment of deans was publicized in a letter condemning the rankings that was sent to every student who registered to take the LSAT from 1995 to 2009 and was published on the Law School Admissions Council's website. This letter, signed each year by about 90 percent of the deans, pointedly rejected the legitimacy of ranking sys-tems and denounced the *USN* rankings in particular: "Several commercial enterprises promote 'ranking' systems that purport to reduce a wide array of information about law schools to one simple number that compares all 192 ABA-approved law schools with each other. These ranking systems are inherently flawed because none of them can take your special needs and circumstances into account when comparing law schools."[7] The measured tone of this letter contrasts with the harsher views of many deans we inter-viewed. One told us, "We hate them. And we hate *USN*'s [annual] book." Another kidded, "I wish al Qaeda would make *USN* their next target."

It is easy to understand why deans are so critical of the rankings. As the LSAC letter suggests, the data and methods used to create the rank-ing scores are highly controversial. To take just one example, most deans believe that respondents to the reputational surveys are ill informed about the schools they evaluate and that their evaluations are often strategic. One dean said: "The data on the reputational survey are so bad. . . . There is clear consensus of the ten or twelve schools that should get a five [where five is "outstanding" and one is "marginal"]. . . . Anyone who doesn't put Yale, Harvard, Chicago, Michigan, NYU, or Berkeley as a five is either being instrumental or is an idiot."

Many deans reported that they knew so little about all but a handful of law schools that their evaluations are meaningless—as, they suspect, are those of most of their peers. The LSAC letter makes the same point:

> According to the magazine, 40 percent of the rankings is based on each school's 'reputation.' The reputation ranking is derived from a survey of a modest number of legal academics, lawyers, and judges across the country which asks them to rate comparatively all ABA-approved law schools. Reputation is an important factor in choosing a school, but schools with excellent reputations within their communities, states, or regions may not be well known in other parts of the country. None of us has adequate knowledge about more than a tiny handful of law schools so as to permit us, with confidence, to compare them with each other.

These indictments of the rankings echo the criticisms of other scholars as well as our interviews in which administrators consistently raised methodological issues about every measure—from faculty size to placement statistics to library budgets—used by *USN*.[8]

But deans have reservations about more than methodology. Many questioned the very act of quantifying law school quality. This uneasiness stems from two arguments. First, as the LSAC letter points out, many characteristics of law schools are hard to quantify, and a single indicator cannot fairly compare all law schools to one another. This sentiment is expressed by many administrators. For example: "[The *USN* rankings] don't—and they can't—measure real quality because real quality is subjective. So they measure a bunch of surrogates for real quality and they're not very good surrogates." Second, rankings leave unmeasured many characteristics that determine a law school's reputation. Missing from rankings are the quality of teachers, faculty scholarship, racial and gender diversity, the size of first-year classes, the strength of alumni networks, student satisfaction, and even cost.[9]

Deans also criticize the qualifications of journalists to evaluate legal education. Deans feel that their experience makes them far more qualified arbiters of quality. Many constituents use the rankings as a barometer of success for schools and demand that decisions should be made with an eye toward future ranking achievement. These demands, heeded or not, often conflict with deans' own judgments about what is best for the school, especially in the long term. But because rankings seem objective and disinterested, deans cannot disregard them, because powerful constituents take them seriously.

Rankings add unwelcome complexity to a difficult job. One dean explained: "Whatever the validity of the methodology, it's difficult to pretend that the rankings don't matter. I mean, prospective students use them; employers use them; university administrators use them. So whether we in legal academics think they're valid or not, whether they're reflective or not, the truth is that I don't think you can just ignore them." This is, for this dean, the "pragmatic reality" of rankings.

With every decision made about personnel, curricula, school policies, and budgets, deans must ask themselves, "What will this do to our ranking?" in addition to, "Is this best for our school?" The answers to these two questions often diverge, pitting professional judgment and expertise against the effects of rankings. One dean told us that after a decline in her school's ranking, "I had alumni writing me left and right, I had my board of directors asking me what had suddenly happened that [our school] had suddenly [dropped].... It was an irrational response because the people writing mostly actually knew about the school. I had my student body protesting, and they're here and they know in the course of one year that nothing had happened. But they all essentially were saying, '*What did you do?*'"

Deans' responses to rankings were not unanimously negative. A few argued that rankings had positive effects, and some others, when pushed, acknowledged some benefits of the rankings. Some of the benefits mentioned were that rankings provide a disinterested and informative measure of relative quality, that they hold schools accountable to their constituents for their performance, and that they might encourage some schools to identify and work on eliminating weaknesses. As one dean contended:

> In the past a dean could pontificate about how great his program was, but now it's harder to pull the wool over people's eyes. With these numbers, you can't just talk.... Our job and our career goals haven't changed, but now we have metrics. I think it's just like *Consumer Reports* for cars. You can quarrel with individual things, you can quibble with the formula, but we have a wonderful product, and it's good for people to know that. Most deans think all this is horrible—I'm a real outlier on this. No one would argue that *Consumer Reports* is a bad idea, just that what we provide is more complex and has more variables that what [*USN's*] formula shows.

While acknowledging rankings' weaknesses, supporters believe that rankings offer important information to prospective students. David Van Zandt, the dean of Northwestern University School of Law from 1995 to 2010 and perhaps the most vocal advocate for the rankings, wrote in 2010, "I strongly believe in them [rankings]. Rankings offer prospective law students an important source of consumer information with which to evaluate law schools. . . . As I have argued for many years, the rankings help applicants make more informed decisions by supplying information about a school's objective performance and perceived reputation, rather than relying so heavily, as in the past, on the advice of friends and relatives, which can be less reliable."[10]

RELATIONS OF ACCOUNTABILITY: MANAGING IMPRESSIONS ACROSS CONSTITUENCIES

One of the most prominent effects of rankings is that they provide a powerful and simple cognitive framework that organizes how interested parties think about law schools and their relative standing. However flawed they are, few deans can afford to ignore rankings because others take the rankings seriously. One director of admissions explained:

> [We] experienced a drop of two positions, and the dean really kind of went into overdrive to send out letters to alumni and in their alumni magazine to make a very elaborate explanation of that. And you say, "Why would anybody care? It doesn't mean a thing. It's just one of those minor statistical variations that is always going to occur from time to time." But that sort of tiny little change was seen as very threatening to the school and really required some sort of emergency program to combat it.

Providing such accounts is common practice at law schools. Rankings have remade accountability by making it public, annual, and available to many. Deans are now at the center of a web in which pressures can be activated and radiate from all sectors. There are multiple audiences for a school's ranking, including internal audiences and powerful external constituents.

Governing Bodies

Deans are subject to a number of governing bodies: the boards of trustees, regents, state legislators, and university administrators that oversee their policy decisions and budgets and judge their overall performance. These audiences generally pay close attention to the school's rank, so—especially because they hold so much power—their expectations must be carefully managed. One dean told us:

> The pressure the surveys are creating is a lot higher than it was ten years ago. Just more people are paying more attention to them, [and] by more

people I don't mean just student-consumers, but boards of trustees, central administrative officials, legislators, and everybody else. I think they all understand that these are imperfect instruments, but there are so few measures of output that these things just count more than they should or than they ever did before.

Rankings offer distant overseers a simple benchmark for comparing one law school to other schools and programs within the university, or even to itself over time. Several deans reported that there is always a ranking question in every oversight committee meeting. One dean described as "a glutton for punishment" by his staff scheduled his board of visitors meeting every April, just after the rankings came out. Every agenda included a discussion of the school's ranking, what went right or wrong, and plans for fixing any problems. From another dean:

> Law school faculties and the smart administrators all say, "This [the rankings] is a bunch of hooey, we don't care about this," until the [ranking drops] and the board of trustees says, "Hey you're dropping; why should we give you more money?" And the board of visitors from the law school say, "Man, your school's really going to pot and you haven't changed a thing. . . . Big changes need to be made here." And your monetary support—the alumni— say, "Well I'm not sure I want to support a school that's going in the wrong direction." And your money starts to dry up, and you go, "We have got to have the money; we can't afford to lose funding or else it *will* spiral downhill and we will be a worse law school."

For university administrators rankings are the rare metric that permits them to compare one unit with another in ways that seem disinterested and plausible. Even as recently as the late 1990s and early 2000s it was rare and was seen as somewhat distasteful for candidates applying for open dean positions to discuss strategies for addressing the school's ranking. That was then. Now it is assumed that such discussions will take place. In fact, presenting a plan for dealing with a school's ranking is a necessary part of an interview. One administrator explained, "It was a huge issue in the search. I would say that it was the number one issue in the dean's search. The rankings—because there are just those rankings, that was really what people were talking about when they talked about reputation and visibility." Many deans, especially those with longer tenures, ruefully noted that this focus on managing *USN* has changed both who gets hired for open positions *and* how these new deans view their work. There is more focus on short-term goals, actions are more constrained by quantitative assessments, and being savvy about marketing is now a very desirable characteristic. In fact, it is not uncommon for contracts to include explicit ranking goals or bonuses for improvement.

How much, and how, overseers and top administrators use rankings varies from school to school. Few deans reported that these constituents gave no weight to the school's ranking, and many believed that the ranking was a very important factor in the evaluation of the dean's job performance. One dean told us, "We have a new president and when he came in he met with all of the deans of all the schools. He was pretty clear that reputation as measured by rankings was important to him, and that it would be part of the way in which I was evaluated." The dean of a third-tier school described a memorable meeting:

> [During] my second year here, I was meeting with the president and the executive vice president for academic affairs . . . about an entirely different matter, and all of the sudden the president rears up, he says, "And I want the law school's strategic plan for how it's going to get into the second tier." . . . I told him, "We're going to work on that next year." He said, "No, you're going to work on it now, and I want it in six months." What happened was the trustees were chewing on him, so he did what any president would do: he chews on the dean.

Another put it more succinctly: "I would like to ignore the rankings, but I work for a president who won't let me."

The use of rankings as barometers of a dean's ability is not confined to contracts or official meetings. They can also become part of a dean's unofficial professional biography and for some, how he or she is remembered. For example, when Kenneth Randall retired as dean of the University of Alabama School of Law after twenty years, the university's president, Judy Bonner, recounted to reporters as one of his accomplishments that he had helped the school reach "unprecedented levels of recognition," including being ranked in the top twenty-five law schools by *U.S. News and World Report*. The tribute paid to the dean of Stetson College of Law when he died stated, "Under Dean Vause's leadership, Stetson University College of Law recently earned another first place ranking for its trial advocacy program from *U.S. News and World Report*."[11]

Alumni

Alumni are not indifferent to rankings, since they offer a vehicle for bragging rights, a way of keeping score about the value of one's degree, and a way to categorize colleagues. Alumni realize that rankings help define their status. One associate dean remarked, "Since I've been here emails [to alumni and other constituents] have gone [out] that say, 'This is where we are and this is what's happened, and we're very proud about what we've accomplished. This is what we've accomplished, and all we can do is stay the course and move ahead.' "

In the case of upwardly mobile schools, the value of graduates' degrees improves along with the school's rise. Happy are the New York University alumni who attended a less than stellar law school in the 1970s and have evolved into graduates of a top-five school. A successful lawyer described how closely rankings were monitored by alumni at his firm. Those whose schools dropped could expect ribbing. Some (although not all—opinion is split on this issue) administrators believe that rankings affect alumni giving. What is clear is that alumni pay attention to rankings. One dean described how, if rankings go down, "they write angry emails, make telephone calls, and are generally disgruntled. My guess is that it has some impact on annual giving." And rankings play a role in first impressions among lawyers. Having attended a higher-ranked school can encourage a sense of superiority, or the opposite in those from lower-ranked schools. One young lawyer described how, whenever his firm hired a top-ten graduate, "You just knew they felt superior to guys like me from 'inferior' schools. So you just have to prove them wrong."

The Media

Rankings are news. Another crucial audience that deans must attend to is the rapidly proliferating number and types of media outlets that report on rankings. For journalists hungry for copy, rankings offer an easy annual story about how local schools compare to other nearby schools and to themselves over time. Many of the deans we interviewed recount the unpleasant experience of having to explain to a reporter why their school dropped this year. The *Chicago Tribune* recently ran a story under the headline "University of Chicago Law School Beats Northwestern in U.S. News Rankings Again." The *Lawrence (Kansas) Journal World* headlined a story "KU's Law School Drops Again in National Rankings, While 12 Programs Make the Top 10." Worst of all is a story like the one that appeared in the *Boston Globe* with the headline "New England Law Head Draws Scrutiny for His Pay: A Princely Paycheck for Dean of Unheralded School." The $867,000 salary of John O'Brian, the dean of New England Law School, a fourth-tier law school, was reported to be more than that of the deans of the Harvard and Yale law schools.[12] More than one dean suggested to us that it would be better if journalists stuck to reporting news rather than making it. But *USN*'s success in marketing and disseminating the rankings has reinforced the rankings' perceived newsworthiness.

Social media have introduced new forms of news and accelerated the spread of rankings news. Along with all the websites devoted to getting into law school there are a number of popular blogs dedicated to law and legal education that regularly report on rankings. *Above the Law*, a prominent blog that is often critical of legal education, regularly reports on rankings and began to produce its own version in 2013. A recent post, "Responding to the New U.S. News Rankings: The Parade of Butthurt Deans Begins Now," mocks the efforts of deans to "spin" their ranking, some doing so even before they are publicly released.[13]

The 2008 recession created a sharp drop in demand for lawyers; the market began to improve only recently. Consequently, there were many law school graduates who had borrowed heavily, only to face unemployment in a terrible market and debilitating loan repayments (the average debt of graduating law students is over $100,000 and often is as much as $200,000). It is hard not to be bitter when facing such bleak prospects, especially if you read that your school had inflated its placement numbers. The Internet has made it easy for angry people to retaliate in so-called "scam blogs." The most notorious site, *Third Tier Reality*, the title inspired by the chat room slang term "third tier toilet," combines vitriol with graphic photographs of filled toilets. According to this blog, law schools dupe students with inflated employment statistics, "exploding" scholarships (scholarships that will be revoked if students do not maintain a high grade-point average or class rank), and other promises for the benefit of fat-cat faculty and administrators. People posting at this blog especially criticize lower-ranked schools, claiming that they bilk students who they know will probably never be employed as lawyers.[14] Some of these charges are fair and are supported by a growing number of law professors and administrators, but they are presented in the crudest possible way.[15] Anyone who defends the status quo or makes a case for going to law school may become the subject of abuse.[16]

Other blogs that are critical of rankings include *The Irreverent Lawyer, Inside Law Schools, Temporary Attorney,* and *Subprime JD,* the motto of which is "If I can stop one person from going to law school through this site, my work is done."[17] It is hard to assess the effect of these sites, but clearly, they are very popular. The sites have received millions of hits, are the subject of much commentary, and have done much to publicize the bad job market for lawyers and lousy jobs that many are forced to take.

Students

In addition to these important consumers of rankings that deans must manage, there are crucial inside audiences for rankings, including students, faculty, and staff, who see their careers and status hinging on a school's ranking. Students worry over how rankings will affect their job options and sometimes express their anxieties forcefully and belligerently. One dean, when asked if current students discuss the rankings, remarked: "Oh yes! I hear it all the time, and sometimes they're a little snotty about it. I wanted to give an award for I guess public service. And I asked students to nominate other students and I got one form back that said, 'Well this is all nice, but what are you doing to get us out of the third tier? We don't need awards, we need results.'" Students' anxiety skyrockets when their school's rank falls. Even if they have witnessed no appreciable changes in the quality of the school from one year to the next, they fear how rankings will affect the views of others. After a fall in the 2013 rankings, students at American University circulated a petition that began:

> Current 3Ls at WCL began their tenure at a law school ranked 45th in the nation by US News and World Report and now attend a school ranked 56th. Part-time 4Ls began in a program ranked 4th in 2009 that now ranks 10th. Aside from the likely unemployment and crippling debt they face, they now will also be graduating with a degree from a "second-tier" school. The administration has allowed the ranking of this institution to slip more than ten positions in a span of three years. Dean Grossman has refused to take measures necessary to maintain not only our position within the rankings, but also our prestige amongst the nation's law schools, firms, and other employers.

The petition ends with students' "demand[ing] the termination of Dean Claudio Grossman's employment."[18]

It is not uncommon for deans to lose their jobs as a result of this type of unrest among their constituents. It is not surprising, then, that some deans change how they allocate resources and make decisions in response to this pressure. Describing the fallout from just this type of situation at his school, one administrator said, "The student body took a very aggressive stance with the dean and said, 'There is absolutely no reason why we should suffer in our job prospects and salary outlooks because of this phenomenon, and we want you to do something about it.' So she invested in areas where the school would tend to get points [in the rankings]." Rankings give students the space to confront administrators and demand explanations in ways that would have been unthinkable before rankings, a change that exemplifies how public measurements transform the relationships and power dynamics inside a field.

Faculty

Faculty members worry over rankings, too. Most faculty, like most deans, think rankings are either inappropriate, are poor measures, or both. Nevertheless, they take them seriously. According to one faculty member, "It takes about four seconds after the new rankings come out for them to circulate through the whole law school." At many schools, it would be hard to ignore rankings, since they come up routinely at faculty meetings, in conversations among colleagues and with friends and acquaintances at other law schools, and in the classroom. In addition, some schools appoint committees that include faculty members to recommend policies about how to improve their ranking. This occurs most often after a decline in ranking, when a new dean is appointed, or when efforts to improve its ranking become part of a school's strategic planning.

Opinions vary a great deal as to how much rankings permeate the lives of faculty members. While some report that colleagues are "obsessed" with rankings or that it is difficult "*not* to think about rankings," others suggest that the annual release of rankings generates buzz for a week or so, and then interest in rankings fades. Those who serve on admissions committees or have held administrative positions are often more attentive to rankings than others. None of the people we spoke with were unaware of their school's rankings, and most could describe in some detail how their school compared with other schools on at least some rankings components. One law professor believed that faculty care about rankings because of their own experience as students at highly ranked schools: "The schools that faculty went to are all top-five schools, and many of them really do want [the school where they teach] to be Yale. . . . It's kind of interesting to watch. They all think they should be teaching at a highly ranked school." Even schools at the top of the rankings feel their effects. Several professors told us that they enjoy "the luxury" of not fretting about rankings but admit that if the ranking dropped a notch or two, that would change.

However broad their views, faculty do not shy away from voicing their concerns about rankings or suggesting ways to deal with them. One dean related:

> This year the school slipped from third to fourth [tier]. I firmly believe that it was nothing more than a statistical aberration that had no meaning, but

nonetheless it was very difficult to communicate that to the students, to the faculty, and to other constituents. Some members of my faculty became very, very anxious about this and believe that it just spelled dire consequences, and that we have to do everything we can to somehow have an impact. And the only way that anyone could think of to have an impact was to somehow increase the LSAT scores of our students.

These complaints are not always leveled at deans. Lower-level administrators, especially those in charge of admissions or career services, report that they often take the brunt of faculty criticism. One director of admissions told us,

Frankly, most admissions people don't have the time to create a furor over something like this [drop in the rankings], but these guys on the faculty do and they will. So if you're in the school where the faculty has got the dean's ear and you get some people on that faculty who are very vocal and who see [rankings] as a goal, that's the schools where you'll see just incredible amounts of foment over the *USN:* "Who's doing what?" and "Is career services hurting our ranking?" and "Is admissions hurting our ranking?" I'm lucky I'm not at one of those schools. . . . But, I think that [faculty have] more to do with ranking pressure than anything else. If faculties would just lay off, just get a grip and go out and do what they're supposed to do, most of the places that I know where there is an extreme amount of pressure, the pressure would be relieved.

Another administrator said that rankings "induce some constituencies— particularly the faculty—to be very anxious, to focus admissions on students with high LSAT scores." We followed up this remark by asking if he thought that faculty were the biggest source of rankings pressure, and he replied, "Absolutely. At least at the schools I've been associated with. I believe at some other schools, the pressure comes from deans and the administration."

Faculty are affected by some of the general consequences of rankings such as problems of morale, student reactions, and changes in how decisions are made within the school. In addition, there are two rankings-related issues that are particularly relevant to them: the recruitment and retention of faculty and publishing.

It's hard to say precisely how much rankings influence recruitment of faculty, since employment decisions are complex, candidates rarely fully disclose their reasons for selecting one school over another, and the reputation of a given school is only partly a function of rankings. Nevertheless, many of our respondents believe that rankings affect their ability to recruit candidates for faculty positions. Several deans we interviewed were convinced that rankings informed their candidate's decision to decline offers from their schools. For example, one dean of a law school in a large urban center believed that their candidate weighted school rank higher than lifestyle preferences in choosing between offers:

> Last year we recruited an individual to be a faculty member who was living in [a large city], [who] had a brother that lived in [our area], and to all appearances this was a big-city person. And I think if this person could choose a place to live, he would choose [a large city]. He ended up going to [a school in a much smaller, more remote city] because it's a more highly ranked school. That's really what it came down to. Our offer was actually ... higher than what he got from [the other school].

It was not uncommon for faculty members to admit to us that they had considered a school's ranking when evaluating employment opportunities. One professor, who described himself as someone who "hates" rankings, confessed to consulting them when he was considering overtures made from another law school. He believed that faculty would most likely be too embarrassed to admit that they considered rankings in their decision-making. Others described how rankings were invoked when colleagues or advisers advised them about what jobs to apply for or take. One recently hired assistant professor described how colleagues had tried to dissuade her from choosing the school she wanted to work at because it was not highly ranked. "When I was thinking about coming here, there were people who discouraged me. . . . They said, 'You shouldn't do that. It's academic suicide. It's third tier.' The rankings were invoked directly, 'Don't do it. You shouldn't go to a third-tier school.' "[19] One dean reported that he had never had a faculty member leave for a lower-ranked school.

Some faculty members believe that their school's ranking influences their success in publishing in law reviews via the "letterhead effect" (named for the school's letterhead on which the cover letter for journal submissions is written). The argument goes that inexperienced students are poorly qualified to evaluate the scholarly merit of many manuscripts, especially those in highly specialized areas. So instead, they evaluate the letterhead. That is, student editors rely heavily on the ranking of the author's law school as shown on the letterhead as a proxy for scholarly quality. An assistant professor described his concerns:

> It's a publish-or-perish industry. I enjoy writing and I enjoy the intellectual pursuit, but there are those who do say that it is much more difficult to

land a piece [get it accepted for publication]—even if it is a quality piece—if it is coming from a third-tier school than something that is incredibly mediocre coming from a top-twenty-five or -fifty school. Students who work on the law reviews pay attention to that ranking process, so even though you have some sort of great paper, if you are coming from a school that doesn't have a good ranking the competition is much more stiff. They look at where it comes from; it's not blind at all. People talk to me about strategies; they recommend that if I have a coauthor, I should send it out under the name of the coauthor's school, or if you have affiliations elsewhere, to send it out under the name of the outside affiliation. So I'm constantly aware of that. We want people to publish well, so it adds even a greater pressure.

This uneasiness was echoed by faculty members at all career stages and in a range of schools. We did not systematically interview student editors, but those with whom we discussed this issue strongly agreed that the school reputation of submitters shaped the chances of manuscripts' getting accepted at their journal. These editors reported that, given the high volume of manuscripts they receive and their limited knowledge, they often consider an author's institutional affiliation in making decisions. We spoke with editors at several schools. They believe that it is standard practice at most law reviews to use institutional reputation as a signal of the manuscript's quality, and that rankings shape their views of an institution's reputation.

Rankings play a more important role in judgments of institutional prestige of less elite schools, since there is broad consensus as to which are the "best" schools. Some faculty members also use the rankings to decide where to publish their articles. If their manuscripts are accepted by several law reviews, they consult rankings when deciding where to publish—partly because bonuses are awarded to those who publish in top law reviews. One professor told us, "Where you publish in those law reviews means everything to your career, everything. They influence where you get hired and where you are asked to visit. So you have twenty-five-year-olds determining how much of a bonus you are going to get. . . . So when I am deciding where to send something that has been accepted at two different places, I do go by *USN*."

In general, the rankings provide an avenue by which constituents, both external and internal, can question their deans' priorities and decisions. This pressure forces deans to offer explicit accounts of and justifications for the decisions they make that affect the school's rank, the reasons the school ranks where it does, and, at times, the reasons the school fell in the rankings.[20]

REACTING TO RANKINGS: DEANS' EFFORTS TO MANAGE RANKINGS

Two core job requirements for deans are to raise money and help decide how to spend it. Many deans are quick to point out that high rankings are correlated with big endowments. A dean of a third-tier school told us:

> It is so clearly the case that rankings track resources. They really do. It just comes down to how much money a school has. It's not difficult to understand why schools are ranked where they are. I went from the fourth tier to the third tier. I'd love to be a second-tier school, but I know what the second-tier schools are spending per student, and they're spending another five or six thousand dollars per student more than I am. I'm spending somewhere around sixteen, they're all up around twenty-two or twenty-five. When you take that times six hundred students, that's six million dollars. If I had six million dollars, I could be a second-tier school.

The connection between money and ranking was an obvious point of frustration for many administrators. The constraints imposed by limited resources are not only a stubborn reality of their school's position—an administrator at a second-tier school said, "The money fairy isn't going to fly in the window and drop a bundle in our dean's lap; it isn't going to happen"—it is also a reality not often fully appreciated by the constituents with which deans must work. Several deans complained about unrealistic expectations from trustees, alumni, students, and faculty about what was possible for the school and the failure of these groups to recognize that the actions of deans are restricted by the resources available to them. Speaking about his conversations with faculty members, one dean remarked:

> They really believe that if you just run a tight ship, it is just going to happen. That's really not true at all. They also think that if you set your standards really, really high, if you only admit a certain kind of student and you only hire a certain kind of professor, then it will happen. Well, it is true that we could just admit a better quality of student than we are admitting right now, but then we wouldn't be able to fill the class, and we wouldn't be able to fill our budgetary needs because we are tuition driven. People don't live in the real world with this. Whereas I have to live in the real world with it, and I constantly feel like I am in dialogue with the faculty as to what is realistic here.

These financial constraints are particularly acute for schools outside of the relatively resource-rich schools found in the top half of the first tier. Deans at lower-ranked schools are blunt on this point. A dean at a third-tier law school said, "We need more resources. I frequently say to people that if they give me fifty million dollars, I will get us into the second tier overnight." Another told us that when alumni question him about how to improve the school's ranking, "The answer involves their getting out their checkbooks."

Money comes up a lot when rankings are discussed. Many deans mentioned that they had either completed, were in the middle of, or planned to initiate capital campaigns to raise money and increase the school's endowment through alumni and philanthropic donations. Others raised tuition or created part-time programs, for which student statistics were not required until recently.[21] One dean explained:

> We're more willing to actually encourage some people who we might think are marginal to go part-time at first. Ours is a school where you can switch from part-time to full-time. Now, again, there are a couple of issues here. One is that it still allows you to get students to take courses in the summer and that is income that I get to keep. The tuition for the semesters doesn't come back to me—I get the same budget no matter how many students we have. I increased by $100,000 my discretionary money, which for me is significant.

Developing an LL.M. program or increasing the size of an existing one is yet another way for schools to generate additional revenue. LL.M. programs are one- or two-year programs of study comprised mostly of international students who pay hefty tuition for introductions to American law or specialty areas. A dean of a school without an LL.M. degree program told us, "We've certainly looked at LL.M. programs as a possibility ... simply because that can be a cash cow." Although the money raised by these and similar efforts is used for a wide variety of purposes, several administrators made it clear that they earmarked a large portion of the "extra" money generated by these programs to increase funding for marketing or other rankings-related purposes.

Along with cutting class size, not reporting scores of "special" admits, and buying high test scores, a common tactic of redistribution is the drastic increase in expenditures on marketing and public relations.[22] Nearly every law school administrator we interviewed noted that one of the most obvious effects of the rankings is the exponential increase in the amount of promotional material that law schools distribute.[23] To try to increase their school's reputation rating among their peers—the most heavily weighted criterion among rankings factors—law schools "paper the world" with brochures and other marketing publications that are distributed to those who vote or might have a vote in the *USN* survey.[24] Deans know that surveys are sent to all deans and associate deans and the most recently tenured faculty (which is why some schools collect *USN* surveys and fill them out strategically, systematically downgrading close rivals), but *USN* has never explained who gets the practitioner surveys. Most federal judges seem to get them, and they are sent to prominent partners at big law firms. But schools don't know for sure who gets them, so they feel compelled to target a broad audience with their literature. Administrators note that these brochures arrive in a steady stream throughout the year and literally clog their mailboxes in the weeks before the *USN* reputational surveys are sent out each October—what one marketing director referred to as "sweeps week." Most report that these mailings usually end up in the garbage unread. "I don't read the ones that are mailed to me," one dean told us. "My secretary has instructions to throw them away upon arrival. Who reads those things? I don't. I don't keep them—they literally go from the mail room to the trash can."

In the zero-sum game of budgeting, money spent on glossy brochures is money not spent on new faculty, programming, research, clinics, libraries, placement, or scholarships, purposes most administrators see as more worthy targets. Not surprisingly, this is a hot-button issue for deans. One dean, holding up a glossy brochure for a specialty program, said,

> We have things like this that we would not have had before [rankings]. It wouldn't have happened. Money would not have been spent for that purpose; it would have been spent for other, more educational purposes, frankly. Whether it would be not having to raise tuition, or better salaries, or more faculty, or more research resources, I'm not sure. I don't know what is being cut out because of it but I do know that an enormous amount of money is being spent on this. It's just a huge waste that would totally be unnecessary if it weren't for *USN*.

If so many deans see this type of rankings-related marketing as a waste of money, why, then, do they do it?[25] Deans offer two answers to this question. First, they need to demonstrate to their constituents that they are doing something to improve or maintain the school's rank because not doing so would leave a dean vulnerable should the school's ranking fall. One dean explained, "We're doing that not because we think it will do any good, but because we think that if we don't do it, it is probably not good. So, it's kind of a case where everybody's doing it everywhere." The second explanation is that since tiny changes in a measure can produce such big swings in a school's rank, administrators are, they say, "afraid" that if these brochures *do* have even a small effect, their ranking might suffer if they choose not to produce them. For two deans:

> There are more [marketing] publications for a broader audience, and the reason for that is you are afraid not to. Because if you don't, then you're afraid that some guy in Utah or Montana will think that they haven't heard anything about you, so they'll put you in the fourth tier.

> I know why we moved down to the fourth tier: I did not spend money. I thought that we had all of these wonderful programs and we had four Supreme Court speakers in here and we did all this stuff, but I made the strategic mistake of not sending out magazines and brochures about all of our programs to the immediate world.

Brochures are tangible public symbols deans can use to demonstrate they take rankings seriously. Also, refusing to participate in this arms race of advertisement could matter at the margins, and margins matter for rankings. It is a testament to the power of the rankings that so many resources are used on activities that most see as a waste of time and money.

Administrators told us of other tactics used to boost rankings. Some changed hiring strategies to improve faculty-student ratios. A faculty member at a top-fifty school told us that his dean "actually very strategically looks at his faculty-student ratio for ranking purposes. If he can get two junior faculty for the cost of one senior faculty, he may pursue the juniors in order to lower the faculty/student ratio." Some schools reallocate money in order to increase their "expenditure per student" numbers, while others employ consultants to help them manage rankings more effectively. A number of deans now discourage fall sabbaticals since fall is when faculty members are counted for *USN* purposes.

Money is the most prominent resource that is redistributed due to the rankings, but the reallocation of other, less tangible, resources such as time and attention is also consequential. One administrator told us, "Almost everything we do now is prefaced by, 'How will this affect our ranking?'" A faculty member described how a meeting devoted to curriculum development included discussions on possible effects of proposed changes on the school's ranking. Even the compilation of statistics for *USN* can be time-consuming, and it becomes even more so as administrators scrutinize their numbers to make sure they cast the school in the best possible light and to ensure the accuracy of the submitted numbers. One administrator told us that rankings stats are checked far more carefully than budgets. Another dean described how she found herself paying increasingly close attention to the intricacies of the numbers submitted to *USN:*

> I actually found myself this year for the first time looking at what are the elements of faculty resources.... I actually sat down and quizzed the person who is primarily responsible for doing that document. I actually found myself saying, "Lisa, now when we do the instructional budget, we do include the money from the endowment that goes into instruction, right?" Because I am finding myself thinking that we have never thought about the elements of it in terms of *USN* and then I realized that, "Oh, God! I'm getting the disease."

Several deans told horror stories of schools dropping precipitously in the rankings as a result of reporting errors. One emphasized that they must be extremely "careful to respond to their questionnaires accurately and not goof something up so that you shoot yourself in the foot." Another said, "I feel pressure to keep a close eye on what other schools are doing; I feel a lot of pressure to watch very carefully where all of our administrative offices—our admissions office, the career services offices, etc.—where all of these student services offices are in relationship to our peers, because you can see precipitous things happen."

The scrutiny that rankings evoke is not just directed toward one's own school. Deans acknowledge, albeit a bit sheepishly, that rankings encourage them to analyze other schools' statistics in much the same way they analyze their own. Dedicating so much time and attention to these statistics frustrates many deans.

Proponents of the rankings might point out here that the adoption of strategies like these may be good for legal education. After all, spending money to improve the faculty-student ratio, increase expenditures per student, or even to broaden the visibility of the school through marketing all seem like beneficial changes. The rankings, according to this argument, provide administrators with comparative information about where they are lagging behind their peers, and this information can then be used to target a school's weaknesses for improvement. Indeed, some deans made it clear that their attempts to optimize their school's rank through changes in spending were guided by genuine needs. For example, if a school's career services department is doing poorly both in real terms and as measured by the rankings, a dean might reallocate more money to this department in hopes of addressing both concerns simultaneously.

Much more often, however, deans emphasized the constraints that rankings introduced in their decisions. One dean said,

> I think that for schools like ours, it does drain significant . . . resources that I hate to see used for these purposes. . . . So it takes the energy away from the development of a better curriculum and smaller classes and exciting pro- grams and all of those kinds of things that would do the students really good and would be fun for the faculty. . . . So resources of all sorts get diverted into worrying about how *USN* is going to have an impact on that rather than all the other things about legal education that you're trying to provide a very talented group of students who have the capacity to do a lot.

Another dean explained,

> This is the kind of pressure this brings to bear: If you need $100,000 for a new academic program that will really help your students become better lawyers, and you also need $100,000 to improve physical facilities, and you also need $100,000 for merit scholarships to maybe raise your LSAT score one point, how do you decide what to spend that money on? Whatever the right balance of decision-making is, it's clearly been tilted a long way towards spending that money on the things that will help you in the rankings.

Another dean who refused to spend resources on rankings summarized her dilemma this way:

> I don't feel badly that we don't waste our money that way. I do have fears that someday it is going to come back to bite us. And that's why March is such a scary time. . . . I just feel badly that they are wasting their money in that way. They could hire another teacher, they could serve a hundred more clients, they could do something good for the world with that. But for those that have the status, they want to protect it; and for those that don't have it, they want to get it.

SELF-DEFINITION AND SCHOOL IDENTITY

Rankings not only encourage schools to change how they manage resources, they also pressure many schools to reconsider how they define themselves and how they educate their students. If issues of identity and purpose are less tangible than resource allocation, their effects still are powerful and exemplify how rankings penetrate and transform core components of law schools, including the schools' missions and the specialties they cultivate.

Rankings threaten schools' missions because they create self-fulfilling prophecies by encouraging schools to conform to what rankings measure, a process that then reinforces the validity of the measures.[26] Rankings impose a standardized, universal definition of law schools that presumes they all have the same goals and motives; hence, comparisons among them are fair. This squarely contradicts schools' notions of themselves as unique institutions. One dean explained,

> The devastation of the rankings is this: Each institution has its own niche, things that it does really, really well, ambitions and goals for what it wants to be and the students it wants to admit and the kinds of students it wants to graduate and the kinds of things it likes those students to do. In terms of the whole identity process, each school is really unique. And what USN does is come in with a template, and it lays it on all law schools and says, "Well, you're a shitty school because you're not in the first tier." Well, that's not true.

Because USN has created such a powerful definition of what a good law school is, many deans claim that they have less latitude to promote values that are not rewarded by USN's conception of school quality.

Deans at schools with missions that diverge from the "ideal" law school as defined by USN—missions that emphasize access to legal education, accepting under-represented students as well as those with high LSAT scores and GPAs, or commitments to public interest as opposed to, say, corporate law—are forced to decide whether they should modify their missions so as to fare better in the rankings or stay true to their missions and risk the stigma of being perceived as a "bad law school" by those who use the rankings uncritically. One dean said, "It's wrong for a school that has a mission that's not Harvard or Chicago to be slapped and say, 'Why, you're a crummy school, because you're not doing what Harvard is doing.' So that's the devastation." A dean of a third-tier law school discussed this dilemma in concrete terms. She described the mission of her university as always having has been that of "an access university," that "gives students opportunities that they would not have had elsewhere." She continued,

> A student can have a very high GPA but a very low LSAT score. That student is not going to help us in the rankings. But let's assume for the moment that

that student is a minority—that's the kind of student we like to admit and to give an opportunity [to], even though that's going to adversely impact our rankings, and even though that student is not going to pass the bar exam the first time around. And that is our mission. We are going to have [to] change our mission and change our thinking if we are going to take that student's place and give it to a student with a higher LSAT score—if we are going to be driven by the rankings. Our problem, and our challenge and our opportunity, is that we are poised at the top of a tier. So it is almost impossible to resist the temptation to move into that [next] tier because then that becomes a self-perpetuating situation.

When asked if her school would still admit students with the lower LSAT scores along with the higher-scoring students, she replied, "It could be that for a couple of years we don't give that student the opportunity. Or we say to that student that we used to have a place for them in the day program but now we have a place for you in the night program, which is part-time and which doesn't count as much toward the rankings."

These same homogenizing pressures may also encourage schools to change programs or even to change the ways they train their students. Because the rankings do not recognize organizational goals that do not conform to their definition of a high-quality school, deans must consider whether to continue to fund programs and specialties that are not rewarded in this framework. Speaking about his school's commitment to clinical education, for instance, one dean explained:

There are other things that are very much part of our mission that aren't captured [by *USN*]. We have a very strong public interest program, including clinics. Clinics are a very recent invention; they started up in 1986. And now it's been a tremendous focus over the last twenty years, and now we have quite a large clinic. We do that because it is at the heart of our mission in two ways. One is that I think it is critical to train people to be lawyers . . . clinical education, where you actually learn by doing, is actually much more important [now] than it was. And then it is also part of our mission of giving back, we try to show students that this is part of their mission and role of a lawyer, to help other people. That's not captured in *USN*. The reputation variable is attuned much more to academic reputation and to scholarship. So to the extent that you put resources into clinical education, it doesn't help you in these other areas.

This is a clear example of how the rankings create pressures for law schools to adopt organizational goals that correspond comfortably with ranking criteria but actually undermine the schools' educational goals. Schools and their deans, of course, can choose whether or not to make changes in response to these pressures, but they are fully aware that resisting this pressure will likely hurt their ranking.

USN's ranking of eight specialty areas also influences programming. These specialty rankings encourage schools, especially those in lower tiers, to concentrate resources in these highlighted subfields in order to create a market niche. Schools with high-ranking specialty programs but lower composite rankings often build marketing campaigns around these specialties in an attempt to attract good students who might not otherwise consider the school ("Tout them to high heaven," said one faculty member). Deans of these schools noted to us that high specialty rankings are appreciated by trustees, university presidents, and boards of visitors, and such rankings allow these deans to defend their practices and sometimes even the mission of the school.

School responses to specialty rankings go beyond advertising their successful programs. Deans told us that they are developing curriculum geared to be ranked in specialty programs. Some schools pour money into specialty areas in which they feel competitive. A dean at a third-tier school noted,

> Now we're making strategic decisions; we've decided, for example, to invest huge resources in our intellectual property program because it's attracting students who come to us who turn down [other more highly ranked schools] . . . because it's such a fantastic program. We're going to make decisions this fall about what other areas we want to build on that model, so that we can attract a core of excellent students who come for particular programs who might not otherwise consider [our school]. So . . . we think more strategically about what we're about, and the rankings are a definite part of that.

Others spoke explicitly about moving resources away from unranked specialties into fields they believed they could "leverage" in order to "define their place in the market." A few deans even described starting programs in specialty areas that they thought were less competitive than other fields that are hard to break into, such as tax law and international law.

Exploiting a comparative advantage or a market weakness is, of course, a savvy strategy, but it is sobering that these decisions are so dependent on *USN*'s decisions about which specialties to rank. As one dean said, "Schools that have a potential for getting into the top five with the program are going to allocate resources to that program rather than to something else." This dynamic can produce surprising unintended consequences as well. One dean admitted that a ranked program at his school was completely moribund as a result of a loss of faculty, was now useless to students, and should be cut. However, he felt obligated to keep it going and continue spending money on it that was needed by other programs simply because the high ranking was valuable for attracting students. He nodded to his window where we could see a banner publicizing the program's ranking, quickly noting that this was the work of the marketing department.

INSTITUTIONALIZING AND INTERNALIZING RANKINGS

So far we have focused on how pressures from law school constituencies drive policies and practices. But some of the most pronounced rankings effects are those that operate on how people understand themselves and their colleagues. Deans have many reasons for internalizing the judgments made by USN and, as one dean put it, "catching the disease": they feel emotionally tied to these public assessments because they are arbiters of performance; because their jobs have become increasingly bound up with ranking performance and their ability to craft convincing strategies about how to manage them; and because of the hypercompetitive structure embodied by the rankings.

How are rankings internalized by deans, and what role do deans play in institutionalizing the rankings' influence in legal education?

It is hard to disassociate what the world thinks of you from what you think of yourself, so rankings can evoke strong emotional responses. Students, faculty, administrators, and even alumni see themselves in the rankings.[27] When the University of Pittsburgh School of Law dropped from the second to the third tier in the late 1990s, their dean told a reporter, "It's hard to quantify precisely the injury that was done to the school's reputation. But I can tell you it is heartbreaking to see faculty, staff, and students at a truly high-quality school so thoroughly demoralized by such an unfair assessment."[28] The words "demoralization" and "devastation" came up often in references to a drop in rankings.

Given deans' investment in their schools and their ambitions, they may feel these emotions most acutely. Deans told us about feeling distraught when their rankings dropped, about colleagues who had lost their jobs for not meeting ranking expectations, about the trauma of angry students and disappointed colleagues. And when there are changes in the leadership, even if they are not publicly attributed to the numbers, speculation is rampant and the temptation to scapegoat can be powerful. As one dean put it, "You can almost feel the faculty muttering." Sometimes the blame for rankings is directly and publicly attributed to a dean's performance.

One well-known dean who purportedly lost her job because of falling rankings is Nancy Rapoport, formerly of the University of Houston Law Center. During the six years of her tenure as dean, the school dropped twenty spots in the ranking, five of them in what turned out to be the final year of her deanship. Angry students and faculty wrote harsh critiques of her leadership in blogs, bulletin boards, and emails that were widely circulated. At a faculty meeting attended by a hundred students, Rapoport famously teared up when she realized no faculty member would defend her. A week later she resigned. Afterwards, she attributed her forced resignation to the school's drop in rank, and wondered in her blog if she had become "the poster child for why *U.S. News and World Report* rankings are bad." But one reporter reflected, "It's perhaps more accurate to say Rapoport's Houston ordeal scares the bejesus out of deans. Her tears are emblematic of the nerve-shredding power *U.S. News* rankings hold over deans, faculty, and students."[29]

Not surprisingly, rankings also play a key role in deciding who is hired to be dean. In its search for a new dean in 2013, Southern Methodist University Dedman School of Law understood its task as "charting the law school's long-term future," although different groups disagreed about what this meant. According to the *Dallas Morning News*, some members of the search committee "believe their school should focus on capital fundraising and improve its standing in the *U.S. News and World Report* rankings, which would help graduates get jobs at firms outside of Texas."[30] One recently hired dean at a first-tier school admitted that his proposed approach to rankings was crucial to his hire: "It was a huge issue in the search. I would say that it was the number one issue in the dean's search." According to the long-serving administrators and faculty whom we interviewed, only a few years ago, rankings were rarely mentioned by candidates when they were being considered for the dean position; now most candidates are expected to offer carefully considered strategies for improving a school's ranking. As an associate dean at a top-tier law school recalled a search in the mid-2000s: "I was on the dean search committee, and I think everyone we talked with talked about it. But they all tended to talk about it in different ways. Everything from, 'I think rankings are very important and I'm going to move you up,' to 'I've reverse-engineered *USN* and this is what I think you need to do,' to 'I don't believe in rankings,' so not everyone said the same thing but most people addressed them."

The last response would no longer be acceptable. Many of our respondents lamented the dramatic change in the role of the dean. This change was most sharply drawn by those at schools that had recently replaced well-established deans:

> [Our previous dean] was sort of an academic's academic, [someone in] an ivory-tower position where the world should support us because we think big thoughts, and we will improve the human condition over time, and you have to have a millennium-long perspective and *USN* doesn't fit well into that. [Our new dean] takes much more of a perspective that we live in the real world, the budget depends exactly on where we stand and where we are going, our ability to attract students and to attract donors depends on that, so *USN* is what they are worried about.

> We've had a change of deans recently, and our old dean . . . was pretty much a saint. He would say, "The numbers are the numbers are the numbers." He also had the expression, "The world doesn't need another Harvard." His view of the world was that we are who we are and we are not making any apologies and that's it. The new dean's mission is, I think, to take [our school] to that next level. Whether that means a top-twenty school or a top-fifteen school, the question remains, how are we going to measure that? The most obvious way is by using *USN*.

It has become increasingly difficult for deans to take the view that "the numbers are the numbers." The expectations of what the dean's focus should be, and therefore the activities that constitute her or his job, have changed because of rankings.

A former administrator who now works as a consultant with law schools trying to improve their reputations said his advice about how to manage the rankings is most welcomed by newish deans: "They are fairly young deans and that makes them more receptive to what I'm saying, more interested in changing it. They have a recognition that their [school's] reputation isn't as high as it should be, and that's why they were hired." If true, these claims point to the institutionalization and naturalization of the rankings as a permanent actor in this field. According to this view, newer deans take the rankings into account not only because of the practical effects that the rankings have on their schools but also because these deans take for granted that the rankings are an external force that must be managed.[31]

GAMING THE RANKINGS

The ongoing institutionalization of rankings among deans highlights another important aspect of the rankings: they are seductive, even to those who object to them. This ambivalence toward the rankings is not so surprising. Deans are driven and successful people, and rankings, fairly or not, are often taken as a measure of their competence. The desire to control rankings, to make them seem less like an imposed fate, is alluring because it reasserts some of the discretionary power that rankings have removed. Regardless of outside pressures, deans can easily get caught up in the competitive aspects of rankings.

The line between gaming and managing may be blurry. Gaming can be understood as a more or less cynical effort to manipulate the rankings data without addressing the underlying condition that is the purpose of the measure. It's about managing appearances without really changing anything. Gaming offers a chance to protect one's school from the penalties of a poor ranking, to *do* something in the face of great uncertainty, to reassert some control and maybe even save your job.

Law schools have been creative in their gaming strategies. An early blatant example entailed schools' reporting different numbers to *USN* than to their accrediting body, the American Bar Association. The 1995 rankings issue of *USN* lists 29 schools that reported higher median LSAT scores to the magazine than to the ABA (out of a total of 177 schools surveyed). Detroit Mercy and the University of Alabama were two of the schools that had four-point differentials between their *USN* and ABA medians.[32] More recently, admissions directors at Villanova University School of Law and the University of Illinois School of Law were found to have reported fraudulent LSAT scores to *USN*.[33] Meanwhile, a number of law schools have been or are being sued by graduates charging them with inflating their employment statistics.[34]

Other gaming strategies include defining employment as being employed in any job, no matter how low-paying, rather than as being employed in a legal position, encouraging under-qualified applicants to apply in order to boost selectivity statistics, "skimming" top students from other local schools to keep entering first-year cohorts small, rejecting qualified candidates to protect yields, and "tracking" students with lower LSAT scores into part-time or evening programs, which until recently were not included in *USN*'s statistics.[35] Such gaming strategies have prompted *USN* to engage in counter-gaming strategies such as including part-time students in its selectivity statistics and developing more explicit rules about how to measure rankings criteria. They now also monitor information more closely.

With rankings, one person's climb requires someone else's descent. It is a zero-sum game. Many deans have told us that rankings have exacerbated competition among law schools in ways they find disturbing. Legal education becomes less of a joint national project and more of a desperate attempt to distinguish one's institution from the others. One dean told us, "I think it puts a kind of unwholesome kind of competition between institutions of higher learning; there shouldn't be any competition between lighthouses, and I think we have that." Robert was even blunter in describing how some respondents manipulate reputational surveys:

> Anyone with half an analytical mind knows that the only thing that gets rewarded in the rankings are those who rank out of stupidity or out of evil self-interest. Just because the reputation rankings—which are the largest determinant in the system—because of the way they create those rankings, there are people out there in the country who believe a school like Virginia is not one of the top law schools in the country, or a school like a New York University is not even in the same category of excellence as Penn, or that Harvard is in a qualitatively different position than Stanford. While each of us might have a preference between those schools, no intelligent person could believe that they are not among the top thirty or twenty-five law schools in the country.[36] Yet someone is making that decision in rankings and . . . that gets credited in the ranking. That's just completely and utterly irrational, and we reward that behavior.

A focus on gaming the rankings means not just more competition but also paying less attention to other issues, including disputes with *USN*.

The psychology of gaming is complex and evolving.[37] For those who "live and die by the rankings," anxiety and even panic are natural responses. For many, resorting to gaming tricks feels unseemly, something hard to reconcile with claims about the dignity of the legal profession. No one likes feeling coerced into doing work that they believe is stupid, so resentment suffuses work related to rankings. But rankings also evoke an ambivalence that encourages gaming. If rankings are contemptible, gaming them is more defensible; if everyone else seems to be doing it, it appears less shameful. And if gaming rankings means capitulating to their power, it also offers a response that simultaneously grants some measure of agency to those they rank while simultaneously undermining their legitimacy as accurate measures.

Gaming the rankings demands expertise in the production of the numbers that compose rankings. The game can be seductive. Much like the game of "making out" created by the machinists that Michael Burawoy studied in which workers competed with each other and themselves to meet steady production quotas, the gaming of rankings is also seductive, pulling deans into the excitement of competition.[38] Rankings present a clear goal, reward ingenuity if the goal is met, and punish the failure to meet it. Gaming encourages a literal-mindedness in conforming to the letter rather than the spirit of the enterprise, a familiar part of learning to "think like a lawyer." And gaming rankings ensures that players have a stake in the outcome, which further naturalizes rankings and eases their incorporation into people's sense of themselves. As law school rankings become taken for granted, people are less aware of their influence and less critical of their effects.

The line between pragmatism and capitulation can be blurred. One dean said, "We're not going to get rid of them so we *have* to adapt." Many administrators commented on the hypocrisy of their colleagues. This comment was typical: "I think schools spoke out of both sides of their mouth very early on. They said that [rankings] weren't important publicly, but then would get together with their staffs and do two things: rail on the process of the rankings but stress how important it was to go up in those rankings."

Gaming, as its links to game theory implies, suggests rational actors maximizing self-interest in an evolving and joint project. And that broad characterization fits our findings. Yet it is unsatisfying as an explanation for all that it leaves out: motives, consequences, and the ways rankings become internalized as reference points, norms, values, or even forms of conflict. If gaming challenges the scientific authority of rankings as accurate depictions, it also reinforces people's investments in them, rendering them simultaneously alluring and coercive.

In sum, rankings keep deans awake at night. They pressure deans to make decisions they otherwise wouldn't make. No one feels very noble trading potentially vibrant academic programs for brochures that no one reads or seducing star students from cross-town rivals. "The rankings made me do it" is an embarrassing and diminishing deflection of agency. One dean described the feeling as "being occupied by a foreign power."

Because rankings intensify competition among schools, it is easy to become paranoid. We've had deans request us not to mention particular manipulation strategies to others. Deans have described rivals as lying about admissions statistics and placement rates and feeling as though you should be "looking over your shoulder." And some deans do encourage, at least tacitly, unethical behavior. As a rule, deans of law schools are extraordinarily accomplished and ambitious people, people who haven't failed much, people who believe that talent and hard work will carry the day. But rankings offer an alternative view: one of constraints, impotence, and even shame. Not everyone feels this way, of course. Some deans are frank about their focus on boosting rankings and publicize their successes. But there is no escape from the pressure, and no one wants to feel they have let colleagues or students down; no one wants to have to account for what is sometimes impossible to control.

But this is the situation in which contemporary law schools' deans find themselves, and understanding this situation helps explain the contradiction between deans' behaviors and opinions, their active pursuit of optimizing their rankings despite their disdain for them. Exploring this contradiction sheds light on the constraints, often hidden, created by accountability measures. These measures can, as in the case of law school deans, take judgment and control out of the hands of those who know best by pressuring them to pay fealty to processes that they find unproductive and sometimes even irrational. Expertise gives way to measurement. This process is all the more striking, and demonstrative of the power of accountability measures, when one considers that the people caught in this contradiction are not low- or middle-level managers, but some of the most powerful people in legal education. If even the people at the very top of an organization feel as though they must capitulate to the pressures created by these measures, it is difficult to imagine others without their status or organizational standing resisting the demands of public assessment.

Chapter 6 | Career Services and Employment

OUR INTERVIEW WITH Jane, the director of career services at a first-tier public law school, began like most others. Invited into a neatly organized office, right on schedule, we were politely greeted by a well-dressed woman in her mid-forties. To break the ice, we asked about her background and which parts of her job she most enjoyed. Like many we spoke with, she was thoughtful and articulate. She explained that she has worked in career services for about fifteen years at three schools whose stature and job titles rewarded her experience and expertise. Jane had held this particular position at a large public law school for five years and "loved it." It was exciting work. She especially enjoyed working with students, helping each find the job that was right for her or him: "I always find it an honor to work for students at this point in their careers." Jane's reflections promise a rich interview. She had firsthand experience at schools of different ranks and profiles. She could help us disentangle how rankings, over time, may have influenced the work done in career-services departments: "How, if at all, have rankings affected your job?"

"Well, I was fired last week," she said. "The dean decided that I was responsible for the decline in the rankings from thirty-six to thirty-eight. So, how has *U.S. News* affected my life? Pretty badly."[1]

Less poised than Jane, we could barely mask our shock. Even though we had become accustomed to hearing the many reports of how rankings had complicated administrators' work and made it less enjoyable and of colleagues who had been forced from their jobs due to disappointing numbers, this was the first time we interviewed someone *as* she was being fired "because of the rankings." We marveled at Jane's grace and candor with intrusive sociologists at this difficult time. But she told us, "At first I thought of canceling, but then I thought this is probably the type of stuff you're interested in learning about."

Perhaps Jane's account should not have been so surprising to us, because hers was hardly a rare experience. Nearly every career-services administrator we interviewed spoke of friends and acquaintances who had been fired for "their numbers." The numbers that matter in career services are the employment rate at graduation (accounting for 4 percent of a school's overall ranking), the employment rate nine months after graduation (14 percent), and the percentage of graduates to pass the bar exam (2 percent).[2] Rankings direct administrative high beams on placement statistics with an almost blinding glare, which can produce immense pressure on personnel to raise their employment numbers. Most career-service directors have explicit or implicit targets, which are set by the administration. These target numbers, thresholds, or trends may affect bonuses, salary, and security.[3] One director stated, "I know quite a few career-services deans and directors who lost their jobs over this. Deans who didn't quite understand what was going on and thought that, 'It's *your* fault. You're not getting the numbers, it's *your* fault.' And it wasn't their fault."

Such recounting, if taken at face value, might reflect a few famous and oft retold cases, a circling of professional wagons, or even apocryphal horror stories of the sort that colleagues tell to scare themselves over drinks at a professional meeting. Our evidence suggests otherwise. Jane's immediate predecessor had lost her job for the same reason after just one year.

Consider the headline over a 2013 post on the popular *Beyond the Law* website.[4] Referred to by many educational insiders as a "scam blog," the site announces in big, dark type "Some Students Want Their Deans Fired After Poor Showing in the U.S. News Rankings (and One Head That's Already Rolled)." The "head" in question, according to this posting, belonged to Camille Chin-Kee-Fatt, formerly the director of career services at Brooklyn Law School, who was forced to resign because employment numbers were blamed for a drop in the school's rank. In an email to the "Brooklyn Law School Community," Dean Nicholas Allard wrote, "Today, Camille Chin-Kee-Fatt submitted her resignation as Director of Career Services, and I have accepted it. On behalf of the entire community, we are grateful for her service over many years and her commitment to Brooklyn Law School. . . . Finding jobs for our students that are meaningful continues to be my highest priority." *Beyond the Law,* suggesting that *USN* seems to have become even more powerful in a tight legal job market, noted that Chin-Kee-Fatt was an "easy scapegoat" for a relatively new and no doubt anxious dean looking to show constituents that something is being done about a drop in the rankings. It is informative to look more closely at the process by which one administrator comes to be blamed for rankings disappointment.

The backstory: In 2012, the American Bar Association changed its reporting rules for counting who is employed. This was in response to growing public outcry about suspect employment statistics, including charges of "lying with statistics," lawsuits filed by angry unemployed graduates, and prominent and unflattering stories in the *New York Times*.[5] The eventual outcome was a new, more complex classification system that breaks down employment into subcategories with additional instructions and definitions. This proliferation of distinctions, this hairsplitting, is actually a ratcheting up of bureaucratic meticulousness. The reasons for and the consequences of this creation of precise distinctions are worth careful scrutiny for what they reveal about bureaucratic disciplining and the contested, evolving dynamics it involves.

The development of more fine-grained measures follows the typical unfolding and expansion of bureaucratic logic, a process made famous by Max Weber in his classic historical analyses of rationalization and its relation to capitalist and political development.[6] This expansion of bureaucratic practices helps explain the proliferation of standardization, rules, calculations, offices, and many of the other familiar features of bureaucracies that we associate with modern life. Large organizational bureaucracies tend to become ever more articulated in response to challenges like the ones created by the ABA and *USN*: conflicting interests, politics, a desire to look or be efficient, pressure for clarity or fairness, evolving complexity or ambiguity, gaming, economic and professional power, or some combination of all of these. As Weber and other scholars have noticed, this proliferation of bureaucratic practices is hard to contain, partly because these practices become imbued with status, purpose, and power. It is difficult to curtail this expansion unless the groups who have become fluent in these same features of bureaucracies voluntarily surrender these enticements. Naturally, they are reluctant to concede organizational turf, expertise, or even professional identities to others without a fight. Sometimes the burden of such bureaucratic edifices becomes too cumbersome for the bureaucracy to maintain its usefulness—the brokenness of the apparatus is too publicly obvious to ignore—opening the possibility for reform. In the case of employment statistics, the ABA could not buffer itself from the threats of lawsuits, congressional oversight, the *New York Times*, or the conflicts among law schools about gaming and reporting, so change was necessary.

Changes to bureaucratic practices, however, are much more likely to be incremental than fundamental. This was true for the responses of the ABA and *USN*. They made small changes in existing practices, a conservative process but one that made sense in light of their past successes and the uncertainties of more wholesale change. In this way, core processes, the main business of an organization, are buffered from dramatic structural changes.[7] Small shifts seem less likely to result in surprising and undesirable big changes. So, the ABA's response to gaming was to fiddle. No overhaul of embedded classificatory schemes, no abrupt shift in power or duties, but rather more of the same kinds of logic and processes deployed in carefully contained locations in direct response to the gaming problems it was trying to curtail.

The new rulemaking that was the ABA's vehicle for responding to the fury created by suspect employment statistics was a protracted process. The legitimacy of these actions—actions that were politicized because they directly affected so many institutions and people and created new winners and losers—hinged on their being participatory, deliberative, and scrupulously procedurally correct. The upshot of this reform in reporting standards is that it precluded certain kinds of manipulation and gaming or, at a minimum, made these practices more difficult to engage in covertly. *USN*, which relies on these ABA statistics, was able to integrate these new distinctions into its own formula and now, like the ABA, can distinguish between graduates employed full-time and part-time, temporarily and permanently, and between those working in jobs that require a J.D. and those who are not. Notice that this accumulation of constituencies for these numbers, from the ABA to *USN* to applicants to law schools, propels them and their uses, making them more durable. Rules beget rules. And rules beget people with interests and expertise in those rules.

The creation of more specific categories is intended to impede schools' ability to obscure real differences in employment success and to make this aspect of legal education more transparent. They may succeed in doing so, at least for a period of time. But in career services, as in admissions and the dean's office, gaming is a moving target. Schools had constructed their public employment numbers to make themselves look as good as possible under the existing rules, so the new reporting rules were a threat to the many schools whose rank had benefited from the definitions and the manipulations that were possible using the old classifications. The new system will make some of these schools look as though they are doing worse, even if nothing has changed except how numbers are reported.

And that is why Dean Allard of Brooklyn Law School had every right to be anxious and likely why Camille Chin-Kee-Fatt was forced to resign. Before the new categories were in place, Brooklyn Law School's ranking was sixty-five. The first year after the change, the school "failed to submit" its employment statistics, likely in anticipation of a bad outcome. It is *USN*'s practice to estimate unreported employment statistics, and these estimates are believed to be very conservative so as to discourage schools from withholding data from *USN*. The school's ranking dropped to eighty. Brooklyn's administrators may well have anticipated that their rank would drop in light of the more detailed reporting categories that were introduced and may have bet that even the conservative estimates made by *USN* would be higher than their rates under the new regime. In other words, they could game the new numbers, too.

What can we learn from experiences like Jane's and the story about Brooklyn Law School? Most obviously, their crises exemplify the risk of rankings. Jane is not a one-off casualty. Again, it is clear that jobs are at stake in the race to improve *USN* indicators. The small change in the ranking of Jane's school was most likely not capturing any important change in the law school; the measures are too crude, the variation in them too compressed, and the gaming too rampant for that. But that the difference between thirty-six and thirty-eight was not statistically meaningful was not relevant to the decision about Jane's job. When the numbers decline, deans must demonstrate that they are doing *something* to deal with it. One clear signal is to fire and hire. Even if Jane's dean was strategically using the change in rankings as a pretext to replace Jane—which seems unlikely— what matters is that this was what Jane was told and what she and others believed. That she was fired for "her numbers" is certainly how colleagues and potential employers would understand her record as well. Indeed, we spoke with several other professors and administrators at Jane's school, and all of them told us, when we asked them about this, that she had been fired because of the employment numbers.

Supporters of rankings argue that the market discipline imposed by *USN* rankings produces informed consumers, which is good for what many see as complacent, wealthy, and self-serving organizations that should do better by their students. Law schools have plenty of critics, including many inside the academy who believe legal education is in the midst of a crisis (although these "crisis" arguments are a source of great contention within the legal education field).[8] It is not just disgruntled students but faculty, staff, and even deans who worry that students are no longer viewed as the priority they should be. And certainly it is easy for faculties and schools to lose sight of student needs in their competition for status—now powerfully mediated by *USN* rankings. The production of more measures and more precise measures is likely not the answer to the "crisis." The accountability produced by these particular employment numbers, some version of which have long been collected by the ABA and incorporated into rankings, often does not productively redistribute energies and resources in ways that directly benefit students' job searches or their well-being.

THE WORK OF CAREER SERVICES

Rankings have changed the day-to-day work of career services. Tasks revolving around "the numbers," the term of use that confirms their power, now absorb big chunks of the resources dedicated to career services, while other important tasks such as career counseling and individualized help attract less attention and fewer resources than in the era before rankings.

Ideas about what is exemplary work in career services have also been transformed by rankings. A narrow focus on the numbers makes those in career services easy scapegoats when rankings expectations go unmet. As a result, career service professionals, like their counterparts in the admissions office and sometimes even the dean's office, now have less discretion in their work, are more accountable to imposed standards, and find that their jobs are more tenuous.

Traditionally, the main task of career services has been to help students find good jobs that are interesting and well compensated and that match their interests. Ironically, most who work in this field became interested in career services because they were unsatisfied with their own employment after law school. Nearly all of the career-services personnel that we spoke with had first practiced law; one had taken a career-services position right after completing her M.B.A. Those who practiced law realized, most within two to three years, that "this wasn't for me" and found themselves attracted to the lower pay but more reasonable hours of law school administration. They consistently told us that they were especially drawn to the idea of helping students find the right jobs in launching their legal careers and many cited their own career counselors as inspiration—as negative models. They knew what it was like to be in the wrong job.

In a career-services office on a typical day you will likely find a diverse, although disproportionately female, staff comprising a director, at least one assistant director, and, depending on the resources of the school, an assortment of other full-time, part-time, and student personnel. Before rankings, these employees divided their time between advising students and maintaining or strengthening relationships with current and potential employers. During the school year, schedules are also filled with individual meetings with students; one director told us, "I am in constant contact with students." In these sessions, counselors offer a wide range of personalized mentoring. For first- and second-year students, career counseling might involve helping them figure out the type of legal career they are best suited for and helping them secure summer internships, often a step toward a job offer. These meetings might also offer students a safe place to vent frustrations or get a reality check if their job expectations are out of line with their academic performance. For third-year students, these meetings are for pressing issues such as assessing their immediate job prospects, polishing résumés, discussing how to present themselves at interviews, and sharing tips for negotiating offers. Although career-services personnel complain about students wanting them to "solve all of their problems," they also acknowledge that this mentoring is what they enjoy most about their job.

A second key part of the job has been to develop and maintain good relationships with employers. This involves keeping in touch with the firms that have historically hired from the school, arranging on-campus interviews (sometimes referred to as OCIs—a key junction in the job process), and making sure that alumni are doing well and are willing to lend a hand to budding lawyers from their alma mater. It also entails seeking out new employers and trying to convince them to do on-campus interviews or to broaden the pool of applicants that they will consider, such as interviewing those with a GPA of 3.2 rather than 3.3 or those who rank in the top 30 percent of the class rather than only those in the top 20 percent.

At schools from all tiers, rankings pressures change the rhythms of the job, priorities, and the use and distribution of resources. A director at a first-tier school captured the sentiment of many when she said, "From the career-services side, the rankings are just the bane of our existence." Rankings have become so disruptive in career services in large part because this administrative unit is directly responsible for factors that make up 18 percent of the school's overall score. Even this percentage significantly underestimates the associated pressures generated by this factor because deans believe they can exert more influence on placement numbers than they can on more nebulous factors such as the school's reputation among practitioners. Administrators also recognize that small improvements can produce big payoffs for their rank because employment statistics are so compressed. The most heavily weighted factor in the employment statistics used to calculate this portion of the ranking is employment nine months after graduation. The median employment rate at nine months after graduation for all schools is about 93 percent, so that "the entire game of this variable [is] played out in the remaining 7 percent."[9] A few more jobs for a few more students can make a big difference. These placement statistics, especially employment nine months after graduation, are a driving force in career-services offices.

MAXIMIZING EMPLOYMENT NUMBERS

Without exception, the career-services personnel we interviewed reported that they were pressured to raise their employment numbers. How they do so is an iterative exercise in adopting new tactics depending on which statistics the ABA requires in its annual report, which indicators and weights USN uses, what others are doing, what the dean and faculty demand, and how much one can stomach. Because positions in career services are relatively low-status in the administrative hierarchy of law schools, they are particularly vulnerable—an unhappy condition that magnifies the influence of rankings in the work that gets done and even who is hired. Many see themselves as "very easy targets" for blame when their school's ranking does not meet expectations, due to the prominence of the numbers produced by their office and because, in the words of one administrator, "People in the career-services area certainly are not at the top of the heap in their law schools."

The extent of this pressure varies according to recent performance, the status of the law school, and how local rivals are doing. Schools at the very top with enviable reputations and rankings—say, Yale, Harvard, or Stanford—hardly face the same intense pressures as those experienced at Brooklyn Law School. The dismal job market since 2008 has complicated the task of finding good legal jobs for graduates of all schools, but this task is a greater challenge for those at the margins, who can only envy the resources and networks of those at the top. Often pressure comes straight from the dean's office. For one director of career services at a school that had recently risen in the rankings, improvement in the rankings "is a continuous—this is all confidential, right?—it's a continuous theme and mantra of sorts that I hear from the administration. There's a great emphasis put on them, particularly since our school moved up from the third tier to the second tier recently. It's stressed frequently."

But faculty anxiety can also be directed toward the career-services office. When asked if she felt pressure because of the rankings, a director of careers services at a third-tier school responded:

> Definitely I do. I go to the faculty meetings, and they want to know why we don't have more people employed or what's up with the numbers or why we can't get them higher. And sometimes it's not even directed directly to me, but just comments like, "You know, we wouldn't be in the third tier if we could just get that employment up. What's going on with employment?" . . . It just so happens that we are the lightning rod, we are the last stop for everyone.

Commenting on the pressure he feels at his job, a career-services administrator at a second-tier school also mentioned pressure coming from the faculty:

> It's not really been the dean so much; mainly it has been all faculty. It never fails that they will say, "Why can't you get these people jobs? I got ten students jobs." And all of these students are, like, the top of the class. It's that bottom ten percent that is hard to employ. As a community, all of our end goal is the same: to take entering students and send them out into the world as employable professionals. It should be a cooperative effort. It shouldn't be: "What can you do to raise the rank?"

And no one scrutinizes employment statistics more keenly than do law students, who read them practically as if they were tea leaves forecasting their futures. Like deans and faculty, they want answers from career services. When the numbers drop or compare unfavorably with those of peer schools, students can be scathing in their criticisms. Unemployed students, many of whom are deeply in debt, look for someone to blame. Their anger and sense of having been duped by the placement numbers and the marketing machines of law schools are shared in emails and in phone calls. Sometimes they withhold vital information about their employment status, even if it might be in their best interest to provide it. And of course, the anonymity of cyber space makes it a locus for some of the most scurrilous comments about career counselors. A quick glance at a few blogs yields adjectives too ripe to reproduce. More temperate criticism is also easy to find. The words "appalling," "furious," and "liars" are common.

In 2013, unhappy law students at American University's Washington College of Law launched an online petition in which they demanded the dean's removal and "a complete overhaul of the Office of Career Development." They cited the following employment figures:

Washington College of Law's employment at graduation rate, according to *US News,* was an abysmal 36.4 percent. For comparison Catholic University Columbus School of Law came in at a 37.5 percent employment at graduation rate, George Washington Law School managed to get 81.7 percent of their graduates employed, Howard University School of Law had an employment at graduation rate of 48.4 percent, and Georgetown University Law Center mustered up a 63.7 percent employment rate for their graduates.[10]

Career-services personnel, then, feel the heat of rankings expectations from all sides. Disappointing rankings demand an explanation, and explanations often demand a culprit. The combination of low status, seemingly clear numbers, and the importance of their mission to help students find jobs encourages finger pointing at their department. Everyone we spoke to believed their job conditions had worsened since rankings had become so influential.

MORE OR LESS TRANSPARENCY?

Numbers create transparency, which in turn produces accountability, incentives, and improvement. So goes the argument of those advocating quantitative evaluation systems like the rankings. In other words, the public comparisons of employment rates provide motivation for lagging schools to push harder and work better, middling schools to raise their standards, and outstanding schools to maintain their excellence. All law school personnel care about getting students jobs, especially in light of the cost of their legal education. Employment rates seem like a straightforward and simple measure: either one has a job or not, so employment numbers seem to provide a strong case for the value of rankings and similar accountability measures. Everyone agrees that career-services personnel should be doing everything they can to help graduating students find jobs and that those who underperform compared to their peers—something rankings make evident—should face the consequences.

What is wrong with this thinking? To answer this we return to some of the practices that precipitated the ABA reforms of employment measures used in rankings.

Because measures are never an exact representation of the underlying qualities they are designed to assess, it is almost always easier to improve the number than the underlying qualities. One unanticipated consequence of emphasizing employment rates is that the definition of what counts as employed has changed as schools have tried to climb in the rankings. The "employment rate" may seem like a fairly objective "yes or no" measure. In fact, its ambiguity can be exploited. The most striking example of this was the rankings-inspired practice of counting those working in any non-legal job as "employed" in the *USN* survey. For years, *USN*, following the official ABA classification of employment, used a broad definition of what it means to be employed. As one administrator said, "When they ask for the employment figure, employed means full-time or part-time, temporary or permanent, legal or non-legal. It means doing nails."[11] More experienced directors described to us how they have had to adapt their counting procedures to the ABA's new rules. One administrator explained:

When I first started, the NALP [National Association for Law Placement] form asked for the number of students who have received offers. That is how you calculate these numbers for them. So when I first started that is how I calculated these numbers for *USN*. So even if they were a night student who worked full-time, if they didn't get an offer, then for NALP purposes I would count them as unemployed. That would then translate over to *USN* as unemployed. The same with students who were working in a nonlegal capacity. If they didn't get an offer, then they were considered unemployed. But in the years I've been in this position and in talking to other schools about how they've been doing it, that's not necessarily the way that people report it. You know, as long as they are working, they are counted as employed. . . . So in the four years that I've been here, I've seen our numbers dramatically increase because of those differences in reporting in terms of who's employed and who's not employed. Which is great for me because they are like, "Wow, you are doing such a great job."

Although we came across a few schools that did not calculate their employment figures according to these loose standards, our interviews suggest that this strategy became a nearly universal practice. While some expressed misgivings about not following the spirit of the rule—"They want to know any job that people get, and so in one way that means McDonalds, and that is no success for us"—others justified this practice by explaining that, as well-trained lawyers, they followed the "letter of the law": "You know, we're lawyers. We are trained to say if that's the rule or there's the line, I can go up to that line; and as long as I don't cross the line, I'm acting appropriately. In the instructions it just asks you whether or not a person is employed, and you try to be as smart within the rules as you possibly can. So I think, initially, people weren't quite sure whether they should do that but then they realized that employed is employed is employed."

Whether or not schools felt comfortable adopting this strategy, it became pervasive because schools feared the consequences if they failed to exploit the ambiguity about who counts as employed as their competitors did. If you don't use this less stringent criterion for counting who is employed, your employment numbers will sink and your job security will become precarious. This is the burden of relative measures such as rankings. A long-term director told us of how she was urging a younger colleague at a nearby school to adopt this method of counting so that this colleague could keep her job. Despite pressure from her dean, this younger colleague had stuck by her principles and had refused to count those in nonlegal jobs as employed. Relating the advice she had given, the experienced director said, "I told her that she should start thinking about it. It's not that we are simple or innocent, it's just that we never cared particularly about how far we could go with definitions because our primary concern was if students were finding the kind of job that they came to law school dreaming of . . . I agree with taking the high road, but it is probably an unnecessary high road."

The spread of attitudes like this exemplifies what one administrator called a "race to the bottom," where schools are pressured to conform to a lowest common denominator of standards in order to remain competitive within the rules established by rankings.

USN measures encourage schools to be much more concerned about *how many* of their students are employed rather than *how well* they are employed, a focus that creates still other perverse incentives. Several career service administrators noted that each year they face dilemmas about whether to advise students to accept job offers that these students feel are not right for them—because the salary is low or the job is not at a firm or in a city that the student prefers—so that they will count as "employed" on the *USN* survey, or to encourage them to reject these offers and hold out for better opportunities, with the risk that they will be counted as "unemployed" on the survey. A director of career services at a first-tier school told us, "In the past there have been lots of instances where I have told students not to take a job, but even I have [become] more guarded in giving that kind of advice. You feel a conflict between the perception of what's best for the student and [what's best] for the numbers, and ideally both of those things will coincide. But in that context that's not necessarily the case."

At the extreme, this logic prompts staff to urge students to take any job during the period when employment surveys are filled out. One director lamented, "Now it's like, 'Can you get a job in the beauty salon painting nails until these numbers are in?' " Rankings pressure rewards schools for adopting strategies that improve numbers without improving the results that matter and that the measures are supposed to convey. Instead of increasing transparency, this seemingly straightforward measure is creating something that is more dangerous: opacity in the guise of transparency, accountability undermined by accounting.

Employment statistics are manipulated not just by misleading definitions but also through more creative forms of gaming. These range from generous rounding practices to overt lying, with the aim of closing both small and large gaps between reality and the desired number. As with other locations inside law schools, the overarching impulse in career-services offices is always and relentlessly to maximize the numbers. Part of the dynamism of rankings, especially in their unintended consequences, arises from evolving modes of inventive gaming that offer valuable, albeit temporary, advantage. Innovation in gaming tactics is most useful before competition encourages broad diffusion of a new tactic and comparative advantage dwindles: once everyone is doing it, the premium is lost. This perspective helps make sense of remarkable employment rates during a recession.

People shared with us many strategies schools use to improve their numbers. Employment statistics make good objects for manipulation because they are hard to verify. Verification would require the same onerous detective work that schools must perform to collect the data from graduates in the first place. Several interviewees from different schools accused others of sending letters or leaving phone messages for hard-to-contact graduates saying, in effect, "If we don't hear back from you, we will assume you are employed."[12] A few career-services directors admitted receiving vague demands "to do something about the numbers" that made them feel like they might be expected to do something ethically questionable. A director of career services at a first-tier law school told us,

> What I saw with faculty was that they would never be willing to do any-thing unethical, but they would be perfectly willing to have me do something unethical if it were to mean an increase in our rankings. . . . I was struck by the fact that within the career-services committee, the faculty members on the committee—who I am sure themselves would never engage in any unethical behavior—ask me why we have to be so lily-white. And I tell them that I am responsible for the numbers, that's why.

A faculty member at another school related to us that a former career-services director was looking into filing a wrongful dismissal suit, claim-ing he was fired within twenty-four hours of refusing to submit what he believed were false numbers to the reports that were to be sent to the ABA and *USN*. In a different case, we were contacted by a lawyer look-ing for information on behalf of a client who was considering suing her school for wrongful dismissal because she refused to jimmy the numbers. During our interviews we heard numerous reports from administrators about similar activities at other schools. There is no question that some feel pressure to, in the words of one director, "phony up the numbers," although we do not know how common such practices are.

Another common gaming strategy is for the school itself to hire unemployed graduates on a temporary basis to bolster employment numbers.[13] Students are typically hired for one or two months at a mod-est rate of pay to work as research or teaching assistants, library aides, or mail clerks at the law school so they can be counted as "employed" on the *USN* survey. This practice seems most prevalent among schools in or near the top fifty—they have the money to adopt it. One faculty member at a first-tier school told us, "We did what I think is the worst thing we've ever done related to rankings, and that was . . . to hire all of our own graduates who were unemployed in the first thirty days fol-lowing graduation so that the first number ["employed at graduation"] would be absolutely great."

This person saw the hiring of graduate students as dishonest and as a poor use of resources, but others pointed out some benefits from this practice. A dean who had previously served as an administrator and faculty member at a school that hired its own graduates (and who claimed credit for the idea) maintained that "there are very rational rea-sons why you would have a program where you would hire students who are unemployed at graduation. One of the biggest problems of being unemployed is the psychological dignity and issues." Regardless of the indirect benefits that students may receive through their alma mater's adoption of this strategy, it is clear that its primary purpose is to raise these schools' at-graduate employment figure and, they hope, influence their overall rank.[14]

Such gaming strategies highlight the ambiguities that reside within all measures. There are analogous strategies for nearly every measure used by *USN*. Even such an apparently simple question as "How many of your graduates are employed?" can be finessed in a way that puts its accuracy and meaning in doubt. One director of career services remarked, "I think the biggest frustration with the rankings is that there is ambiguity about what counts as a job. What counts as a job and what doesn't? And schools can take whatever interpretation of that and use it."

Gaming changes professional relations, too. When third- and fourth-tier schools report better numbers than Stanford and Yale, it is hard for career-services professionals who read this not to be skeptical and resentful. One administrator said, "The other thing we reward in ranking is lying, cheating, stealing, and otherwise not telling the truth. Because one hundred law schools in the country don't have 95 percent of their graduates employed." Another said,

> Sometimes you look at the numbers and all you can say is, "Really! Wow, look at that, 100 percent of their graduates are employed and the economy's in the tank!" Now how can that be? They have an assistant dean for career services and admissions and we have five full-time career-services people in one of the largest legal markets in the United States, and ours is this and they're in Paducah, Kentucky—I'm just making that up—and they're 100 percent employed. So, some of the numbers to me come across as disingenuous.

Manipulation or disingenuous responses reduce the numbers' usefulness, and this is the opposite of transparency. Morriss and Henderson found that employment at graduation for all law schools rose from 62.6 percent in the 1999 rankings to 73.9 percent in the 2006 rankings.[15] During the same period, employment nine months after graduation rose from 83.9 percent to a remarkable 91.6 percent. This stunning change is less about advances in placement than about advances in gaming.[16] The precipitous drop in the ranking of schools such as Brooklyn Law School after *USN* changed its reporting rules clearly demonstrates this.

And the recession took its toll. Nine months after graduation, the employment rate of 2012 graduates was 84.7 percent, down from 91.9 percent in 2007. Even more disconcerting for students, however, was that "the percentage of graduates who found full-time, long-term employment in jobs requiring bar passage remained below 60 percent."[17] Many law students accumulate enormous debt with the idea that they will pay it off comfortably once they start earning large salaries at their virtually assured jobs.[18] As the job market for those with law degrees has deteriorated over the last several years, however, students have begun to recognize this discrepancy between the reports and the employment reality.[19] This awareness has prompted unemployed graduates to file at least twenty class-action lawsuits against law schools, claiming that the employment statistics that law schools published constituted, in effect, fraud.[20] The result is not just bad publicity for schools. Students crying "Fraud!" have also galvanized lawmakers such as Senator Barbara Boxer of California to intervene.

HOW RANKINGS CHANGE WHAT CAREER-SERVICES PERSONNEL DO

Changing the definition of employment is not the only unintended consequence of this new emphasis on employment measures. The measures have also transformed the actual work of career-services personnel: how they spend their time, energy, and resources. Attempts to maximize employment numbers have led to a focus on a few narrow aspects of the job at the expense of others. While increased attention to determining the employment status of students may improve some aspects of career services, the overriding effect is to jeopardize the quality of services offered to students.

Tracking Missing Students

To improve their numbers, most schools now devote ample resources to learning the whereabouts of their recent graduates. They are especially eager to track down—and count—any who might fit into the "employed nine months after graduation" category. For every four graduates a school cannot account for, USN assumes that three are unemployed.[21] This is likely to be a very conservative estimate of their graduates' employment status, because the likelihood of their graduates being employed is much greater than 25 percent when, as we have discussed, any job counts as being "employed." So finding "unknowns" so that they become "knowns" is an obvious way to improve a school's employment rate. Thus, differences in employment rates have long had as much to do with tracking former students as with tallying actual job opportunities.[22] After unpacking this measure, Theodore P. Seto concludes that given the tiny differences among the top hundred law schools, the most important factor in determining this figure was "the amount of staff time each law school was willing to devote to managing this figure [by tracking down graduates]. From an educational perspective, this time was completely wasted."[23] Another administrator explained, "Even though, in any rational sense of the world, the rankings don't have any relationship to reality, we know that if one of your students doesn't report one year, your employment ranking will go down, not because your student's unemployed but because the students wouldn't report. And that will have an impact on how the school's ranked."

Each year schools bounce around in the rankings as a result of minor oscillations in the number of students that they are unable to track down. The overall ranking of the University of Texas School of Law dropped from eighteen to twenty-nine from 1997 to 1998, reportedly because a small group of recent graduates failed to return their employment surveys.[24] Makau W. Mutua, the dean of the SUNY Buffalo Law School, contends that small changes in one factor should not lead to such disproportionate shifts in how schools are perceived:

> The big part of our problem with *U.S. News* had to do with integrity of their system. To give you a sense, in 2007 we were ranked no. 77; in 2008, no. 100; in 2009, no. 85; today we are ranked at 103. Surely, that kind of volatility speaks, in my view, to the lack of integrity of the process. The one thing that really affected us this year was that last year we reported one unemployed (graduate) and this year we had nine unemployed, and it is those nine who cause us this problem. It seems to me, in terms of weighting, nine unemployed people should not cause this much volatility.[25]

Fair or not, the dramatic effect of these fluctuations in employment numbers on a school's overall ranking explains why the pressure is so intense.

Every person we interviewed in career services complained about the "tremendous amount of time" dedicated to maximizing their employment numbers. One director of career services explained, "Now we expend a great deal of resources keeping track of that kind of information so that we can give it to *USN*. I spend at least one day a week on this, and my assistant spends at least two days a week." Another told us, "The first time we really reach out to them after May [when they graduate] is sometime in October, and then again in November, and then again in December. During this time we are inputting surveys into the program. And then I usually turn towards it in a very concentrated way in January and February, and I search through each and every [student] record."

Many described how, in the months before their numbers are due—primarily, January and February—most of their time is devoted to trying to learn the employment status of as many graduates as possible. One office reported that each member of its six-person full-time staff dedicates two entire months to this work each year. When asked how much time her office spends tracking down this information, another administrator replied, "We don't calculate how much time and people-hours we put in because it would be too upsetting."

In addition to the time investment, the lengths to which those in career services go to find out whether or not graduates are employed is eye-opening. One director told us: "I track them down, and I track them down any way I can. . . . I call old boyfriends. I call parents. I am not ashamed to do that. I go on the Internet and look up whatever I can on www.what evername.com, you know? I do it all. I hunt them down. I have never been below 96 percent in response, and I never will be." Several directors admitted that if a classmate said, "person X has a job," that was enough verification to count them as employed. In this way, career-services staff come to resemble private detectives; indeed, one administrator admitted, "We've actually talked about hiring a private investigator to go through all federal documents, W-2 forms, etc. to find out whether that person is actually employed or not."[26]

It is not surprising, then, that many in career services also note that this is the most stressful and least enjoyable aspect of their job. One director echoed the sentiments of many when she said, "It's awful. I would say that for me personally it is by far, hands-down, the most stressful part of my job. . . . I dread February. I dread that period of time because it is so bad." This dread is easy to understand, given that a great deal of their effort in this last month before the numbers are due is aimed at finding students who do not want to be found, and activities such as cold calling recent graduates bring to mind comparisons with telemarketers.[27]

But do these activities improve outcomes for students? Do they lead to better career services? A few administrators and faculty did see these redoubled efforts at tracking down students as beneficial. One administrator at a school that had moved back and forth between the first and second tier explained: "Now, the good news about what [this emphasis] has done is that it has pushed law school people to find every one of their graduates. And that's one of the good outcomes, because that is not that easy to do. And I can tell you that our career-services director has devoted herself to finding every single person. . . . So it has encouraged people to stay in better touch with their alumni and to find their graduates. There's a plus side." The implication here is that the better the communication between schools and their graduates, the more likely it is that schools will continue to provide assistance to these alumni, especially those who are unemployed, or underemployed, after they graduate.

Most staff, however, thought otherwise, saying that the time spent gathering employment information kept them from helping students as much as they used to. Now, staff simply have less time to help former students find jobs or find better jobs because they dedicate so much time to determining whether or not the students have a job. This is why the vast majority in career services believe that these activities do nothing directly to improve the actual quality of career services. Accounting for the employment status of students is not the same as helping them find employment. One such comment:

> The time I spend tracking down those thirty-three students who don't respond I should be spending on strengthening employer contacts, developing new programs to help students be successful in their searches. [Searching for missing graduates] is the most aggravating part of my job— but the dean wants those numbers. It is a huge amount of effort and what is unfortunate is that we spend so much time trying to collect that data that there are two or three weeks straight through that Susan and I would block out our calendars and not take any appointments because we had to be focusing on these numbers, and it ultimately affects the efficient running of our office.

These cuts in services are especially dangerous because they are hard to measure: students are often unaware of the services they are not receiving as a result of the attention being paid to the rankings.

The students, of course, are not the only ones affected by these changes. By altering their day-to-day work routines, the emphasis on numbers has also transformed how career-services personnel think about their job and profession. Tracking down students is far removed from the student counseling that most see as the most valuable purpose of their work and the reason why they initially entered this occupation. An administrator at a first-tier school explained:

> The best piece of this job typically is when you are helping people, and that's why most people go into it. When you are helping people figure out what they want to do or helping them get a job, that is the piece of it that sort of makes up for everything else. And it is sort of becoming much more statistically oriented; we're a big school to begin with so our resources here are stretched a little bit and the more resources that we spend on USN and on the statistics, the less time we have for the students.

Many in career services are unhappy at the conflict between their professional view of what good career-services work entails and the requirements that rankings impose. They feel less helpful to students and worry that such a concerted effort to maximize employment numbers will affect their efforts to help students find the "right" job instead of "a" job. Although not all respondents expressed this worry, almost all agreed that the services they provide are compromised by rankings pressures.

EMPLOYERS

As in most professions, the job market for lawyers is not one market but many. The legal profession is stratified by the type of law practiced, the status of one's clients, and the status credentials of the lawyers working in the organization. One big status divide is whether one serves corporations or individuals—corporate work has more status. It also matters a great deal whether one works at a large international law firm, in a smaller "boutique" firm, as a solo practitioner, as corporate counsel, or in government. The work of an attorney at a large firm and that of the solo practitioner differs significantly, not just in what they do but also in how they are judged by other professionals. Far more lawyers work as solo practitioners, in smaller firms, and in government than in the biggest law firms. There are important status differences within each of these categories of lawyerly employment. Others factors in attorneys' status are the law school attended, the kind of law practiced and, for more local status, one's regional and community ties.

As social critics and social scientists have shown repeatedly, those on top of a social order have the resources and power to define worth and success in terms that benefit them, even if these terms are neither exhaustive nor uniform. In law, this means that success, broadly construed, is determined by those who make and police its crucial boundaries. Elite universities and colleges, law schools, practitioners, clients, and the media all play their role in defining the "best," and this includes determining what most people consider to be the best jobs. Powerful bodies such as the American Bar Association, the Law School Admission Council, *USN,* and others certainly play important roles in the machinery of professional education, and sometimes they exert independent influence. Yet entities and organizations would not be able to sustain their practices if they were rejected by elite members of the profession, or if the notions of success that are embedded in these practices did not conform to the ideas and practices of most of the professions' powerful players. The "best" jobs within any profession are culturally constructed categories that are marked by distance from what lies below and around, a distance and filtering that rankings reproduce, formalize, popularize, and sometimes reconfigure. Elite law firms require "elite" lawyers, and in the United States, the legal profession depends on elite schools to signal merit. For a status system to work, access to the elite must be strictly policed in order for distinctions to remain legitimate. A recruiting attorney offered the prevailing view: "Number one people go to number one schools."[28]

As we have argued in earlier chapters and elsewhere, there is variation in how rankings affect law schools and legal education. How rankings affect students' employment, of course, also varies according to factors such as the location of their school, its rank, whether it is private or public, and the types of networks it is part of. After first noting some of the important patterns in how rankings shape perceptions of employment, we will say a bit more about how they do or do not matter for different kinds of employers. While much of our analysis focuses on practices *inside* law schools and *inside* the field of legal education, employment is obviously one of the most important arenas in law for understanding how status and inequality are produced and arbitrated through rankings.

The Legal Labor Market

It is useful to describe briefly some of the broad features of the structure of the legal profession as it affects new lawyers, especially in light of the Great Recession. In 2012, about 760,000 lawyers were employed in the United States. Of these, 22 percent were self-employed. The median annual wage for lawyers was $113,530. The bottom 10 percent earned less than $54,000, and the top 10 percent earned more than $187,000.[29] Big Law, that ubiquitous and ambiguous symbolic placeholder for large corporate law firms, gets the most media attention and, for many, symbolizes success— this despite the fact that there is no consensus on just what "big" means, which is precisely why it is such a useful rhetorical sign. A broad definition of "big" would be firms of over one hundred attorneys, including part-timers. The mid-eighties saw the beginning of a trend of a higher proportion of new lawyers going to work for firms of over one hundred employees. In 2008, the peak of Big Law hiring, about 43 percent of recent graduates were hired by such firms.[30] Thus, even at the peak, these firms were never the source of the majority of jobs. This trend shifted abruptly starting in 2010. By 2014 only about 35 percent of graduates were hired in firms of over one hundred attorneys. This cohort, part of the so-called "Lost Generation," whose life chances as lawyers were marked, perhaps permanently, by the recession, saw only 34 percent of its new J.D.s entering firms with more than one hundred attorneys. In 2014, for the first time since 1996, only about 51 percent, "a bare majority," were being hired by *any* type of law firm. In 2010, only 68.4 percent reported having a job that required passing a bar exam, the lowest numbers since the mid-1970s.

But the most important feature of the market for new lawyers is that some ten thousand jobs disappeared during the downturn. The employment rate for new lawyers dropped every year from 2007 until 2015. The class of 2011 faced the worst job market in post-recession years, and the market for the class of 2014, the latest year for available statistics, looked only slightly better: the number of jobs shrank by 3 percent, but the employment rate rose because of a decrease in the number of law school graduates.[31]

An important part of what scholars, journalists, and employers have variously called "retrenchment," "paradigm shift," and, repeatedly and emphatically, "crisis" has been the effect that these labor market changes have had on law schools.[32] Scholars do not agree on how unusual this "crisis" has been—whether, for example, it is simply a cyclical downturn or reflects a more enduring shift that demands a rethinking of the dominant model of legal education in the United States. Nor do they agree on whether it is still worth getting a law degree unless you go to a top-ranked law school. However it is labeled, it is nonetheless a huge crisis for those who are unemployed, underemployed, or sinking under the weight of their student loans. This backdrop is crucial for understanding recruitment.

Most accounts of the economic hardships faced by young lawyers concur, not surprisingly, that the trauma born of the terrible post-recession market was disproportionately felt by students graduating from lower-tier schools, students who took on the most debt, and students with weaker records in terms of typical admission criteria that the *USN* rankings powerfully reinforce. These characteristics often go together and may reflect multiple forms of disadvantage such as being a first-generation student, an immigrant, someone without family support, someone *with* a family to support, or a member of an under-represented group.[33] Increasingly, these groups are among those being discouraged from attending law school by critics of the current model of legal education. For example, Brian Tamanaha, a law professor at Washington University Law School, is deeply critical of the structure and rewards for law school faculty. He believes that law schools underserve students and that rankings play an important role in producing competition and administrative costs that get passed on to students.[34] Another of the harshest critics of contemporary legal education, Matt Leichter, has gone so far as to say, "Regardless of what *U.S. News* wants us to believe, the onus is on law schools to demonstrate they are adding value for their costs, and their resistance to doing so indicates they are no longer worthy of access to federal student loans and public subsidies."[35] Leichter suggests that prospective students may find it almost impossible to appreciate how fully the odds are stacked against them. He argues that attending law school is bound to be a losing proposition for all but a few.

The view that there are way too many lawyers, way too many law schools, and way too much student debt is shared by many in legal education and also among practicing lawyers. Many also agree that more must be done to help students fully comprehend the investments and risks they are taking when they go to law school, especially to one that is not highly ranked. And, naturally, the distribution of this sentiment and what to do about it is powerfully mediated by where one's law school stands in the rankings.[36]

But it is important to point out that many students have heeded the message that law school may no longer be a good investment. They understand that the market is bad and law school is expensive. The number of law school applicants has dropped dramatically since 2009. This has been a key feature of the "crisis" or "retrenchment" that law schools face, and one that has been prominently featured in many mainstream media and blogs.[37]

How Employers Use Rankings

As we discussed in the previous section, the obsession with employment rates that dominates career services and is spurred on by the rankings is one important way that *USN* has affected career services. Another significant way in which career-services offices are affected by rankings is through *USN*'s ability to shape the perceptions and practices of employers. Many in law schools believe that employers use a school's rank to help them decide which schools they will visit to conduct on-campus interviews, whether they will consider applicants from certain schools, how deep in a school's class they will interview (that is, only those who rank in the top 10 percent of their class or those who rank in the top 25 percent), and whom they ultimately hire. Data published by the National Association for Law Placement (NALP) suggest there is reason to be worried. In the NALP's non-random survey of 221 law firm representatives from 139 different firms, *USN* rankings were the resource most often consulted by these employers: 83.6 percent reported using the rankings. Moreover, 72.1 percent of respondents said that the rankings affected or changed their perception of law schools. The only factor that mattered more in employers' perceptions of law schools was the performance of recent graduates from a given school—77.9 percent of employers reported this as a factor.[38] Other evidence supports the widespread practice of consulting rankings either formally, as part of well-established organizational routines, or informally as an occasional heuristic used to defend one's decisions. A number of employers we spoke with reported that they kept a recent copy of *USN* rankings nearby, especial if they worked extensively in recruitment.

There are several reasons why employers might use the rankings to help with hiring decisions. First, rankings are an efficient means for employers to sift through an almost overwhelming amount of information, a cultural and cognitive process that mimics the one used by prospective students. For those at law firms charged with hiring, the rankings offer a seemingly objective, or at least defensible, basis to develop criteria for screening applicants. This point was highlighted by several administrators:

> It's a tough nut to crack because employers, too, are in the business of making their jobs as simple as possible. They want to find the best person possible with the least amount of effort expended on their part. So they are going to use whatever tools and whatever instruments they can to try to define where those people might come from. So I think there is a big temptation for some to rely on some external rating to narrow the field for them.

> Law firms definitely use rankings to decide where to conduct onsite interviews in order to establish the first cut for applicants. It is important to appreciate from the vantage point of employers how heavy the demands are on them: they must sort through thousands of résumés and OCI [on campus interview] programs, and what else are you going to use? Firms must find a way to decide whom to interview.

In short, the rankings provide a convenient and work-saving justification for deciding where and whom to interview. Several of those we interviewed reported that when they worked at law firms or for federal or state judges, they used rankings in just these ways to evaluate candidates.

Second, law firms use the rankings because they know that their clients pay close attention to the credentials of the lawyers working at their firms, and the rankings shape these perceptions. One administrator said, when asked if employers use the rankings, "To some extent, yes. I mean it's a quick thing for employers to do to see what kind of snob power they can, if I can be pejorative, have at the firms. Although it is beyond that because given what the top [clients] are paying, they've got to be able to tell those clients, 'Look at the schools we're drawing people from. You've got these tier-one folks who are going to be servicing you.'"

Echoing this sentiment, another administrator in career services said that it was explained to her when she started in the field many years ago that "if you are going to be perceived as an elite firm, you must have elite lawyers." Understood this way, status depends on a chain of influence in which rankings shape the perceptions of law-firm clients, clients' perceptions affect the hiring practices of law firms, and the demands of these law firms play a powerful role in determining how law schools organize their career-services work. The length, influence, and sturdiness of the links of this chain will vary, of course, a process that we examine in detail later in this chapter.

A student who transferred from a lower-ranked school to a top-ten school relates,

> When I started participating in my current law school's fall recruitment, the number of employers participating was more than six times the number of employers who participated in my old law school's fall recruitment. It was extremely eye-opening: at my new school, firms fought over us, took us to dinner and drinks during on-campus recruiting, while at my old law school we were lucky to get interviews with top firms. At the new school, employers sent us emails inviting us to events, and inviting us to apply to the firms, while at the old school I never heard from a single employer. The employment opportunities my new school afforded me immediately paid off my decision before classes even started.[39]

But not everyone was as worried about the effects of rankings on their job prospects. Some insisted that they had not experienced changes in employer behavior because of the rankings, nor did they believe that the rankings have substantial influence on employers generally. Some administrators and faculty pointed to the importance of existing relationships between schools and particular employers in determining how many of their students found work, and where. They believed that networks and past experience with graduates of the school outweigh the influence of the rankings. The NALP survey findings suggest that this view is also widespread, but it is a perspective that depends on status, location, and specialty.

Employer Perceptions of Rankings

Because those who actually hire lawyers may view the effects of rankings differently than those inside law schools, it is important to get a sense of their perspective on the rankings. Our evidence, as well as evidence from other scholars and journalists, suggests that many employers (although certainly not all of them) *do* use rankings in the ways that career-services personnel and others in legal education described to us, and that these uses reflect and mediate the status system of the legal profession.[40]

There are good reasons to believe that people working inside law schools have an accurate understanding of how employers use the rankings. Those in career services often worked in law firms as attorneys before they started their administrative careers in law schools and had firsthand experience in the hiring practices of law firms—experience that led them to seek employment in law schools. Even more, it is their job to keep current on hiring practices for a broad range of legal positions, especially at places that are more likely to hire their students. If they do not know how rankings matter in the firms with which they do business, they will have a harder time placing students and, likely, keeping their jobs. They feel enormous pressure to improve placement, and to do this, they must have a pulse on how employers think and what they deem important.

Many of the faculty we interviewed also had worked at law firms at some stage of their careers and still retained close ties to employers of various sorts. Most also consider helping students find jobs to be an important part of their jobs. None of the law faculty or administrators we interviewed were uninformed or callous about their students' job prospects. How they expressed their concern, what they did about it, and whom or what they blamed for a poor record in placement varied. Given the strong criticism that law schools have faced recently, including from many faculty and others inside law schools, this is worth emphasizing and elaborating.[41] Those we interviewed (and likely the majority of professors at law schools) write numerous letters of recommendations each year; many employ students as research assistants, make calls on their behalf, give job-seeking advice, or share contacts. How much help they give depends primarily on their relationship to a student and that person's performance, but most schools have, since the financial downturn in 2008, made extraordinary efforts to try to mobilize faculty and alumni to help students navigate the terrible job market for attorneys. In short, we found most professors to be very attentive to how the rankings might affect their students and their students' job opportunities.[42]

Rankings Among the Very Elite

The symbolic salience of one's law school is so paramount that it can outweigh other important criteria for employment. William D. Henderson and Rachel M. Zahorsky describe a successful senior associate at a regional law firm who was shocked to learn that he had been rejected for employment by a more prestigious firm.[43] The candidate was among the top 10 percent of his law school class, a member of the law review and moot court, and had a stellar undergraduate record. Even more important, he had successfully managed many litigation cases and was among the top 5 percent in his firm in billable hours. According to his recruiter, his rejection hinged on the fact that he had graduated from a second-tier school: "We don't typically recruit from [School X].... We'll pass."

It is difficult to overstate just how elitist elite law firms are. As the sociologist Lauren A. Rivera shows in her eye-opening book about elite professional recruitment, recruitment at the very top law firms (as well as consulting firms and banks) is a protracted, rigorous, and not very rational process. One attorney at a top firm described it this way:

> It's very hard to get a job at a top firm if you are not coming from a handful of schools. . . . I heard this unbelievable story from a girl who worked at [my firm] when I started there. . . . She came from the University of Connecticut Law School [then a top-tier school] . . . and she had to literally jump through hoops. She had to do all these insane things just to get her résumé to the right people at [the firm]. Whereas, you know, coming from Columbia . . . it was the easiest thing ever, you know? Everyone came courting you.[44]

Courtship is a good word to describe relations among elite firms and elite schools. Firms invest extraordinary resources in sustaining close ties with what they call their "core" recruiting schools, actively pursuing law students from their "golden pipeline of three or four elite schools" with activities, perks, and connections that only accumulate over time.[45] Rivera provides an insider's view of how this works from the employers' and the applicants' perspectives. Among the many advantages for students at these "feeder" schools are endless proposals to consider these top firms, multiple opportunities to meet with firm recruiters, and reminders to apply. There are lavish receptions and networking events, practice interviews with firm personnel, repeated notices of internships and job opportunities, advance résumé screenings from recruiters, networks of recent graduates employed by the firm who are happy to explain the process, and even cool, branded "swag" doled out by firms. As the transfer student quoted earlier noted, all of this is invisible to applicants who do not attend these schools. And this is only the beginning of how elite credentials give students a leg up in the courtship dance.

Getting into a top-ranked law school is a necessary condition for employment at a top law firm, but it is only the first step of screening. According to Rivera, in addition to a degree from the right law school, what most firms care about is an applicant's "pedigree." Successful applicants will more often than not share similar economic and educational backgrounds, and usually the race and ethnicity of most of the firm's lawyers and its clients.[46] The reproduction of these broad categories is negotiated in the veiled language of nuance. "Fit" is one of the master tropes firms use in explaining to themselves and others how this works.[47] What are the features of "fit" in this world? Being good at small talk, being enthusiastic but not overeager, confident but not arrogant. Intelligence is signaled by the reputation of one's school more than one's grades. In addition to comportment, "fit" includes the right hobbies (tennis, golf, and crew are better than team sports such as baseball, basketball, or hockey). And having a partner or even a junior associate vouch for you can make a crucial difference in getting an interview.

The chance that a candidate from a lesser school will get serious scrutiny at the most elite law firms is remote. Exceptions do occur, most often when someone in the firm shares a similar background (rare but not impossible) and champions an applicant, or, less often, when a client intervenes. As Rivera explains, merit often looks like whoever is defining it, and the power to make one's definition stick often reflects enduring social and institutional inequalities. One law firm, proud of its breadth and open-mindedness, only considers the "top" student at every law school. How many of these "number one" students from a third- or fourth-tier law school go on to get jobs at elite law firms is hard to isolate. But even a quick glance at the attorney profiles of elite firms suggests that very few do. Being the best is not enough if you made the mistake of attending the wrong school. Or, as one of Rivera's attorneys put it, "There are many smart people out there. We just refuse to look at them."[48]

Law firm recruiters admit that, given the volume of applications they receive, they almost never open the ones that are sent in electronically from applicants not coming from a "core" school. Absent such an affiliation or absent sponsorship from someone in the firm or an important client, the odds of the file even being opened are very slim. The attorneys who are charged with screening and interviewing applicants are even more pressed for time than the recruiters and tend to scan the already culled résumés from piles put together by the recruiters even more cursorily than the recruiters did. They do not look forward to the extra work that hiring entails. Attention is one of the greatest assets conferred by pedigree and, perhaps, one of the hardest to redistribute, as the woman from Connecticut Law School could attest.

A career-services dean at one of our focus schools, a second-tier school, told us about a phone conversation he had with an alumnus about one of the school's star graduates. This alumnus had somehow managed to land a job at a regional office of a Big Law firm. When the dean asked the alumnus what he could do within the firm to help similarly able students, the attorney was blunt. He told the dean he could not squander his credibility or capital within the firm by sponsoring an application from outside the top tier. He needed it for other battles.

Outside the Very Elite

If rankings matter at the very top to the extent that they correspond with and reproduce the categories of "core" or "target" schools for recruiters, they matter differently in other segments of the hierarchy of schools. For schools that occupy the bottom half of the top ten, rankings are read differently by recruiters than are those from schools in, say, the top five. In fact, a new tier-talk expression, the "top fourteen," has been invented to include the clump of schools that hover near the top-ten threshold and jockey, sometimes ferociously, to join that exclusive top-ten club. Since applications from outside the "top fourteen" may have little chance of even being glanced at by elite law firms, fifteen becomes an unhappy position.[49] We cannot say precisely how firms react to top-fourteen schools compared with schools slightly lower down in the rankings, but this boundary has slipped into the vocabulary of recruiters and is invoked at least occasionally in deliberations about whom to hire. The most elite law firms might occasionally hire an applicant from one of these schools, but they cannot do this too often without risking their reputation. After all, the pedigree of their attorneys is how they justify their high fees to their clients, and rankings are a very prominent marker of excellence. Schools jockeying within the top five or top ten or top fourteen are very attuned to how such differences might matter to employers.

These concerns about the effects of changes in rank are felt all the way down the rankings hierarchy. Because this is a dynamic system, one in which small changes in rank occur every year, these concerns about employer decisions are extremely anxiety-producing for schools, students, and job applicants alike.

Without trying to parse the entire distribution of law schools too precisely, there are other patterns relevant to the relationship between one's school's ranking and getting a job. Since Big Law employs a minority of law graduates, the matching between pedigree and professional placement is most stringent for the biggest and best-known firms. Firms sell their often very expensive services to clients who want to be assured that they are getting the best representation and that their money is being well spent. Hiring overlays and reinforces broader assumptions about distinctions between schools—and law firms—as elite, top, good, average, and mediocre.

For new graduates, one of the most prestigious and useful positions one can attain is to clerk for a judge. There are many different kinds of clerkships at the federal and state levels, in courts of appeals, district courts, or specialized courts. The most coveted and competitive positions are generally clerkships with federal judges, the pinnacle being the Supreme Court. Rankings can play a powerful role in some clerkship decisions. Typically, judges are free to hire law clerks according to any criteria they choose; efforts to standardize the hiring of clerks have mostly failed. Some judges use rankings explicitly, some consider reputations, now mediated by rankings, and some use political or more idiosyncratic criteria. A former clerk at a federal court who helped screen applications stated, "Rankings absolutely matter." Her judge considers stellar recommendations as the first criterion in selecting a clerk, but rankings feature prominently in the culling of the applicants whose résumés the judge sees. This judge receives several thousand applications a year. Most of these are eliminated by an administrative assistant who uses rankings of schools as one of the main filters. Neither the judge nor current clerks ever see the vast majority of applicants. Virtually all applicants who did not go to a top-twenty school are rejected unless there is something extraordinary about their application that catches the eye of the administrator or unless they are "sponsored" by someone the judge knows. The culled applications are then sent to the clerks for further winnowing. The clerks get a spreadsheet that includes some basic characteristics of the applicants, including the name and rank of the applicant's school. Our informant said that clerks would winnow the names on this list, usually about twenty, down to ten, and give the judge the spreadsheet of those names. Of these, he would invite six to eight for interviews, depending on whether they were hiring one or two clerks that year. The lowest-ranked law school that one of their clerks graduated from during this person's four-year tenure was 23. Most clerks for this judge were graduates of Harvard, Yale, University of Chicago, and occasionally Berkeley or NYU law schools.

Not all judges decide in this way, of course. Some favor applicants from their own law school or those who come with recommendations from people they trust. Some seek out people with a variety of political perspectives. Some judges focus most on the rankings of the students and less on the school rank. But rankings do appear to set parameters for many clerkships. We interviewed a staff attorney at a federal appellate court who supervised twenty-seven staff lawyers. Her court used rankings in similar ways as employers did. She said, "Rankings did matter. It was like a sliding scale. The higher in the pecking order of rankings, the deeper in the class we felt we could go. That said, the standards were still pretty high. The top quartile is the lowest we would go." She reported that she kept a copy of the latest rankings with the hiring file and said, "I take the rankings with a big grain of salt, but to set aside the rankings themselves, who is number one and ten—there is something to be said about the real-life ability of people who come out of these places, especially for people who come out of the top quartile." She also reported that if a graduate who was top-ranked in his or her class came from a third- or fourth-tier school, "We would be very hard-pressed to offer them an interview. Not because of our own snobbishness and desire to exclude those schools, but because of our credibility with the judges." Like the alumnus who refused to recommend a fellow alumnus, social capital must be carefully deployed.

As a witness to the hiring of many law clerks, she had seen similar patterns in the judges' decisions. To have credibility with the judges, applicants must have good grades from a good school.

> I don't want to leave the misimpression that rankings are destiny. They are helpful. But I'm a graduate of a state school myself, and other things can get you noticed by judges who are looking for clerkships or by prestigious law firms looking to hire. Law review editorial board, publishing law review articles, your class rank. If, like me, you couldn't afford to go to a private school, and you go to state school, you can get yourself taken seriously and focus on those kinds of accomplishments.

Our interviewee also described the impact of rankings on hiring for academic positions. At her school, a top-tier school, she reported, "Applicants are cast in piles of top ten as *USN* ranks them, the next tier, and a big chunk of schools that are also-rans. This drives and is tied to school rank. If [my school] wants to move up, they don't want to hire [their own graduate]; they want a Yale graduate.... It's kind of ironic. You wind up as a graduate being rebuffed by your own school, even if they know how good you are, because everyone is looking up the food chain, trying to climb up themselves."

VARIATIONS IN EMPLOYER EFFECTS

Because so much effort is invested in managing and interpreting rankings at most law schools, how *other* schools and *other* employers respond to rankings becomes an exercise in projection for many in legal education. These projections are not always accurate. Many of those we interviewed expressed the belief that rankings have had little effect on the relationship between employers and elite schools with strong national reputations. We have just argued that that is not necessarily true. Rankings do matter for employers, even at the very top, but they are a reinforcing backdrop for elite hiring rather than a recipe or heuristic for hiring. The reputations of elite schools are firmly established among employers, regardless of their location and size, and small oscillations in their rankings don't seem to matter. One administrator at a top-tier law school who had once worked as a hiring partner at an elite firm explained:

> You have ... the normal suspect schools, the Harvard, Yale, Stanford, Michigan, the University of Chicago, Berkeley, Columbia, NYU, Georgetown, Duke, Penn, whatever—you have your network. And at the very best law

firms you really are only thinking about the really elite schools. That's what we'd do at the D.C. firm. You'd basically shut out all but the elite schools, and as to whether Michigan is third this year or sixth this year, you don't pay any attention. I mean, it's Michigan. You don't worry about that.

For elite schools, their longstanding and general reputation is much more important to employers than small changes in their current rank; it is, indeed, their broadly recognized reputation that distinguishes them as "elite."[50]

This correspondence between general reputation and the ability to attract employers was one reason why some administrators were skeptical of the effects of rankings on employer perceptions and actions. These administrators, most of whom were from elite schools, tended to instead emphasize the importance of past experiences and established relationships between the school and employer. For example, one career-services director from a top-ten school argued, "I think [employers] look at whom they have hired and who has done very well and who has excelled and who has a personality that is geared towards personal development, which in a service industry at some point is going to be critical for their survival." Nearly all who addressed this issue, no matter their school's rank, underscored the importance of established networks in determining where firms elect to conduct interviews and how many students from a school they are likely to hire. In general, when employers have a lot of firsthand experience with a school, the evaluation of an outside arbiter such as *USN* is going to have far less influence.

Unfortunately for schools outside this elite circle, their networks of employers are usually smaller and more fickle. Administrators and faculty from non-elite law schools, whether ranked lower in the first tier or in one of the tiers below, are quick to point out that in order to establish positive first-hand impressions, one must have the opportunity for firsthand relationships. Many of those from non-elite schools contend that the rankings influence the opportunity of their institutions to gain such access. One administrator from a second-tier school who had worked in a private firm explained:

I think from the employers' side from when I worked in a firm that it did really matter for the firm if they had positive experience with the school in the past—whether that be that one of the partners there went to school there or if they have hired one person from a school and they turn out to be a star. That will make them focus on the person rather than the rankings. But I think it is true in regards to picking schools to interview at, [the ranking] makes a difference. We would love to have Baker [a prestigious law firm] do interviews here—but they won't. And if you look at the schools at which they do interviews, they are all top-tier schools.

The general pattern for non-elite law schools is that they are able to place their students in local and regional law firms but have trouble convincing law firms outside of these areas to conduct on-campus interviews or consider their students.[51] It is with these extra-regional law firms that rankings become a more important factor in the relationship between law schools and employers.

One striking aspect of the effects of rankings on employer decisions is that even first-tier schools with very good national reputations experience them. One might expect that these effects would be minimal for law schools ranked in the top fifty, but administrators at these schools don't see it this way. One dean said, "If you are top ten in the first tier, they are going to take you no matter what—you are as good as gold. But in the lower schools in the first tier, that is not as true. People definitely give a lot of weight to those rankings." We spoke with several administrators in the first tier who had been told by law firms that small differences or small changes in ranking affected their decisions about where to interview and whom to hire. When we asked whether firms pay attention to rankings, the views of administrators from two first-tier schools illustrated the point:

> Oh yes. I'm sure they do. They all tell me that they do. Number one, they decide where they are going to do on-campus interviews based almost exclusively on the rankings, and you can drop out [of] on campus interviews if you fall too far in the rankings. And all of my graduates are afraid of this. And it makes a difference in how far down [prospective employers] go in the class as well, they [will accept] a lower GPA if the students come from a higher-ranked school.

> I've had discussions with people on hiring committees and from three firms in particular—two based in Washington, D.C., and one based in L.A. One said that because we had dropped [two positions within the second twenty-five of the first tier], his firm was cutting the number of interview days from two to one here. It's just lunacy. Another one told us that the way they make decisions about which schools to visit and which students they interview within schools is that they take the school's ranking and then they multiply it by—they have an algorithm—they take the school's ranking and the student's class rank and they come up with a number and that number determines whom they are going to interview. So the rankings have a very direct effect on employers.

One reason why rankings have such strong effects, even for well-regarded schools, is that law school rankings create seemingly objective hard lines of distinction between schools whose quality is virtually identical.[52] For example, a school ranked 26th is virtually the same as the school ranked

25th, but it is not reified as a "top-25 school." The 11th-ranked school is not part of the "top 10," and the 101st-ranked school is not part of the "top 100." In the absence of direct experience, it is efficient for firms to use these constructed boundaries as justifications for their interviewing and hiring decisions. Another administrator at a first-tier school described this type of strategy as follows:

> In effect, it's completely irrational behavior on the employers' part because they have to have a cut-off someplace and have to draw the line some way or otherwise they're just going to be inundated. The problem is that it doesn't force them to look at the merits of the place; they use an external device and they say, "If it's from this kind of school, this is who we'll look at; if it's from this other kind of school, that's who we'll look at," without making much of an individuated determination as they prescreen.

This is one reason why schools that fall even one position below a recognized cut-off point—such as the top twenty, top twenty-five, top thirty, or top fifty—worry about the consequences. Employers may use these cut-off points as shortcuts to decide where and whom to interview.

These constructed boundaries become even more critical as one moves down the ranking hierarchy. Many law firms believe that it enhances their prestige to not hire from schools outside the top fifty. The alumnus from a bottom-tier school described earlier risked losing face within his firm for supporting a stellar candidate from a poorly ranked school, even if it was his own school. An associate dean at a second-tier law school related that in a meeting with a representative of a major national law firm he was told that his school would need to get into the top fifty before the firm would consider interviewing their students. To add insult to injury for this school, recent graduates of a competitor school in the region that in the past had been generally considered inferior to this school were now getting interviews and job offers at this firm because the school had climbed into the top fifty. A director of career services at a third-tier school expressed a similar sentiment: "I don't know if they would know we were in the third tier, but they definitely would know that we're not in the first tier. I don't know if they pay attention after the first tier. . . . They really pay close attention to the first tier."

Considering the emphasis that many firms place on hiring from highly ranked schools, it is not surprising that administrators at schools outside the first tier agree that employers use rankings when making interviewing and hiring decisions. Here is where the effects of the rankings on employers are most evident and powerful. When asked whether employers pay attention to the rankings, several deans and career-services personnel reported that employers had told them directly that they do. A dean at a second-tier school told us, "Quite a few employers would tell us that they would actually utilize those rankings when they decide what schools they're going to visit for on-campus interviewing or even what schools they are going to accept résumés from. They look at the rankings first. . . . I think it's pretty prevalent. I really do. I think that it has a very strong effect, especially if it's a school that isn't as well known, if it's a smaller school." In the absence of existing relationships, employers are more likely to rely on the rankings to determine whether or not they are interested in graduates from that school.

The influence of rankings on employers has an important geographical component. The very elite schools possess a strong enough national reputation to attract employers of all types and regardless of their geographic location, but less well-known schools do not have this clout. Administrators from these schools noted that rankings became particularly salient when they tried to make connections with employers outside their own region. A number of administrators at schools in or close to major metropolitan areas often reported not being concerned about the effects of rankings on their ability to place students at nearby firms but thought that the rankings had a big impact on how employers in more distant cities viewed their graduating students. An administrator of a second-tier school on the east coast said:

[We do] very well in New York and we are now trying to go beyond New York. If we dip a little bit, it doesn't mean that we are going to lose employers in New York; we have enough alums there. If we dip three or four years in a row, I think it would be a major problem. I think it has more of an impact when we are trying to convince firms from, for example, Chicago to come to campus. The law school is tied to a relatively weak university, I mean [the university] is not what you would call a powerhouse on a national level. So a lot of people don't know [it], and it is hard to convince that firm from, say, Chicago to come here if we have dipped in *USN*. There are enough good schools in Chicago and they will go to the top ten schools in the country, but they may not see a lot of reasons to come here.

Chicago is pretty secure; we have a thousand graduates up there. But New York and Los Angeles are really tenuous markets for us. We always send people there, but they really watch the rankings. There is a very clear kind of effect there.

The regional character of a large portion of the marketplace for legal jobs also means that the rankings are less consequential for the employment opportunities of graduates whose schools are predominantly regional or local. These schools, with their strong but circumscribed network ties, are far less worried about the influence of the rankings than other law schools.[53] One attorney at a boutique, specialized law firm in a mid-sized midwestern city almost laughed at the idea that rankings would influence hiring. In his firm, networks, grades, and specialties all mattered more for candidates than the rank of their law school.

Region matters in other ways, too. Schools with strong regional ties can become "feeder" schools for regional firms, for practices specializing in certain types of law, or even for some branches of government. Thus, if one intends to stay in the region, attending a regional school, even if it is not highly ranked, might be an *advantage* compared to attending a less local, more highly ranked school. A steady stream of alumni, especially if they perform well, reinforces a preference for local graduates with local connections. Law firms doing lots of business with local firms, say, in Mississippi, might do better to hire someone from the University of Mississippi Law School than someone from a higher-ranked school. This advantage can be especially clearly demonstrated in the realm of local politics; some law schools display this regional advantage on their websites. The University of Mississippi School of Law on its website touts itself as the alma mater of "10 of the state's 25 governors, nearly a third of the state's lieutenant governors, half the justices on the Mississippi Supreme Court and nearly two-thirds of the presidents of the Mississippi Bar."[54]

Finally, it is important to note that for a handful of schools the rankings have improved employment opportunities. Most generally, these are schools that either rank unexpectedly high in *USN* or who make notable moves upward in the rankings. One new administrator who previously worked as a headhunter for firms looking for new employees said that rankings were a good way to convey information about potential employees if employers were unfamiliar with the schools from which the students had graduated:

> I think that the way that we would market a candidate from, for example, [a school ranked in the twenties and outside the region of the employer] over a candidate from [a school ranked in the thirties but located within the region of the employer] would be to say that [the former school] is ranked twenty-four or whatever, and that's ten spots higher. It would be a way to sell a particular candidate, something you would remind law firms about. Because I think the law firms are very conscious of the rankings; they know who the top ten are but then it gets murkier after that.

The schools that are best positioned to benefit from the rankings are those that attain a high ranking in *USN* or cross over one of the important cut-off boundaries despite not having a strong national reputation, at least among employers:

> I think that if you talk to career-services people, I think they will tell you that it makes a difference. Particularly with employers who don't know your program well, then that [higher ranking] may put you on their radar screen when you wouldn't be otherwise. Whether they came to campus, how well they'll respond to somebody sending in a résumé blind, how deep in the class they'll look if they do go to your campus or if they do go to a job fair that you participate in—that [higher ranking will] play a big role.

Here we see how the emphasis on boundaries created by the rankings can benefit schools if they are able to climb into the first tier or top twenty-five. These schools can shed misconceptions or create new identities for their schools by moving into a category of which they were not previously a member.

Supporters for the rankings have argued that the rankings have changed the employment process for law schools only at the margins, if at all. They contend that a school's reputation has always been the decisive factor in determining which schools employers choose to hire from and for the most part the same employers are hiring from the same schools. This position describes the situation of elite schools and possibly regional schools that rely primarily on local markets and are satisfied to continue doing so.

However, our interviews show that rankings clearly do matter for most schools in their relationships to employers. Administrators at these schools confirm that rankings are an influential resource for employers when deciding where to interview and whom they will consider hiring.[55] The information produced by *USN* is most salient to employers when they are not familiar with a school, and in these cases the hard boundaries created by the rankings are often decisive. It is hard to know if these changes are marginal or more substantive, but schools that have been hurt by these effects definitely do not view them as marginal, even if advocates of the rankings would like to characterize them in just this way.

Lost in this argument, however, is the fact that law schools, because they are aware that employers heed the rankings, adapt their own behavior accordingly. Because they believe that employers take the rankings seriously, they commit resources, often considerable resources, to maximizing their position in the *USN* rankings. So, the real changes in employment created by the rankings matter. So, too, do perceptions, especially when they are fueled by competition and anxiety.

CAREERS IN CAREER SERVICES

Jane spoke at length about how rankings are changing the nature of career-services work and the effects that these changes have had on those employed in this area. Putting her own job loss into perspective she told us:

> I would say that probably half the positions like mine across the country are vacant right now. We've always had some attrition, but nothing like you see today. I always wanted to know when I was growing up how people figured out what they wanted to do. . . . The decision process has always fascinated me. I see that with a lot of people in my profession. We're in it because we love the job search, we love helping people present themselves as well as possible, and to do that well you have to figure out what people are excited about. This is true of most of my colleagues. However, we are definitely being diverted from those kinds of activities in favor of things that will have an immediate gain [to the school's rank].

As Jane explained at the end of her interview, these changes have convinced her to leave career services and return to practicing law. "I really love this work," she said, "[but] I will never do it again."

The rankings have transformed what it means to do career-services work and what it means to do it well. Expectations about how time and other resources are allocated within the office have changed dramatically; tracking down hard-to-find graduates is more important than getting to know students and finding the right kind of job for them. It is worth noting, too, that as the skills associated with career services change, so too will the type of people who are hired for these positions. Knowing how important these numbers are, law schools are more likely to move away from those with backgrounds in career counseling and toward those with bottom-line orientations to "manage" this department, as is the case also for admissions departments and deans' offices. Moves in this direction were already apparent at a few schools we visited. Personnel changes such as these institutionalize the focus on numbers and ensure that the career counseling aspects of the job will become even less of a priority.

Rankings have not only changed job expectations and demands, they have also reduced the standing of those who do this type of work and the power relations within the organization. Measures such as rankings are purported to increase transparency, but, as the case of career services demonstrates, only phenomena that are easily quantified can be made transparent in this way. The measures have made career services a more mechanical job, a job in which managing numbers outweighs more nebulous interpersonal skills. This focus on numbers not only reduces the discretion of career-services personnel but also increases their vulnerability: the numbers become the only aspect of their work that matters, and they are judged—feted or blamed—on how these numbers turn out. So although it is true that the rankings have made career-services personnel more "accountable," they are only accountable for their ability to produce acceptable employment rates. Meanwhile, they are more susceptible to external evaluation, they have less autonomy, and they are responsible for outcome measures over which they have only partial control. The rankings do not make them accountable for student satisfaction with their placements or the quality of guidance students are given in their career choices. The rankings, then, only provide "selective accountability," an accountability that, at least according to our respondents, has deteriorated rather than improved the state of career services in legal education.

Chapter 7 | Rankings Everywhere

The more any quantitative social indicator is used for decision-making, the more subject it will be to corruption pressures and the more apt it will be to distort and corrupt the social processes it is intended to monitor.

—Donald Campbell

RANKINGS ARE PART of a dramatic global shift that has culminated in a transnational "evaluative culture," one that is obsessed with ratings, indicators, and performance measures of all sorts.[1] We rank high schools for the number of advanced placement classes they offer; companies for their benefits for women; philanthropies for their spending on social programs; cities for their murder rates; and countries for corruption, ease of doing business, and maternal mortality rates. The numbers and scope of performance indicators have exploded, creating a new lexicon for types (leading, lagging, input, output, process, practical, directional, actionable, and financial) and systems (new public management, key performance indicators, operating index, balanced scorecards, hits) of indicators. These indicators are promulgated by groups ranging from bloggers measuring the hottest neighborhoods to consultants assessing progress and shaping business plans ("What gets measured gets done") to global organizations, such as the World Bank and the United Nations, evaluating international development, health, safety, and human rights.[2]

Again, we need to ask: How did we get here? Is this genuine accountability? Big questions, these, and no single study can offer a satisfying answer; performance measures, like other cultural practices, are mediated by their form, contexts, and histories. But our detailed study of law school rankings offers insights into the patterned ways that individuals and organizations respond to quantification. The identification of these patterns can help us understand the effects of quantitative accountability more generally, across settings and in other social realms, and suggest hypotheses for future research.[3] In this concluding chapter, we discuss the implications of our findings for law schools and then show how these insights generalize to other types of educational rankings, focusing most closely on the growing influence of global rankings. We also use these comparisons to discuss factors such as how assessment is structured, the existence of competitor rankings, and the opportunity for resistance that lead to variations in the effects of rankings. Then, drawing briefly on examples from law enforcement and health care, we move beyond the field of education to examine how the reactive processes we identify in our study unfold when quantitative assessment is implemented in other contexts.

We conclude by returning to the questions with which we began: How do numbers accomplish the transparency, accountability, and rationality that we desire from them? Why do they inevitably introduce changes we never intended? What dangers accompany such a powerful mode of valuation?

BROAD PATTERNS OF CHANGE IN LEGAL EDUCATION

It is clear that rankings have changed legal education. We have shown how rankings shape the entities they measure. They have become the backdrop against which members understand themselves and others: they define law schools as certain kinds of organizations, populated by individuals with particular identities, embedded in a field of a very specific nature. And as *USN* has become a powerful player in this field, one that mediates the relations among the people, organizations, and units that the field comprises, the influence of rankings has become increasingly institutionalized and has intensified the pressure on schools to fashion themselves after *USN*'s conception of quality.

Throughout this book, we have provided evidence of the many ways, both subtle and obvious, these developments have transformed perceptions, behaviors, and organizational decision-making. Taken together, these effects help us to identify three broad patterns of change in this field brought about by rankings. Rankings have altered:

1. Relations of power and authority
2. Organizational practice both within and among organizations
3. The distribution of opportunities and status in legal education

These patterns all highlight how rankings have insinuated themselves into the fabric of legal education. Not only have they changed the behaviors of individuals and organizations, they have also transformed the structure and dynamics of the field of legal education itself.

Changes to Power and Authority Relations

One way in which rankings have transformed the power relationships within and among law schools is by changing the terms under which law schools are held accountable. Spawned from an algorithm, rankings are highly formalized evaluations produced by supposedly disinterested outsiders—a reputable magazine with no stake in legal education other than to profit from its evaluation. Consequently, rankings seem to be more objective than the self-interested accounts that law schools prepare about themselves. Rankings make possible two valuable kinds of comparisons: a precise comparison of every school to every other school and longitudinal evaluations of the same school. This is information that produces trends and comparisons that administrators who allocate budgets across schools and evaluate deans find useful. As broadly available and simple assessments, rankings are vehicles through which members and external constituents can judge decisions made by the administration.

Rankings are an effort to popularize specialized knowledge. Making it easy for outsiders to evaluate complex institutions shifts power relations. Much has been written about the disadvantages that individuals face in trying to obtain information from large organizations. This is hardly surprising given that most organizations rely on highly specialized staff with vast resources to work full-time on organizational matters, including public relations departments that are expert at protecting organizations from interference and mediating how others perceive them. Organizations also have longer time horizons than individuals, so they can easily wait out conflicts with or challenges from individuals. The relationship between organizations and individuals is deeply "asymmetric." Consequently, many view rankings as helping to mitigate the unfair advantage that organizations have.

Most law school administrators do not see it this way. Although rankings simplify and circulate information about schools, they are also crude, standardized measures that may promote harmful short cuts in students' decision-making by excluding important distinctions while manufacturing trivial ones. But because students and other powerful constituencies act on rankings, administrators and faculty are forced to attend to them. Rankings both reduce and displace the discretion of administrators. Rankings have emerged as an omnipresent pressure, one that acts as a powerful constraint on administrators' discretion. Deans and their staff must now vet all decisions for their potential impact on their school's ranking. Instead of feeling free to construct their own version of excellence or to devise their own organizational goals or missions, they are now publicly evaluated by out-siders under terms they do not control. Instead of defining the missions and profiles of their schools, administrators now tinker with ways to interpret the ranking categories into which information gets slotted: How can fac-ulty resources be maximized? Do nonlegal jobs qualify when calculating employment rates? What counts as a book?

In addition to imposing a uniform definition of excellence on all law schools, rankings also make it easy for almost anyone to hold law schools accountable. A drop in rank can generate widespread demands for explana-tions and strategies for improvement. Formerly these demands might come from the American Bar Association accrediting body, central administra-tors, powerful alumni, or boards of visitors. Since rankings, anyone with an interest in law schools now feels qualified to assess their performance, including those in the media. Monitoring law schools is as easy as watching numbers go up and down. From applicants to state legislators to prospec-tive employees, rankings make possible and legitimate intense scrutiny that makes it easier to "govern from a distance."[4]

Rankings also disrupt power relations inside law schools. As the terms of rankings become more important to external groups, they are more likely to be used to evaluate subordinates. Employees in admissions, career services, and development are rewarded or punished for their perceived impact on rankings. Jobs in these fields are increasingly being redefined in terms of rankings. Just as rankings integrate all law schools, they also integrate the performance of all units within law schools. Departments that are in charge of specific rankings' components now feel extraordinary pressure to boost their numbers, including pressure from their peers. Since these numbers are public, it becomes easy to point fingers when things go badly.

Quantification's capacity to constrain discretion explains its allure for sus-picious overseers and citizens. This also explains why it is usually forced on decision-makers who cannot defend their authority, groups that Theodore Porter characterizes as weak elites.[5] We do not usually view law school deans as vulnerable political actors, but the fact is that they were unable to block the spread of rankings as a widely adopted means of evaluating their institutions despite their concerted efforts to do so. As a result, rank-ings became the standard reference in their decision-making. Increasingly, deans were made to account for themselves in terms they did not control. The kind of nuanced knowledge of an organization that is acquired from sustained intimate experience becomes less important as rankings privi-lege more formalized kinds of information. Rankings diminish profes-sional autonomy.

Even if rankings were not originally intended as a constraint on the discretion of administrators, the mechanical objectivity they construct has proved useful to many groups.[6] As the legitimacy of rankings becomes more accepted—even taken for granted—other ways of accomplishing accountability may seem less appealing or valid. Pressures for mechanical objectivity help explain how rankings change power relations.

Changes to Organizational Practices and Interorganizational Relationships

A second category of rankings effects consists of changes to organizational processes and the relationships among organizations in the field. This matters because, as the organizational theorist Walter Powell puts it, "Institutions are the external memory of society." That is, institutions within and among organizations are largely responsible for that which endures in society. How that endurance is organized across time and place is how practices extend beyond the capacities and lives of individuals.[7]

One way that rankings change organizations is by creating powerful incentives for law schools to deploy resources differently. Administrators change how time, money, and attention are distributed in their efforts to manage their ranking. They may increase marketing efforts to improve reputational scores, allocate scholarships for students with excellent test scores, or encourage faculty to take spring (instead of fall) sabbaticals so as not to affect student-faculty ratios. Simply providing the information that USN uses to calculate its rankings takes a great deal of coordinated work. Numbers must be compiled, checked, and checked again; surveys must be answered and guidelines must be interpreted. To create placement statistics, former students must be tracked down and cajoled into responding to requests for information about their salaries and job status. New ranking categories such as "faculty resources" must be assembled from budgets and statistics, something that often requires extensive elaboration and reinterpretation of existing accounting.

As we have shown, in conjunction with the redeployment of resources, rankings can introduce fundamental changes in the jobs performed within law schools. For schools that make improving their ranking a top priority, quantitative competence may be a more valuable skill than traditional expertise, and some schools have begun to hire professionals with management or marketing training rather than legal backgrounds. Associate deans may focus more on tracking statistics than on improving services. Deans may need to suspend other activities in order to address concerns about rankings coming from students, boards, or central administrators. Strategizing, implementing, and reacting to rankings require coordinated and extensive activity that shapes the content of many administrative jobs and the expertise needed to do them.

Finally, rankings change relations among colleagues. Rankings generate enormous anxiety for many administrators, which makes their jobs less pleasant. Some administrators believe rankings force poor trade-offs between short-term superficial goals and long-term substantive ones. They also think that rankings generate distrust. Because rankings are relative evaluations of merit that magnify fine distinctions, administrators feel as though they must always be looking over their shoulders to see what others are doing. Rankings increase competition among schools and wariness among colleagues.

Our findings also point to the importance of coercive and disciplinary power in motivating many of these changes. The coercive effects produced by rankings take many forms. Most broadly, because rankings are strictly relative, they structure relations among schools as a zero-sum game. The success of one school comes at the expense of others, creating ripples in the rankings that can indirectly affect the standing of many schools. Moreover, if one school adopts a particular strategy for improving its ranking, schools that fail to follow suit are punished.

Understanding the incentives produced by rankings as a form of coercion helps explain why efforts to boycott rankings and other forms of resistance failed, why innovations in gaming and the strategic management of rankings diffuse so rapidly among schools, and why rankings generate such intense anxiety and vigilance. A significant form of coercion associated with rankings is *USN*'s capacity to punish schools that do not submit accurate information.[8] Many of our respondents described how *USN* "estimated" numbers for law schools that ignored *USN*'s requests for information, inserting the average value for each category. These were almost always conservative estimates that yielded a lower ranking than the school would have received had they cooperated with the data collection. Schools quickly learned that they paid a high price for their refusal to participate, and soon every law school provided information to *USN*.

Not all incentives for generating organizational change are as overt as coercion. Organizational change also devolves from more subtle forms of power that members may gradually internalize. Michel Foucault's term for this type of power is "discipline."[9] Disciplinary practices are techniques for surveying, sorting, and measuring that establish people as particular kinds of persons in need of particular forms of expertise. By classifying, creating hierarchies of ability and performance, and establishing what is "normal" and what is not, disciplinary practices turn people into objects amenable to transformation through the application of specialized knowledge and work. This understanding of persons becomes part of their self-awareness, shaping aspirations and assumptions about others.[10]

Rankings exert a powerful discipline over law schools by creating public evaluations of performance that locate each law school in an elaborate status system made up of circulating positions. A relatively stable status system that is derived from ostensibly clear and clustered criteria, but that also yields unstable positions, is perhaps the perfect machine for generating status anxiety. Status is relative; small movements in rank are routine; big jumps, although rare, can devolve from small differences; changes in position are closely scrutinized by powerful constituents; and each year, movement in rank is produced and widely disseminated as "news." Rankings define schools as better or worse and identify parts of schools that need to be improved. The reputations that rankings consolidate circulate broadly and become part of members' understanding of their schools and themselves. Organizational members internalize the values behind rankings and the categories rankings use to express these values, which makes coercion less necessary.

One reason why discipline is such an effective mechanism of organizational change is that it overrides strategies organizations use to manage external pressures. As many scholars have pointed out, formal organizational structures look quite different than informal practices. Organizations often respond to what they see as outside interference by developing symbolic responses that leave core activities untouched. For example, new forms of regulation often result in the creation of formal departments or committees that document responses but often effect little change. Organizations may create offices to give the appearance of legal compliance, implement ineffective programs, or develop policies that may never be implemented in order to appear compliant or legitimate.[11] This "buffering" of the organization from efforts to manipulate it is circumvented by rankings. Rankings prevent buffering by making it easier for outsiders to inspect the organization, by creating strong incentives for manipulating rankings, and by encouraging insiders to adopt the goals implicit in rankings and to internalize rankings as a form of organizational and professional identity. Rankings change perceptions of legal education through incentives that are simultaneously seductive and coercive.

Changes to the Structure of Opportunities and the Distribution of Status

A third category of ranking effects is changes in how professional opportunities are distributed. Rankings produce a new status system that reorganizes how law schools are stratified. This broad change in legal education influences how law schools define their goals, admit students, and deploy resources, and how employers evaluate candidates. These kinds of changes affect who gets to be a lawyer, what kinds of lawyers law students become, their sense of their own status, how they are evaluated by peers and employers, and how legal jobs are allocated among schools and persons.

Because rankings are standardized algorithms applied to all schools, they punish schools that do not conform to the image of excellence embedded in the rankings. One of the deep challenges of measuring social life is finding quantitative proxies for complex relationships. In the jargon of social science, the challenge is to "operationalize" some feature of social life by quantifying it. Like most forms of communication, the value of a measure must be assessed in light of its accessibility and the particular job it is designed to do. We may consider a measure's value in terms of how hard it is to get or make, whether it is valid and reliable, how subject it is to manipulation, whether it is easy to compare across time or contexts, or how much it distorts or leaves out. As Porter points out, sometimes the value of numbers is less their accuracy as depictions of aspects of the real world and more how standardized their production can be.[12] It may be more important for census statistics to be comparable over time and place so as to permit careful tracking of changes than to reflect other meaningful distinctions. An abiding feature in the controversy over rankings is whether the proxies they incorporate are appropriate generalizations of excellence, or whether the distinctions they make and the integration they accomplish obscure more than they illuminate.

In law school rankings, merit and motivation are defined by test scores and grades; spending more money is always better than spending less, regardless of how well it is spent; a higher student-faculty ratio assumes better teaching and more access to faculty; more books trumps more librarians; and the most important assessment of the reputation of a school is the one made by nationally elite practitioners and other academics, not the one made by students, alumni, and those who actually employ its graduates. For law schools whose missions are not captured by *USN* proxies for excellence, rankings evaluate them against a standard they explicitly reject, standards that are incompatible with their goals. A school founded to provide opportunities to low-income students, increase the diversity of the bar, embrace a religious tradition, or cultivate lawyers committed to public interest law or serving needy communities will be punished by rankings for daring to admit nonstandard students as defined by the *USN* formula. *USN* rankings define good students as those who test well and get high grades. These are not necessarily incorrect assumptions, but they are *assumptions*. As such, they necessarily exclude many other forms of excellence. Consequently, law schools that wish to admit students using broader criteria either must relinquish their mission or endure the stigma of a permanently low ranking. These schools face the unwelcome dilemma of either paying a steep price in status and visibility for their principles or abandoning their missions that do not conform to *USN*'s criteria.

Field Changes

These broad patterns of effects all demonstrate that the rankings have not only generated change in individual and organizational practices but also have had a tremendous influence on the organizational field of legal education, an influence that will result in more permanent changes to its structure and practices.[13] *USN* has now established itself as a powerful actor in this field, one that mediates the relations among schools, law firms, alumni, professional associations, and regulating bodies. Rankings have created another important link in how these organizations make sense of the field and how they perceive the relationships within it. Law firms and judges looking for associates and law clerks now routinely consider the rank of an applicant's school in deciding whom to interview and hire. Rankings affect alumni's donations, their expressions of pleasure or disapproval, and their bragging rights.

One of the most important consequences of the field change produced by rankings is that the stratification system of legal education itself has been radically transformed: small differences between schools are now exaggerated and reified while many more schools than before are perceived, at least by outsiders, to be of poor quality.[14] Law schools now monitor themselves much more closely, especially in relation to schools that rank near them. In this sense, a school's location in the ranking now defines with whom that school most directly "competes," and rankings have constructed a status system in which all schools are, in effect, competitors with one another for public distinction. Alternative claims to status now carry less weight, and the terms of competition among law schools are heavily influenced by rankings. The boundaries around legal education and law that rankings help create are of a new stripe—a peculiar conjoining of sameness and difference, of standardization and precise calibration.

In addition to increasing the density and visibility of the ties that bind law schools together and casting those ties as intervals, rankings provided a stimulus for new organizational actors in legal education. There has been a dramatic increase in the number of consultants who advise law schools about how to improve their rankings by means of better marketing, strategic plans, or reputational management.[15] There are more elaborate and expensive consulting services for applicants striving to be accepted by a better (read: more highly ranked) law school. Because rankings render the relative status of law schools transparent, the pressure to attend the "best" law schools has increased. Applicants are now served by a booming industry of counselors and advisers who help them prepare for the LSAT, decide where to apply, choose whether to transfer, and polish their applications. State legislatures, which help fund public schools, are more attuned to the status of law schools and may express their pleasure or displeasure at changes in rank by making changes in their allocations of funds.

The media also play a key role in reinforcing and legitimating the position of rankings in the field of legal education. The annual release of rankings is the subject of extensive media coverage in newspapers, magazines, and on blogs. Reporting on rankings has become so automatic that some call it "easy journalism." Print and electronic media routinely report how national or local universities fare in the global ranking, and rankers continue to innovate in the dissemination of their products.

Rankings are now so intertwined with legal education that it is difficult to imagine the field without them. Even in the face of the dramatic recession-driven deterioration of the legal labor market and applicant numbers, rankings have not lost any of their influence.[16] As higher-ranked schools escape the worst of these effects, schools look to rankings success as a way to increase visibility and show viability in an uncertain time—seeing in rankings a potential solution to their school's financial problems. At the same time, the pressure to avoid the negative publicity of a decline in rankings is greater than ever. "Rankings," more than one dean told us, "are here to stay."

OTHER EDUCATIONAL RANKINGS

How widespread are the effects that we document in the case of law schools? Do we see the same patterns in other forms of educational rankings? How and why might these patterns differ? In other work we have looked at global university rankings and the various rankings of business schools in the United States.[17] In addition, throughout our study we have collected material about college and university rankings in the United States and interviewed a handful of administrators at these institutions. We also sought out examples of fields that have avoided the influence of rankings to improve our understanding of dynamics that might circumscribe their effects. Our interviews with administrators at schools of dentistry represent this effort.

Most generally, we find that the dynamics we see in the field of law play out in similar ways across other fields: rankings change how insiders and outsiders view the standing of schools, encourage schools to redistribute resources and engage in gaming strategies in attempts to maximize their numbers, and transform the organizational priorities, goals, and missions of the evaluated institutions. But these comparisons also point to contextual factors—how the rankings are structured, the existence of multiple rankings, and the solidarity of those being ranked—that produce variations on these general effects. We briefly examine several comparative ranking systems to highlight the consistency in effects across contexts and identify some of the factors that determine the nature and intensity of ranking effects.

Global University Rankings

Global rankings of universities have become a powerful force in higher education.[18] Their influence demonstrates the breadth of the processes we have described and also the ways the stakes change when national reputations become bound up with rankings.[19] Characterized as "the backbone of research governance," these rankings help to coordinate universities across the world into a single global field, perpetuate particular definitions and standards of excellence, and promote competition among universities.[20] The most prominent global rankings are the Academic Rankings of World Universities (ARWU); the World University Rankings (WUR), published by the *Times Higher Education Supplement* in conjunction with Thomas Reuters; and the QS World University Rankings (QS stands for Quacquarelli Symonds).[21] These rankings are very popular: QS claims that it gets 20 million annual visits to its website and that over one thousand different newspapers, journals, and websites report on its rankings each year. In the blogosphere, numerous blogs are devoted to discussion and assessment of global rankings.[22]

Global rankings generate many of the same patterns of effects as the law school rankings do in the United States. In a series of studies, Ellen Hazelkorn shows just how large global rankings loom in administrators' thinking and how much they shape education policies.[23] In surveys and interviews, administrators report that they feel increasing pressure to improve their numbers and to emphasize work that is linked to rankings factors. She writes that despite the existence of seventeen thousand institutions of higher education worldwide, "There is a gladiatorial obsession with the rankings of the top 100."[24]

Hazelkorn provides stark examples of how resources within universities are being redistributed in reaction to rankings.[25] Some schools are diverting funding to areas that are more likely to produce higher rankings according to the criteria used by the rankers. Because research in the natural sciences is best captured in the international databases used to measure publication and citation success, the arts, humanities, social sciences, and areas without the same peer-reviewed article traditions (such as education, business, and engineering) face shrinking budgets or, in several instances, complete elimination because they do not help boost rankings.

Other strategies used to boost rankings undermine substantive educational goals even more directly. For example, some schools have changed hiring practices. Nobel Prize winners are expensive to hire, and most laureates receive the award for work conducted decades ago; nonetheless some Irish and British schools are striving to buy Nobel recipients as faculty.[26] Other schools encourage faculty to publish exclusively in English-language journals, advertise themselves in prestigious journals such as *Nature* and *Science*, cut faculty positions, or change the composition of faculty in favor of older, well-cited members, a practice that may discourage schools from hiring and developing young scholars.[27]

Global rankings also mobilize national governments, stakeholders without an analogy in the United States. World education rankings are an important indicator for some governments because national identities and reputation are tied to education systems and because rankings can serve as symbols of world standing, economic strength, or even "being modern."[28] Many governments use international rankings as a political tool to lobby for and expedite desired improvements. Germany, France, Taiwan, South Korea, India, Indonesia, Denmark, and Japan have all employed international rankings to justify major reforms in higher education; they have explicitly tied these reforms to the indicators that are most heavily weighted in these rankings. Some countries rely on the distinctions made by rankings to define other policies as well. Immigration policy in Denmark and the Netherlands now favors graduates from top-ranked universities.[29] Mongolia, Qatar, and Kazakhstan only provide scholarships to students who are accepted at "top 100 institutions," and Singapore's Foreign Specialist Institute restricts collaboration with its local schools to "top 100 universities."[30]

Some countries are fundamentally restructuring their education systems in their efforts to boost their visibility and reputation scores in the rankings. These changes affect the training provided to undergraduates and illustrate a general emphasis on research at the expense of instruction. To compete with the large U.S. universities that dominate the top of global rankings, some concentrate resources by merging departments and institutions to increase their size and visibility or by separating undergraduate from graduate education in order to develop visible research institutions.[31]

Largely because of the distinctive way higher education is organized into independent research institutes in France, French schools have fared poorly in international university rankings compared with those in the United Kingdom and the United States.[32] To redress this, France has undertaken expensive reforms consolidating universities and research centers in order to boost its rankings. For example, France is spending some 6.5 billion euros to create the Université Paris-Saclay from twenty separate universities and research institutes. Dominique Vernay, who chairs the foundation behind the merger, says, "Our ambition is to be among the 'top 10' in the rankings compiled by Shanghai Jiao Tong University," and "The first goal is to be the top university in continental Europe."[33]

Germany's "Excellence Initiative" (Exzellenzinitiative), launched in 2005, also prompted some mergers and consolidations as universities were forced to compete with each other for the designation "Universities of Excellence" (Eliteuniversitäten) or part of "Clusters of Excellence" (*Exzellenzcluster*) and the billions of euros of funding that flows with these designations. Longstanding egalitarian goals for higher education were reversed, and a sharp split between research and teaching missions was created in the effort to produce highly visible (read: highly ranked) universities attractive to international students.[34] The German sociologist Richard Münch provides a sophisticated analysis of how that program has contributed to the production of a "center" and "periphery" among German universities that will only become more entrenched over time. If some of Germany's universities move up in the global rankings a few notches, the cost to the "losers" will be punishing.[35]

Japan has proposed a major overhaul of its higher education system, reforms that, Hazelkorn points out, coincided with the arrival of global rankings.[36] One idea was to recast the role of smaller regional universities such that they will serve less as autonomous institutions and more as support streams to larger universities. These regional schools could face being shut down or being relegated to the category of "teaching universities," permanently subordinate to the more prestigious research-driven universities.[37] Other reforms focus on increasing the numbers of international students. Elite schools designated as "core universities" for purposes of internationalization receive extra funding.[38] Critics fear that policies such as these will foster the development of a caste-like stratification of universities in many countries where longstanding support of equal educational opportunities could be jeopardized by these "winner-take-all" markets that privilege a few select universities.

World rankings have also prompted the redistribution of work. Some universities have created new positions dedicated exclusively to improving the school's rank.[39] Others have beefed up international offices in order to boost ratios of international students, an important factor in the *Times Higher Educational Supplement*'s WUR rankings.[40] Others devise strategic plans aimed at similar improvements. At Shanghai Jiao Tong University, the birthplace of the ARWU rankings, Du Chao-Hui, the head of graduate education, described his university's goal in their 2020 strategic plan to become a "top 100 world university," adding that ARWU rankings would "guide our own goals and target our ambitions correctly." So far, the university's efforts seem to be working. Ranked 401 in 2003, by 2010 the school had risen to 201. Chao-Hui also noted that two Chinese universities, Beijing and Tsinghua, have moved into the top two hundred and that China now has twenty-two universities in the top five hundred, up from eight in 2005.[41] In Malaysia, after two universities' rankings fell in the QS World University Rankings, the prime minister created a national committee to evaluate how the country could raise the stature of its public universities.[42] It is clear that rankings play an important part in defining what constitutes educational value and motivating schools to change their behavior accordingly. Meanwhile, the actual educational value of these decisions can be debated.

World rankings are interpreted and used differently by different constituents. Ellen Hazelkorn's research shows that there are as many different views of the global rankings as there are stakeholders, a group made up of donors, current and future faculty, employers, government officials, students, and alumni.[43] As in the United States, those inside the institutions being ranked tend to be more skeptical of these rankings than external constituents, who are more likely to take them at face value. But there are also key audience dynamics central to global rankings that are less important in domestic rankings. For instance, international students are even more likely to use the rankings to make decisions about school choice than are the students in one's own country. Hazelkorn writes, "When you are recruiting students, in many countries the first thing they ask you is, 'Where are you ranked?' Not being ranked makes you invisible."[44]

The focus on rankings also raises concerns about the homogenizing effects of these global measures. Mayumi Ishikawa sees the ambition of prominent Japanese colleges to rise in the world rankings as threatening Japan's educational autonomy, its distinctive identity, and the "long-cherished traditions" that characterize it.[45] Traditionally, Japan has proudly assimilated Western knowledge through its own institutions of translation and adaptation rather than publishing and teaching in foreign languages, a practice that both reproduced and symbolized its cultural autonomy.[46] Pressure to publish in English and student demand for English instruction, especially in science and engineering, is challenging this tradition. As more elite Japanese students leave Japan to study in American universities and as Japanese universities feel growing pressure to increase the numbers of international students and faculty, Japan, much like American law schools, is losing control over defining what higher education means. The price and pace of globalization is exacerbated by familiar rankings pressures toward homogeneity and sweeping standardization, pressures that Ishikawa depicts as "global" and "hegemonic." For Ishikawa, the most troubling effect of global rankings is that they have increased the dominance of science and engineering at the expense of the humanities, the social sciences, and the arts. They have also encouraged the adoption of certain gaming strategies such as hiring foreign faculty to boost English citations and survey responses among English speakers.

As these examples show, governments care about the rankings of their national universities and about the ranks of the schools to which they send their best students. Their responses to rankings corroborate our core finding that indicators influence rather than merely reflect practices. Most dramatically, they redefine educational quality as countries alter educational systems to conform to ranking criteria and use the thresholds created by rankings to make policy distinctions. This redefinition of quality and goals has in turn prompted changes in how resources are allocated and has set in motion familiar gaming activities. For instance, the rankings encourage many countries to focus attention and resources on the schools that the rankings deem "world class" at the expense of the education system as a whole. More generally, the rankings have transformed the relevant organizational field from nation to world: the winners and losers are now countries, not organizations.[47] This is a profound change in how people think about education. Ellen Hazelkorn may have said it best: "Rankings are less about students and more about geopolitics."[48]

American Colleges and Universities

American colleges are the epicenter for rankings. This is where modern rankings started and where they sell the most. They have become so popular that it is a rare middle-class family that does not consult them at some point during the application process. The market for selective colleges and universities in the United States is a national one, unlike in many European countries, where students are more likely to plan to attend their local university. Many middle-class parents do not expect their children to attend a nearby college or live at home. The high school ritual of families piling into cars for exhausting trips canvassing colleges is a testament to the seriousness with which families treat the college selection process. A regional search limits alternatives such that it is possible to know a lot about the schools in that area, whereas a more expansive national search increases the number of schools in play and makes decisions more complex and overwhelming. A desire for simplicity is, of course, part of the appeal of rankings.

With nearly three thousand four-year colleges in the United States, rankings provide authoritative guidelines in assessing excellence and help determine whether a school is a "safety" or a "stretch" for an applicant. Because applicants and others attend to *USN* rankings, U.S. colleges and universities face the same pressures as law schools, and they respond in similar ways. Many smart people, often with backgrounds in statistics or business, are housed in departments called "institutional research" or "strategic planning" whose job it is to compile, analyze, and disseminate the statistics that define an institution. Much of this work is directed at informing university policy, yet increasingly this policy is aimed toward boosting rankings data. This might include close, coordinated scrutiny of the numbers generated by a school's various units. But the pressure to present a school's statistics in the best light can be intense, and the line between this and manipulation is not always so clear. One college administrator reported, "At some places it's more than just about rounding up."

Potential college applicants are inundated with emails and mailings from schools that have bought their names from test-taking organizations and other marketers. The amount of mail, phone calls, and email generated by colleges and universities marketing themselves to high school juniors and seniors is shocking. During the height of application season a student often gets five or six elaborate brochures a day. This is in addition to ten to twenty daily emails, often generated by consulting firms hired by admissions offices, as well as several weekly phone calls from work-study students using scripts to sing the praises of their schools. Schools have been quick to adapt their marketing to most forms of social media and now field highly polished videos, blogs, dedicated Facebook pages, and frequent Tweets. All this attention, at first flattering to seventeen-year-olds, soon becomes overwhelming. As with law schools, all the money and time spent on seducing applicants is unavailable for other educational goals. If this seduction pays off in more applications for a school, it also generates more work for the administrators and staff who must process these applications and more disappointing rejections for applicants from the schools looking to boost their selectivity factor. All of this marketing to prospective applicants is just one way in which rankings contribute to escalating tuition.[49]

Maybe the best indication of the pressure felt by colleges and universities is the widespread use of gaming strategies adopted to raise their numbers. The same reactive effects that we see in law schools occur here. Some of the gaming strategies are very similar: much like law schools, these schools face pressures to admit those with high test scores and engage in similar tactics to optimize these numbers (carefully monitoring standardized test scores and GPAs, strategically distributing scholarship money, and aggressively pursuing students who score high enough to raise their cumulative statistics). But some strategies are very different, reflecting the peculiarities of the undergraduate ranking algorithm. Because USN measures student satisfaction with their school as the percent of alumni who donate to the school, some schools go to great lengths to solicit even small donations from their graduates. One midwestern university offered its new graduates sandwich vouchers in exchange for donating as little as a dollar. Many schools employ work-study students to solicit donations from alumni, using scripts that often mention how donations boost rankings. One of the more notorious cases of gaming occurred in 2008 when Baylor

University offered bookstore vouchers to admitted students to retake the SAT in hopes of increasing its average score. Schools have also misrepresented their test scores. Iona College and Claremont McKenna College are recent examples of schools caught reporting inflated scores.[50] Bucknell, Clemson, Emory, and George Washington are among other schools that have admitted to sending inflated student statistics in their reports to the Department of Education and *USN* in recent years.[51]

The pressure generated by rankings on colleges and universities is in many ways comparable to that felt by law schools. Craig Tutterow uses twenty years of panel data to show that the general dynamics of how law schools and undergraduate institutions react to the rankings are very similar.[52] He provides evidence that, for both categories, all types of schools adopt strategies in reaction to rankings even though only the highest-ranked schools see tangible benefits from ranking improvements.

However, there are also differences in how rankings are structured that protect undergraduate institutions from some of their pernicious effects. Law school rankings, unlike *USN* rankings of colleges or other graduate schools and professional programs, use the same algorithm to rank *every* accredited school. This means that no school is exempt from ranking pressure in struggles over status and resources. This places enormous pressure on schools with unique missions or niches to conform to the standard law school model. In contrast, *USN* rankings of American colleges and universities are classified into different categories such as "National University Rankings," "Liberal Arts Colleges," "Regional Colleges," and "Regional Universities"; the "Regional Colleges" and "Regional Universities" are further subdivided into four regions, and *USN* also publishes lists of subcategories ("Best Value Schools," "A+ Schools for B Students," "Up-and-Coming Schools"). This more segmented classification scheme recognizes and rewards some forms of specialization, which blunts the pressure to redefine school missions. Even though the existing categories remain overly broad, this classification structure recognizes, at least implicitly, that different types of schools have different missions and are most fruitfully compared to institutions with similar goals and aspirations. Law schools would likely be better off if *USN* made comparisons on the basis of more specific criteria. Narrowing the scope of ranking categories—ensuring that like is compared to like—is a potential way to reduce some of the negative effects produced by rankings.

Business Schools

Just as the structure of a ranking system alters how the effects of rankings are distributed, the existence of competing rankers can change the impact of rankings. One important difference between law school rankings and many other educational rankings is that *USN* is the only ranking that is broadly used and taken seriously by those in legal education. To investigate whether the number of prominent rankers mattered in the effects of rankings, we compared law school rankings with those of another status-conscious professional field, MBA programs. There are at least five rankings that are considered legitimate among business schools. Our interviews with thirty business school deans provide convincing evidence that although business school rankings produce many of the same ranking effects as law school rankings, being subject to multiple rankings matters in three key ways.[53]

Most important is the fact that the results of the different rankers diverge, sometimes dramatically. The ambiguity created by these inconsistent results allows schools more latitude to choose the ranking that paints them in the best light and advertise that ranking.[54] This reputational flexibility is valuable to schools, and they try to leverage it. One dean said, "We look where we do well, and we make sure that people know that we did well there. We do some ads in [a few magazines], and we pick our best ranking to compare with schools that we compete with and show people how we stand compared to them." This approach to rankings is widespread among business schools. One dean went so far as to say that it would be "stupid" not to take advantage of these differences between rankings. The ambiguity created by multiple rankings provides business schools with more control over their reputations than law schools have.

A second and related advantage of multiple rankings is that schools can strategically tailor their programs to excel in the particular ranking that suits them best. For example, one faculty member at a Canadian business school reported that his school set its sights on the *Financial Times* [FT] international ranking of MBA programs. One factor in the FT rankings—constituting 10 percent of the overall rank—is its "research rank," which is calculated on the basis of the number of articles published by full-time faculty in a list of forty-five academic and practitioner journals.[55] Junior faculty were given a list of "suitable" journals for publication and were strongly encouraged to publish in those journals rather than in other journals in their fields, even if these journals were more prestigious. Similarly, other deans we interviewed described how some prominent U.S. schools decided to focus their attention on the *Business Week* rankings, which weigh survey results from recruiters very heavily. These schools lavish attention on potential and active recruiters with impressive lunches, parties, and carefully prepped job candidates in hopes of generating better assessments. In both of these examples we can see how multiple rankings allow schools more opportunity to exploit the ambiguity created by different evaluative formulas.

Finally, the ambiguity created by multiple rankings decreases the harmful effects of small changes in rank while also undermining the legitimacy of rankings generally. The existence of multiple assessments with divergent outcomes makes minor oscillations in any one ranking less consequential in the eyes of external audiences. Moreover, the differing results produced by each ranking system make audiences more skeptical about the rankings enterprise itself. One dean said:

> We're very pleased about every new ranking that comes out that kind of turns the world on its head. . . . Whenever I see a ranking that has Stanford in the forty-fifth spot, [X] spots behind my school, I say that this is good news because it deflates the bubble. It ought to make people think just what the heck this [ranking system] is and what it is that they are really trusting. And whether they should trust the *Wall Street Journal,* which has them forty-fifth, or this other ranking that has them second or whether it has them eighteenth. It ought to open up the eyes of most people who should say, "Ah, I get it now. I could do my own ranking tomorrow and make it come out any way I want, depending on what I think [are] the criteria."

Inconsistent results undermine the validity and authority of the rankings by encouraging readers to notice the many ways in which quality can be defined. The existence of competing ranking systems changes the dynamics of how rankings affect schools. Schools will continue to orient their behavior to the numbers, engage in gaming strategies, and reallocate resources to optimize their positions, but multiple rankings lessen the influence of any one number and help constituents recognize the arbitrary aspects of these evaluations. This buffers schools from some of the harshest effects of rankings such that small changes in rank tend to matter less and there is more freedom to sculpt and control reputations. This stands in stark contrast to the fields in which a single ranker dominates the landscape and schools must pay close attention to any change in their position, knowing that any decision they make may well improve or worsen their value according to that one ranker's definition of quality—whether they agree with that definition or not.

Why Dentists Are Different: Resistance to Rankings

In a few instances, certain types of schools have been able to engage in collective action to derail *USN*'s attempts to rank them. Dental schools, for example, were able to get *USN* to stop ranking them. The dental school administrators with whom we spoke, all of whom had been active in professional organizations, told us that *USN* tried to rank dental schools using criteria similar to those applied to medical schools: test scores, research money, size of faculty, and space. However, the Council of Deans of the American Association of Dental Schools agreed to boycott the rankings by refusing to submit the information *USN* requested in the late 1990s. The boycott worked because the number of dental schools at the time was relatively small (about fifty-five, compared to the nearly two hundred law schools), which meant that deans and administrators were more likely to know one another and trust one another not to break the boycott. One dean told us, "The deans actually got together as a group and made a decision that they would not engage these types of ranking systems at all. They wouldn't fill in the forms; it was sort of group peer pressure where they said, 'No, we're not going to do it.' "[56]

There have been other successful rankings boycotts. In Canada, *Maclean's* magazine is one of the principal ranking mediums. Over twenty Canadian universities now refuse to provide student data to *Maclean's*, including a number of schools that are highly ranked. Motives for joining the boycott vary—some are angered at what they consider an inappropriate rank, others are offended by the practice, and still others reject the methods used to rank. Regardless of the motives, a successful boycott reasserts the power of universities to control the terms of evaluation while casting doubt on the legitimacy of the resulting rankings. The magazine continues to publish its rankings and the rankings issues continue to sell well. But because most Canadians go to university near their homes and because the status difference among universities is not nearly as important as it is in the United States, rankings do not have the same impact in Canada as they do south of the border.

Why have there not been similarly successful boycotts by U.S. law schools? According to some long-term law school administrators we spoke with, there was an informal attempt to boycott when they realized how influential the rankings might become. Although many schools agreed not to submit their data to *USN*, in the end most schools capitulated to the pressure. The schools that didn't send data fell precipitously in the following year's rankings when *USN* estimated their data. One dean whose school had been burned in this process told us that he felt the school had no choice but to comply with *USN* once they saw how much they would be penalized if they refused to submit their information.

Although it is tempting to attribute the failure of these boycotts to the self-interest of these schools, it is important to recognize how the distinctive relationships produced by the extreme commensuration that undergirds rankings make resistance particularly difficult. By creating a zero-sum structure in which there are precise hierarchical relationships, the rankings have intensified the competition among schools. Consequently, quality is relative, as are perceptions of advantage and disadvantage. This makes collective action more risky and difficult. Schools that fail to engage in some new form of gaming will likely be severely punished in the rankings, making the cost of opting out high. In this way, the very nature of the rankings undermines the collective action that is necessary to resist them.

This is not to say that there is no alternative—that all schools *must* comply with *USN*. Beginning in 1995, Reed College, an elite liberal arts college, initiated a boycott of the *USN* college and university rankings; it refused to share its data and also asked *USN* to leave Reed out of the rankings. *USN* retaliated by including Reed in the rankings and "estimating" the missing data with extremely low values. As a result, Reed's ranking has fallen from ninth in 1983 to ninety-third in 2015, despite improving on many measures of academic quality.[57] Reed is widely known for the high intellectual caliber of its undergraduates and its appreciation of independent thinking; its boycott did not seem to damage its reputation. Instead the boycott is now part of its identity as an intellectually independent college. But for many schools, this option is not feasible. When asked by Reed to join in their boycott, the president of another elite liberal arts college responded, "We can't. [*USN*] will just plug in their own data, and we'll drop ten places in the rankings." Another college president said, "The rankings are merely intolerable. Unilateral disarmament is suicide."[58] Few schools possess the reputational resources to risk the repercussions of a rankings boycott.[59]

We do not normally think of law schools or elite colleges and universities as ineffective actors, but despite the deep hostility most legal educators feel toward rankings, their resistance has proved futile in curtailing rankings' influence.[60] Some fields—those with smaller markets (such as dentistry) or less national competition (such as Canadian law schools)—have been able to slow the encroachment of the influence of rankings, but the law school and undergraduate markets in the United States are, paradoxically, too large to rebuff *USN*. Not only does the size of these markets make them too profitable for *USN* to let go, but the diffuseness that is a feature of fields of this size also creates a situation in which collective action is nearly impossible, considering the sway that the rankings have over the perceptions of prospective students, employers, and other constituents coupled with *USN*'s ability to punish noncompliance. This inability to resist is a stark demonstration of the power of quantitative assessment.

OTHER PERFORMANCE MEASURES

Education is just one sphere in which quantitative measures such as rankings, indicators, and performance metrics are changing institutions. It is difficult to find an area that has not been affected by the push for quantitative forms of accountability and evaluation. International organizations are often enthusiastic producers of quantitative indicators and rankings. The European Bank for Reconstruction and Development was founded in 1990 to help command economies become market economies. From 1990 to 2002 its main way of evaluating legal systems was through the legal indicator survey it created and administered, which ranked countries for the extensiveness and effectiveness of their laws. This ranking could affect a country's ability to attract investments from this bank and from other investors. Indicators like these, and others created by international financial institutions such as the World Bank, the International Monetary Fund, and the Asian Development Bank, simultaneously produce and evaluate law.[61] The U.N. has developed hundreds of indicators, ranging from those measuring sustainable development to crime. There is now a series of indicators of human trafficking and compliance with anti-trafficking conventions, including those developed by the International Labor Office, the European Commission, the United Nations, and the U.S. State Department.[62] NGOs are increasingly using rankings as a tool to attract attention to good and bad practices.[63] Transparency International produces an annual Perceptions of Corruption Index.[64] The U.S. State Department and the Walk Free Foundation rank 162 countries according to the prevalence of slavery. The Heritage Foundation has developed a ranking of countries' economic freedom.[65]

A brief examination of the effects of quantitative indicators in two fields unrelated to education—crime statistics and health care—can provide a fuller picture of how public measures outside of higher education produce unintended consequences similar to those we document for rankings.

Crime Statistics

In the mid-1990s, the Department of Justice commissioned a new crime-fighting tool. Evolving from a pins-on-a-map approach, William Bratton, then commissioner of the New York Police Department, introduced CompStat (short for "computer statistics"), data-driven crime-mapping software that helped police departments create precise, precinct-level incident maps that permitted them to spot crime hotspots and trends and to adjust their resources accordingly. Before CompStat, it could take up to nine months for the NYPD to receive crime statistics, which were outdated by the time they were available for analysis. With CompStat, weekly statistics could be scrutinized in regular meetings of district commanders and their superiors. CompStat was widely touted as a breakthrough that helped to drastically cut crime in New York City. Dubbed "the New York Miracle," it was quickly adopted by police departments in most major U.S. cities and is now used by many cities around the world. In making crime reporting coordinated, accurate, and timely, CompStat offered a powerful new tool for using resources more efficiently and for ensuring transparency and accountability. But like all technology, its value is determined by how it is used.

As good management increasingly became numbers driven, including quotas for arrests and pressure to reduce violent crimes, majors and their higher-ranking officers started to place intense political pressure on precinct commanders to improve the numbers. Failure to deliver the numbers risked public humiliation at regular CompStat meetings (memorably dramatized in season 5 of HBO's *The Wire*) or even the loss of their command. The criminologist John Eterno, a retired police commander, explains, "Once you have one 'CompStat' meeting where they're screaming and yelling at you about your crime numbers, . . . you get the hint and then you do what you can to make sure those numbers are looking the way they want them to."[66] So there was a strong incentive to game the statistics and manipulate the numbers.

Manipulation took several forms. One strategy was to dissuade victims of crime from filing police reports. Claudette Jolly, a Bronx resident, reported that after her car was broken into three times in one month, officers still discouraged her from filing a report, telling her, "These are petty crimes" and "Your insurance will go up."[67] Sometimes supervisors would simply not enter crime reports into the system. Another way to "improve" numbers was to downgrade charges of the seven major felony crimes collected by the FBI (so-called "index crime") to misdemeanors ("non-index crime"), which are not reported. So a burglary became lost property, rape became forcible touching, assault became harassment, and robbery became grand larceny, which could then become criminal trespass. If reporting officers did not do their own adjusting, superiors could do it for them, "editing" their weekly reports.

Research conducted by Eterno and another criminologist, Eli Silverman, shows that this pressure to massage the numbers is widespread and that manipulation is systematic.[68] In a 2008 survey of 309 retired police officers, most of whom have served as precinct commanders since the department started using the CompStat program in the mid-1990s, more than half admitted to massaging the numbers. They reported that pressure to improve their numbers was intense. A later email survey of about two thousand retired police officers of all ranks found that 60 percent had little confidence in the accuracy of NYPD index-crime statistics and that this distrust and the manipulation of crime statistics had sharply increased after the introduction of CompStat. According to Silverman, the top-down pressure to reduce index crime is "putting people in an unreasonable position. The public needs to understand that crime can fluctuate. It needs to be less number-driven. You can't just measure [cities] by their crime rate."[69] Eterno and Silverman point out that, inevitably, when crime rates go down it becomes harder and harder to realize subsequent decreases. This can put precincts that have done a good job in helping to decrease crime on the defensive for not being able to maintain similar decreases over time.[70]

Even if crime rates appear to be lower, police must still demonstrate their activity by making their quotas of arrests for lesser crimes. Another disturbing form of massaging the numbers involves increasing patrolmen's practice of "stop and frisk," in which "suspicious" persons are stopped and questioned and patted down in a search for weapons. Eterno and Silverman's respondents reported that pressure to use these tactics had increased since the introduction of CompStat. This practice is disproportionately used on minorities. In 2010, black suspects in New York City were over nine times as likely to be stopped and frisked as white suspects, and Latinos were over three times as likely to be stopped as whites. Richard Rosenfeld and Robert Fornango report that in that same year "the NYPD recorded nearly three stops for every 10 black New York City residents."[71] Such policy reinforces the deep alienation and distrust many minorities feel toward the police, alienation that is a barrier to cooperation.

One extraordinary case, first reported in the *Village Voice*, showed the extent to which commanders would go to cover up their practice of "juking the numbers."[72] Adrian Schoolcraft, a patrolman in the Eighty-first Precinct, in the Bedford-Stuyvesant neighborhood of Brooklyn, was concerned about the misreporting of crime. He went through internal channels to try to bring attention to the issue, but was rebuffed. So Schoolcraft began wearing a wire, and documented supervisors' admonitions to manipulate crime stats. Once his wire was discovered, his house was broken into and documents were removed, he was harassed at work, and he was forcibly admitted to a psychiatric hospital and held there for six days. He sued the NYPD and the hospital (the case was settled in the fall of 2015). Schoolcraft's charges about the Eighty-first Precinct were eventually corroborated in an internal report.

These pressures to manipulate statistics and make quotas are found in other police departments. An investigation of crime statistics culled from about sixty thousand cases by the *Milwaukee Journal Sentinel* revealed disturbing manipulation. Among their findings were that 500 aggravated assaults had been downgraded in the previous three years, 800 additional cases fit the pattern of manipulation but could not be corroborated with public records, and 214 aggravated assaults that occurred in 2011 had been misclassified. The Milwaukee Police Department had reported a 2.3 percent drop in violent crime from 2010 to 2011. The corrected figure produced by the investigators was a 1.1 percent increase in crime. The misclassified crimes included 160 cases of felony child abuse, including that of eighteen-month-old Karmari Curtis, who suffered life-threatening internal injuries from an abusive boyfriend of his mother's. This crime had been classified as a simple assault, a category appropriate for a slap or a shove, and so was not included in the city's violent crime report that year. The boy was later murdered by the same boyfriend.

Similar trends can be seen in other countries. Emmanuel Didier found analogous efforts to manipulate crime statistics in France.[73] Shay Fogelman, a reporter for the liberal Israeli newspaper *Haaretz*, attributes increases in complaints by Palestinians of the brutality of their interrogations at police stations in Hebron to efforts to improve performance ratings for police stations that are generated by a crime-tracking computer program called Menahel. Fogelman reports that police documents contain the management slogan "What is not measured is not managed, and what is not managed is not improved."[74]

Measuring Health Care

Health care, a field inundated with performance measures and public data, is also vulnerable to the reactive effects we see in education.[75] And in health care the stakes are clearly higher: the consequences of reactivity not only can lead to better or worse health outcomes but also can mean the difference between life and death. The Veteran Affairs scandal (discussed in chapter 1 of this volume) exemplifies the problems that performance measures can create: a statistic created to provide incentives for reducing wait times resulted in dangerous misreporting as administrators struggled to meet their numerical goals, a task made more difficult by reductions in their funding. Once again we see how efforts to achieve accountability through measures can be subverted, especially when financial or other motivating incentives are involved.

Reactive effects have also been documented in the measures used to monitor and assess medical practice and treatment protocols. Once measures are created to evaluate the frequency of practice-based problems, there is a risk of medical organizations changing how they report statistics to influence these measures. For instance, in light of significant declines in infection rates in hospitals, Mary Dixon-Woods and Eli N. Perencevich undertook a study to establish how much of this decrease was due to changes in procedures and protocols and how much was due to changes in reporting behavior. They write, "Put bluntly, the more that organizations are incentivized by the prospect of shaming or financial penalties to decrease sensitivity—and thus not to find cases—the less certain it is that they are reporting a valid assessment of their infection rate. As a consequence, some are now arguing that infection rates may say more about willingness to report than underlying harm."[76]

These same dynamics can be set in motion by physician report cards and other types of public comparisons of performance. Health-care report cards—annual reports on the quality and outcome of care by a particular health-care provider or health-care facility—are mandated by law in some states. These measures do provide consumers with potentially valuable information about medical outcomes, but they also open the door to harmful unintended consequences. One prominent study of heart surgeons found that physicians were more reluctant to perform potentially life-saving procedures on high-risk patients for fear of the effects that such procedures would have on their publicly reported mortality statistics. Eighty-three percent of surveyed respondents "agreed that patients who might benefit from angioplasty may not receive the procedure as a result of public reporting of physician-specific patients' mortality rates."[77]

In a different study researchers found, when they analyzed outcomes for Medicare patients seeking cardiac care in New York and Pennsylvania, that in states that require health-care report cards, more resources were used and sicker patients fared worse than in states without this mandatory reporting.[78] Publicly reporting outcome statistics, even when weighting for risk factors, prompted doctors to select their patients more carefully and weed out the sicker patients. Hospitals also screened patients more carefully, which increased the number of the sickest patients that were sent to teaching hospitals. This added screening increased the time it took for patients to receive care and led to the expenditure of more resources. In each of these examples, we see how concerns about public numbers can affect how decisions are made in ways that were unintended by the policymakers who implemented them as a result of strategic manipulations by those being governed by those numbers.

Finally, there is evidence that systemwide regulations and evaluations also produce reactive effects. In a study of "regulatory transparency" among doctors, psychotherapists, and counselors in the U.K., Gerry McGivern and Michael D. Fischer found that these public assessments caused "clinicians to focus less on actual practice, and patients' needs, and more on representing practice in standardised terms to avoid revealing activities that might draw further scrutiny or later be construed in a negative light."[79] These public measures structure attention, change how medical professions present themselves, raise anxiety levels among these professionals, disrupt normal therapeutic practice, and transform how professionals interpret cases and perceive risk.[80] McGivern and Fischer found that these public reports encourage doctors to act defensively (making sure they do not violate any regulations) rather than to proactively improve quality of care. Others argue that these measures encourage collusion between administrative agencies and health-care organizations, which leads to "seeking improvements in reported performance only, and not providing the organizational clout to ask awkward questions about the robustness of those reported improvements."[81] In all of these cases, numbers become ends in themselves rather than symbols of underlying quality and good practice.

THE USEFUL VERSUS THE GOOD

The anthropologist Sally Merry contends that accountability measures "are rapidly multiplying as tools for measuring and promoting reform strategies around the world."[82] These measures are proliferating in numbers and in influence, and their legitimacy is increasingly taken for granted. Proponents are everywhere. The adage "If it isn't measured, it isn't managed," sometimes attributed to Peter Drucker, has—as we have shown—become a mantra for many. For Bill Gates, "Measurement is a big part of mobilizing for impact. You set a goal, and then you use data to make sure you're making progress toward it. This is crucial in business—and it's just as important in the fight against disease and poverty." In his popular book, *Better,* Atul Gawande offers five suggestions for doctors who want to improve their performance, emphasizing the importance of counting to improving medical care.[83]

Statements like these resonate with *USN*'s arguments about why rankings are good for the world. Robert Morse has persistently maintained, "The main purpose of the rankings is to provide prospective law school students with much-needed—and clearly desired—comparative information to help them make decisions on where to apply and enroll."[84] The production of rankings is useful, and that in itself justifies them.

Given that rankings *are* so useful in providing solutions to some practical problems, it is important to remember that useful is not the same as good. One of the primary goals of this book is to question the often unreflective acceptance of and commitment to quantification as the dominant form of valuation. As we have shown, there is often a shadowy underbelly to the numbers used to measure people and social objects. Measures produce unintended consequences, misguided incentives, and misplaced attention. More generally, they transform what they purport to only reflect, altering the social world in unexpected ways: they are constitutive as well as reactive. This means that public measures are not neutral enterprises, nor can they be understood strictly in terms of their utility or technical achievement, as their advocates often claim. They carry with them assumptions about value, merit, and goals, as well as about what is good, normal, and right.

One of the problems of focusing solely on the usefulness of measures is that it encourages us to overlook the personal costs that they levy on the individuals who are forced to manage them. Balancing the demands created by the numbers with the requirements of day-to-day work and professional ethics is a source of anxiety and presents a variety of moral dilemmas. We found that measures produce a great deal of ambivalence, affecting how work is experienced and responsibility is distributed. We were struck throughout our interviews, especially with administrators, by how much they loathed managing the rankings, many describing it as "the worst part of my job." An important reason they feel this way is that their professional discretion has been compromised, replaced by mechanical routines that regularly produce outcomes that offend their professional judgment. This loss of discretion is closely tied to a loss of professional responsibility. Many administrators are now adopting tactics to improve their numbers that people in their position would have found dishonest and unthinkable not so long ago. They lie about their numbers, release statistics that are technically correct but substantively misleading, and allocate money in ways that belie their school's mission and commitment to providing the highest-quality education.

The anxiety that measures produce in those who are evaluated by them should not be taken lightly. For many administrators, the rankings produce a sense of insecurity about what they are doing, concern about increased competition, and worries that others are finding new ways to game them. It is common for people to feel that corruption is rampant under the rankings regime, that colleagues cannot be trusted, and that there is no way to control rankings. Amid this anxiety, it is easier to understand the ethical dilemmas administrators face and the questionable practices in which they sometimes engage. Rankings offer a ready rationalization for deans or schools to justify the actions they choose to take or not take. Even though most find rankings objectionable, the power of the numbers is beyond dispute and can be mobilized to great effect by administrators. In the same way, rankings can be a useful scapegoat when things go badly. At one time or another those we interviewed used a low ranking to justify the job they did not get, the offer a candidate declined, lower admissions statistics, rejected articles, and even dull students. All of these effects promote a "culture of cynicism" about legal education that stretches from law school applicants to the most elite deans. It is easy to become disenchanted when you hear so many say "It's all about the numbers."

The ethical dilemmas that rankings create for those who are subjected to them are even more troublesome. The pressure to produce good numbers encourages the gaming behavior that has spawned bad press, lawsuits, and distrust—all of which undermines the reputations of law schools and the dignity of legal education. Those who engage in such behavior are often labeled "weak leaders" or "bad apples" who are too amoral or immoral to resist cheating to raise their scores. But we should not lose sight of the fact that rankings promote such activities by generating pressures to raise the numbers "at all costs." All schools feel the pressure to game the rankings, whether by changing their policies on what counts as employed, altering the leave schedules of their faculties, offering bonuses for achieving the "right" admissions statistics, or simply lying about particular outcomes. They know full well that not adopting the same strategies as others will lead to lower numbers. Of course not all succumb to these pressures, but nearly every school engages in some activities designed to manipulate their scores. Rankings create conditions that promote tension between doing what is most useful for the school in the short term and what is ethical, and these dilemmas exact a heavy toll on those who must manage the numbers. It is worth adding that one of the great ironies of rankings, and accountability measures in general, is that they can produce uncertainty about who is responsible or should be held accountable when unintended effects are produced. In the case of gaming, for example, do we blame the deans who feel they must capitulate to keep their jobs? The university presidents and boards of trustees who place so much emphasis on these numbers? The students who blindly follow the numbers in making their school choices? *USN* for setting the whole process in motion? Paradoxically, it is difficult to pinpoint who is accountable for the ethical dilemmas created by accountability measures.

Another paradox of "quantitative accountability" is that the accuracy and reliability of such measures is seldom scrutinized. Given the cost and resources devoted to accountability practices, it is ironic how rarely we interrogate our devotion to measuring performance or lay these measures open to the same hard-nosed evaluation that we demand of other accounting practices. We seldom make any attempt to challenge our assumptions about the value of these external assessments in any rigorous way. We have yet to produce the necessary classifications for doing so; for example, the costs of producing a budget, a strategic plan, or benchmarks are seldom included in our budgets, strategic plans, or benchmarking other than in more general categories of administration or management.

But these individual and organizational effects are not the only or even the most important ethical concern associated with the proliferation of accountability measures. Although hidden, ethical considerations permeate their construction and implementation. How accountability systems are structured—for instance, the aspects of social phenomena they measure and in what forms outcomes are presented—changes how these phenomena are perceived and conceptualized. These structures determine who counts and who does not, who is noticed and for what. They also shape patterns of exclusion in politics, education, professions, and other arenas, and they set the terms under which those who are included are allowed to participate. Even more, these structures play a quiet but influential role in dictating how we define good government, good education, good philanthropy, good health care, or any other social institution that is being measured. In doing these things, they disguise the ideological commitments of those who make and profit from them. The political is transformed into the technical.[85]

Those subjected to accountability measures must often decide between adapting themselves to these standards or paying the penalty for deviating from implicit assumptions about what is normal and legitimate. If schools are any example, most choose the former, which leads to greater homogenization among those being held accountable.[86] One final ethical concern about the increasing dominance of quantified measures, then, is that quantification tends to foreclose other modes of creating and expressing value. Valuing is elemental in social life. We value when we make judgments, consider decisions, or reflect on our experiences. What to do, where to go, who or what has merit, what is good or bad, and how to best distribute resources are all efforts to establish and judge qualities. Heterogeneous societies and groups must negotiate competing modes of valuing to effectively make decisions.[87] But quantification threatens a new and more insidious manifestation of Weber's Iron Cage as the growing global consensus about the superiority of quantitative forms imperils other forms of valuation. Especially at risk are those forms of evaluation that are messier and more time consuming and that require deliberation or consensus. This threat is particularly insidious because quantification, cloaked in auras of objectivity and neutrality, takes on the appearance of being "value-less," apolitical, and outside of ethical concern.

Closely scrutinizing how these numbers are created and used is necessary if we are to see the subtle and often unnoticed ways in which ethical assumptions, claims, and outcomes are incorporated into them. Only if these assumptions are brought to light can we decide whether they are desirable and whether we support them. To do this, however, accountability measures must themselves be held accountable and made transparent. Our work aspires to encourage just this kind of scrutiny, including thoughtful consideration about the ethical aspects of accountability measures, so that quantitative evaluations are not assessed solely on the uses they serve. This balance is crucial for well-rounded judgments about how we should value these measures.

Appendix A | Methods and Data

OUR APPROACH

We have been studying the effects of rankings on higher education since 2002. In our attempt to understand the phenomenon of rankings as thoroughly as possible and to stay abreast of this ever-evolving subject, we accumulated an abundance of wide-ranging data, which we continued to collect and update until the submission of our manuscript. In this appendix we document how and why we collected this data.

We conducted hundreds of formal and informal interviews, took extended site trips to focus schools (seven schools that were chosen to be the subject of a more intensive interview process), observed professional meetings and job fairs, analyzed decades of admissions and yield statistics, systematically followed online bulletin boards and chat rooms, analyzed websites and newspaper stories, and accumulated boxes and boxes of organizational documents. In addition to this primary data, we incorporated evidence from two other research projects: an ethnographic study of college admissions and a comparison of the professional socialization of law and business students.[1] Along with these more formal data sources, we also benefited from a network of supportive informants scattered in schools across the country and the globe, informants who have consistently and graciously supplied us with information, material, stories, advice, and referrals.

Informed by the concept of "triangulation of data," our goal in collecting this variety of data has been to see the consequences of rankings from as many perspectives as possible in the belief that this comprehensive approach would generate new questions, encourage a broader understanding, and eventually produce more convincing explanations.[2] The strengths and limitations of different types of data sources mostly complemented one another: offering corroborating evidence, generating reasons to look more deeply into particular aspects, yielding the apt illustration or telling statistic that keeps an account focused and vivid, and enabling us to fill in blanks.

In analyzing our data sources, we had four main aims:

1. Collect evidence that speaks to different units of analysis such as individuals, departments, organizations, or fields
2. Identify important variation in the effects of rankings and the conditions that produce this variation
3. Learn whether or how rankings effects change over time
4. Corroborate findings using sources with different strengths and weaknesses

The careful deployment of comparisons, selected for both theoretical and methodological reasons, helps isolate specific causal relations. So, for example, to learn how organizational characteristics mediate the effects of rankings, we compared the influence of rankings on law schools that vary by rank, region, niche, and mission, as well as whether they are public or private. We also made comparisons across constituencies to show how the uses and meanings of rankings change as they are adapted by new groups for new purposes: employers use them differently than administrators; prospective students are affected by the rankings in different ways than current students or alumni (although they are all affected).

In addition, we made general comparisons between the effects of rankings on law schools and their effects on other educational organizations, focusing most concertedly on business schools, undergraduate colleges in the United States, and international universities. This strategy helped us to identify which effects are distinctive to certain types of schools and which are more generalized.

Finally, we employed our multiple sources as a check of the reliability of people's perceptions, to compare different points of view, to get at processes of institutionalization, and to understand how organizational factors interact with and shape individual actions. Specifically, we compared evidence of the data we collected through our interviews with the data collected through unobtrusive means in order to assess and mitigate problems of reactivity and deception. We also compared accounts grounded in deep knowledge of local practices with broad, standardized data from a range of schools.

Some examples may help clarify our logic. One potential liability of interviews as evidence is that people can be unreliable narrators. They may dissemble, not know, or try to be helpful by telling you what they think you want to hear. Accounts might be censored or self-interested, memories may be sketchy, and individuals in different roles often see things differently. People change their minds, and their doing so may reflect an evolving response of cohorts, as groups with different tenures adapt to new circumstances and the institutionalization of practices in similar ways. Finally, rankings generate endless gossip, and some rankings practices are controversial or embarrassing. Because of this, respondents may be reluctant to speak candidly with strangers or may be tempted to speak poorly of competitors.

To address these possible reactions to interviews, whenever possible we compared what people in different parts of the organization said, what people said in private and in public, what people reported as opposed to what they did, and what subordinates and bosses said about the same practices. We also compared what schools wrote about themselves on websites and in marketing materials with what school staff said, what current and former colleagues said, and what the same person said over time. For instance, when several deans denied hiring unemployed graduates as a way to boost placement statistics, we were skeptical. When current and former employees provided detailed descriptions of this practice at these schools, our skepticism was confirmed since it was unlikely that the deans in question would not have known about this practice. We tried to maintain this skepticism throughout our research. We also tried to learn from such instances of deception. In this case, for example, we gained insight into efforts to conceal practices, whether concealment *by* the dean or concealment *from* the dean. This in itself was evidence that led to new questions about how moral boundaries are maintained or redrawn as a result of operating in the rankings environment.

Our analysis of how students use rankings is another example of our understanding being enriched by the deployment of different data. Most law school administrators and applicants we interviewed told us that students rely heavily on rankings to decide where to apply to and attend law school. Administrators say that when admitted students decide among schools, they almost never lose students to lower-ranked schools or win students from higher-ranked schools. Our statistical analysis shows how much applicants rely on rankings by demonstrating more precisely how movement in rankings affects applications and yields.[3] Students described their use of rankings in our interviews, and our statistical analysis confirmed these accounts and specified their use.

But it was only after reading anonymous postings on electronic bulletin boards where students chat—sometimes with alarming frankness—that we realized how thoroughly and starkly rankings color some students' thinking, and how uncritical of rankings methodology students are. For example, when students in chat rooms bragged or commiserated about the schools that had admitted them, quality was always described in terms of *USN* rankings ("I got into my first top-twenty-five school!"). Some students entertained long discussions of the relative virtues of schools that were separated by minute and statistically meaningless differences; others described themselves in terms of the rankings of the schools to which they had been admitted. They start to become "first-tier students" or "third-tier students" within the relatively safe confines of their electronic relationships. We cannot ascertain how typical of all students the students who use online discussion groups are, but the view of student attitudes we gained by monitoring chat rooms was corroborated by our analysis of Debra J. Schleef's interview data. Her data, which consisted of intensive interviews of students at two highly ranked schools, a business and a law school, showed similar patterns of student investment in rankings.

Likewise, our statistical analysis of admissions data was very useful to us in that it helped us make generalizations about the population of law schools and provided support for some of our claims about causal linkages. This data, however, could not speak to the meaning and construction of numbers that make up rankings and the particular authority that members grant to them. Furthermore, this analysis could not reveal as well as respondents and observations the details about the dynamic and recursive relationships among variables or the mechanisms that help explain causal processes. Again, these complementary data sources produced more nuanced insights into this phenomenon.

Collecting and compiling eclectic data sources generated an at times overwhelming body of disparate types of evidence ranging from admissions statistics to online observations. If our different forms of evidence could not always be neatly integrated, we are nevertheless confident that these sources have provided a more complex understanding of what is going on with rankings by fostering more iterative processes of checking, extending, and interpreting data. We have tried to indicate in our exposition which data we rely on most heavily for particular findings and how the different sources of data are made to speak to one another. Yet the effect of all these sources remains cumulative in ways that are hard to disentangle. The specific influence of each source of data may not always be retrievable in all of our thinking, but each contributes to a body of knowledge that informs—and we believe improves—our judgments in our analysis and interpretation.

DATA SOURCES

Interviews

Our 237 formal interviews were our single most important source of data. These interviews were organized and conducted as four different samples of respondents. This purpose of creating four samples was to help us answer both distinct and overlapping questions. The samples (see appendix table A.1) include deans and associate deans, lower-level administrators and staff, and faculty. For face-to-face interviews, we obtained signed consent forms. For phone interviews, subjects verbally consented to be interviewed. We promised respondents not to identify their names or institutions. We name individuals or institutions only when quoting from public sources. Some respondents offered to have their views attributed to them, but we have opted not to disclose their names for the sake of consistency. The one exception to this rule is interviews with *USN* representatives, who gave their permission to be quoted for attribution and who are public figures with a long record of speaking publicly about rankings. In order to protect the identity of institutions, we sacrificed some precision. Quotes or descriptions are edited to remove identifying characteristics, and we use general terms such as "elite" or "second tier" to indicate a school's ranking or describe its general status if the ranking information is too revealing.

Our first three samples were non-probability samples derived using theoretical and snowball sampling techniques. Theoretical sampling involves selecting respondents to produce variation that may prove theoretically significant.[4] We selected respondents to highlight variation by school ranking (that is, which tier and where in the tier a school is located), ranking trajectory (whether their school's ranking has changed significantly in the past fifteen years), school location (region of the country, location in a large metropolitan area or a smaller city), and the mission or niche of the school (for example, whether it attracts and places students nationally or regionally, whether its goals are to provide opportunities for disadvantaged students, or whether it emphasizes particular types of legal training such as in corporate or public service law). We also sought out administrators who favor rankings (a distinct minority), as well as administrators with varying lengths of tenure. When respondents had worked at more than one law school, they were asked to compare their experiences.

Finding people and places that exhibit our sought-after variation requires expertise, so we relied on snowball sampling to help identify whom to interview. Snowball samples use respondent networks to suggest potential interview subjects.[5] After each interview we asked subjects to recommend others who might have unique or insightful opinions about the rankings and then solicited interviews from these persons. We continued to solicit interviews until additional interviews generated little or no new information about the effects of rankings, what Barney G. Glaser and Anselm L. Strauss describe as "theoretical saturation."[6] For non-random samples, we cannot generalize precisely from our sample to the overall population, or say exactly how much variation is explained by a particular variable from our interviews.

But the variation we built into our samples does permit us to approximate "tests" of the impact of various kinds of conditions or relationships. Our fourth wave of interviews, which focused more narrowly on the relationship between rankings and LL.M. programs at law schools, were drawn from a random sample.

Our first wave consisted mainly of phone interviews. These sixty-five interviews were designed to help us locate the range of effects of rankings across law schools. Our methodological aims for these interviews were to assess the feasibility of this research, develop our research questions, and refine our interviews. Results from this phase suggested that we should obtain more detailed evidence about how rankings alter relations within law schools because it became apparent that different parts of law schools are affected differently and relations among units change with rankings.

Our second sample consisted of seventy open-ended interviews conducted with members of the seven focus schools we visited. Interviews at focus schools were designed to provide information about the effects of rankings in different parts of the organization, including how these effects overlap and interact, as well as allow us to compare and corroborate accounts from people in different positions. At focus schools we were most interested in how rankings effects were distributed across units within schools and how the rankings affected relationships with their various constituencies, other schools, and professional organizations. At focus schools we interviewed deans, assistant and associate deans, and employees charged with administering admissions, career services, public affairs, planning and development, marketing, student affairs, faculty affairs, clinical programs, and writing programs. We also interviewed staff, including administrative assistants and librarians, faculty, and some students.

The selection of the seven focus schools was geared to provide variation in school characteristics that seemed important in light of prior interviews. In addition, the deans of these schools were willing to allow their schools to be part of this study. Given the controversy surrounding rankings, granting strangers access to employees and records is a courageous act, one not all deans were willing to risk. Although every dean we approached strongly endorsed the importance of this research, three deans turned down our requests, so alternative schools with similar characteristics were selected. Of the three refusals, one dean admitted to being too nervous about what we might find to permit access, which confirms that rankings involve high stakes and underscores the controversy and anxiety they generate.

We selected focus law schools to highlight variation in tier, trajectory, geography, and mission. Our seven focus schools are located in four states—four schools in the East and three in the Midwest. All four tiers are represented in the focus schools: two schools have moved between tiers;

two have experienced significant movement within a tier over the past fifteen years; and the ranking of two schools has remained relatively stable. The mission of one focus school emphasizes public service, another embraces a Catholic tradition, and the others occupy more conventional niches. One focus school is in a college town in a largely rural area; the other six are part of major metropolitan areas. One of the seven is an independent law school, unaffiliated with a university, three are private schools, and four are state schools. When possible, we included interviews with administrators and faculty of varying tenure, including those whose tenure predated the advent of rankings, and recently hired assistant professors or administrators. These interviews allowed us to get a nuanced picture of the distribution of effects within and across different types of schools.

Even though our visits to focus schools were constructed around interviews, the visits afforded opportunities for us to observe situations that helped to flesh out the interview data. For example, in-person interviews meant we could attend to visual as well as spoken cues, and they gave us a better sense of the context in which people worked, studied, and socialized. On many occasions, someone would pull a document out for us to look at, check a computer file, or ask a colleague to clarify something. We were sometimes given informal tours by staff or allowed to use a faculty or student lounge between interviews. These occasions provided many opportunities for informative informal conversations about the rankings. We were especially attentive to displays or materials addressing the school's image, status, or performance. So we noted bulletin boards, photos, brochures, or banners announcing student or faculty achievements, displays of positive press coverage, including, in some cases, advertisements of the school's *USN* ranking. Our visits made it easier to get a sense of how many people worked in a department, how accessible or isolated it was from other administrative units, and how fluid relations among staff members were.[7]

Both our phone and focus school interviews were open-ended; typically they lasted forty to ninety minutes. All but five were taped and transcribed. This format provided the flexibility needed to probe responses, adapt questions to the unique experience and expertise of informants, and pursue emerging insights about processes for which there is as yet little systematic empirical evidence. In addition, the high-stakes nature of rankings—many of our respondents felt threatened by them, believing that poor rankings could jeopardize their reputations, bonuses, and jobs—made it especially important that we probe and corroborate ambiguous or suspect information.

Because respondents were not asked identical questions, we coded interviews for themes rather than precisely predefined variables. Our initial coding scheme, derived from the first wave of interviews, focused on the effects of rankings on different organizational units or groups such as deans, career services, admissions, and prospective students, and on broad themes such as encroachment of market ideologies, gaming strategies, positive effects of rankings, and problems of quantification. After the first wave of interviews we refined our coding categories and, using Qualrus (a qualitative data analysis program), recoded all interviews to isolate more precise themes.[8] Rather than representing "findings" or the end point of our analysis, our coding served as a guideline for interpretation or further analysis, revealing, for example, sources of variation, motivations, and how patterns impinged on one another. Consequently, the frequency of themes was only a rough indicator of their significance and is less central to our analysis than efforts to understand the meaning, context, and variations in who makes claims, as well as how themes are expressed or ignored within different units or across different kinds of organizations. Again, the findings we report represent general trends in our data: they are derived from multiple independent interviews and are consistent across sources.

All told, our first two waves of law school interviews include thirty-nine deans and ex-deans; forty-eight other administrators, primarily deans or directors of admissions and career services, but also personnel in academic affairs, external relations, and development; thirty-three faculty members; nine in other positions affected by rankings such as directors of marketing, librarians, and administrative staff. In terms of school position, we interviewed administrators from twenty-one different schools that have been ranked in the fourth tier, twenty-six schools in the third tier, twenty-two schools in the second tier, and eighteen schools in the first tier. In the first-tier schools, interviews include twelve people from schools that had been ranked in the top twenty-five and five from schools in the top ten. (The number of schools in these totals exceeds the number of schools represented because schools were double-counted if they appeared in more than one category of rankings since 1990. For example, a school that had moved between the second and third tier would be included in both the second- and third-tier categories.) We interviewed several deans two times or more, but count these as a single interview. Table A.1 summarizes how interviews from our combined samples were distributed, by a school's ranking, at the time of our interview.

When possible, we included interviews with administrators and faculty of varying lengths of tenure, including those whose tenure predated rankings and recently hired assistant professors or administrators. We found former and retired deans to be especially valuable informants. Interviews in both samples included questions about respondents' professional backgrounds, their job experience, their direct experience with rankings,

Table A.1   Administrators and Faculty Members Interviewed,
by Rank of Respondents' Schools

	Top Ten	Top Twenty-Five	First Tier	Second Tier	Third Tier	Fourth Tier	Total Interviews
First-wave interviews	6	7	13	13	12	8	59
Second-wave interviews	10	10	19	13	13	7	72
Total	16	17	32	26	25	15	131

Source: Authors' compilation.

including whether rankings shape their interactions with colleagues and peers at other schools and their views about the effects of rankings at their own and other law schools. Because these interviews were open-ended, their content varied across respondents. Depending on the interviewee's particular area of expertise, we asked more specific questions about the influence of rankings on that individual's particular job.

Our third sample was made up of thirty deans of business schools. Business schools are comparable professional schools with at least five different major rankings that schools pay attention to, so this comparison allowed us to assess the significance of single versus multiple rankings. Another useful point of contrast is that only the top twenty-five or fifty business schools are ranked, whereas all law schools are ranked. Our sample included deans from schools with rankings ranging from one to fifty, schools whose rankings varied across ranking bodies, and schools that were well ranked by at least one ranking body but were unranked by others. These interviews took on average thirty minutes and were all conducted over the telephone, tape-recorded, and transcribed.

Our fourth sample of interviews, conducted by a research assistant, consisted of twenty-seven interviews with deans or administrators with special knowledge either about a school's LL.M. (master of law) program or about a school's decision not to create an LL.M. program. LL.M. programs grant the equivalent of a master's degree to students who complete one year of coursework. We investigated LL.M. programs because for some law schools they are an important source of revenue, money that, according to a number of our respondents, deans use to try to improve their rankings. We were curious to see if that was true, if rankings are ever a factor in spurring the spread of LL.M. programs. We constructed a random sample of law schools and conducted phone interviews with program leaders at these schools. Along with the random sample of all accredited schools, we also over-sampled schools on the cusp of ranking tiers, either those just above or below the cut-off points used by *USN* to designate tiers. These interviews were conducted by phone and lasted fifteen to thirty minutes.

In addition to these interviews we conducted forty-nine formal interviews with other relevant entities that are part of the world of legal education. We interviewed six leaders of national professional associations—the American Bar Association Section on Legal Education, the Association of American Law Schools, the Law School Admissions Council, the National Association for Law Placement, and the Society of American Law Teachers— many of whom have taken strong stances opposing *USN* rankings. We conducted formal interviews with seven prospective law school students, seven current students, and four recent graduates. To get a sense of the hiring process, we formally interviewed ten individuals charged with hiring for law firms or judges. To supplement media accounts both by and about *USN*, and speeches given by *USN* personnel, we conducted interviews with Robert Morse, who is responsible for overseeing *USN*'s rankings methodology, and Mel Elfin, who was the *USN* editor in charge of rankings for many years. Also, because dental schools organized a successful boycott of the rankings, refusing to send the information requested by *USN*, we interviewed four administrators associated with dental education to learn more about their response to rankings and the consequences of not being ranked by *USN*. For a comparative perspective, we interviewed four administrators at undergraduate institutions. Finally, we also carried out five follow-up interviews with administrators and faculty with specialized knowledge to fill existing gaps in our knowledge.

The Law School Admissions Council Law School Forum Interviews, Survey, and Fieldwork

The Law School Admissions Council (LSAC) is a nonprofit organization that produces and administers the LSAT. Each year, the LSAC sponsors informational events for prospective law schools in about nine U.S. cities. These Law School Forums feature an extensive program of speakers and panels about topics of concern to applicants: the secret of writing a good application essay, how to decide where to apply, how law schools decide whom to admit, financial aid, what law school is really like. In conjunction with the formal program, these events always include an extensive admissions fair where representatives from most accredited law schools supervise tables, hand out brochures, and answer students' questions for two long, intensive days. Typically, schools bring at least one or two admissions officers, occasionally a star student, and, rarely, an actual law professor. Law School Forums are popular events for students, who attend them in throngs. Admissions personnel may grumble about tired feet and long hours of answering the same questions, but one result of what some refer to as "the circuit" is that these admissions professionals get to know each other well while on the road, sharing dinners, cab rides, and gossip.

With permission, the authors and a research assistant attended the Law School Forum held in Chicago over a two-day period. In addition to observing admissions officers talking with students and attending a few panels, we conducted fieldwork in the break room where busy admissions officers retreated for lunch or coffee. As part of this fieldwork we conducted informal interviews with seventeen admissions officers and two current law students. These interviews each lasted about ten minutes, and were sometimes conducted in groups of two or three. The break room turned out to be a wonderful spot, since it provided a respite from the sometimes overwhelming flux of curious prospective students. The collegiality and informality of the setting facilitated frank feedback from professionals who are used to being more guarded in their interactions with students and researchers. The admissions personnel tended to let down their hair a bit with their colleagues, as was indicated by their humor, teasing, vivid language, and shared war stories. These break-room interviews of small groups often prompted more elaborate answers to our questions than did more formal interviews with individuals, as people chimed in to agree, disagree, or elaborate on each other's answers.

Along with these informal interviews, we also conducted short interviews averaging about five minutes with ninety-three prospective students attending the fair. After confirming their interest in applying to law school, we asked students to describe and rank sources of information that they were using to decide where to apply to law schools, whether they had consulted or planned to consult rankings, and whether they had an opinion about rankings. These data were used to help us understand how students use the rankings when making decisions about law schools.

Admissions and Yield Statistics

In order to analyze more precisely the effects of changes in ranking on admissions and yields, we compiled a data set that included ranking information from all the annual editions of the U.S. *News and World Report Guide to Graduate Schools* from 1993 to 2003 and student application information from the 1996 to 2003 editions of *The Official Guide to U.S. Law Schools*, which is now jointly published by the LSAC and the ABA. This data permitted a quantitative analysis of the effects of *USN* rankings on total applications received by schools, applications received from high-quality applicants (those with high LSAT scores and high GPAs), and matriculation decisions. These data allowed us to gain a better understanding of the tangible effects that rankings have on law school admissions across the entire field.[9]

Observations of Electronic Bulletin Boards

To supplement interview and statistical data we monitored postings at the *Princeton Review* pre-law forum for prospective law students. We conducted this "virtual fieldwork" in two main cycles. The first round occurred in the project's early pilot phase. During this pilot period we assessed a range of sites for prospective law students and selected the *Princeton Review* site as the most lively and informative. Although we periodically visited other sites, the popularity of which ebbed and flowed, *The Princeton Review* remained one of the most popular for pre-law students and applicants. During this period we typically visited *The Princeton Review* weekly for sessions lasting forty-five minutes to an hour. Although we occasionally skipped a week during slower periods, during busy "decision" periods we visited the site daily to track how much and in what contexts students talked about rankings. We have continued to monitor these and new sites throughout our research.

Examples of patterns in rankings talk included asking for advice about where to apply ("Should I apply to school X even if it's in the fourth tier?"), the odds of getting into a particular school ("If I scored 160 on the LSAT and have a 3.4 can I get into a top-tier school?"), how much a school's ranking mattered ("If Texas dropped ten places should I try to go elsewhere even if that's where I wanted to go?"), gossip about rankings ("Chicago's ranking is about to drop"), explanations (usually woefully misinformed) of ranking methodology, announcements of outcomes ("Great news, everyone! I got into a top-tier school"), or soliciting advice about choosing between differently ranked schools (ranging from "Always go to the best [top-ranked] school you can get into" to "Don't let an algorithm dictate your life").[10]

The patterns we identified in our initial observations informed subsequent fieldwork, which was conducted by our undergraduate research assistant, who was considering applying to law school. He visited *The Princeton Review* weekly for an entire admissions cycle, keeping his research role strictly to that of observer. In addition to making field notes about his weekly observations, he tracked patterns of rankings talk, constructed a chronological file of examples, and described patterns that he identified in the kinds of decisions and anxieties that students confronted throughout the different stages of the cycle.

One indication of the centrality of rankings was the sheer volume of ranking talk, including the completely naturalized use of "tiers" in talking about schools. Although it is hard to ascertain how representative the students are who are active in these bulletin boards, their often candid discussions about rankings provided anecdotal evidence, collected unobtrusively, about how students use and think about rankings in making decisions about law school. This provided a useful counterpoint to their more guarded responses in interviews.

The Media

The media play a fundamental role in creating and disseminating rankings. To develop a better understanding of how the media report on rankings, we conducted a content analysis of media stories about rankings to learn if and how rankings are treated as "news," patterns in coverage, and whether reporting has changed over time. Using Lexis-Nexis, ProQuest, and traditional archival research to generate articles, a graduate research assistant collected media stories about law school rankings from 1991 to 2005 from national news sources catering to general audiences (such as the *New York Times*, the *Wall Street Journal*, the *Washington Post*, *Time*, *Newsweek*, *USN*, and *Slate*) and specialized legal publications (*The American Lawyer*, *National Jurist*, and the *ABA Journal*). We found 218 articles and coded them according to their type and content. For example, we coded whether they presented favorable, unfavorable, or mixed depictions of rankings and when they reported changes in a particular school's ranking or described law schools' efforts to resist or change rankings.

One of the weaknesses of our interview data is that one must rely on people's memories to construct how reputations were evaluated before rankings were launched. To compensate for this we also used research assistants to find media depictions of law schools that predated rankings, focusing on the period from 1974 through 1990.[11] We found several examples of articles in which newspapers explicitly evaluated (and sometimes ranked) local law schools as well as newspaper and professional journal articles that shed light on how students decided where to attend law school and ideas about the stratification of legal education (for example, law schools' reputations, how to determine the best schools, and the relative status of schools). This media data helped inform our ideas about the changes that the rankings have brought about in news reports about law schools.

Informal Informants

Sometimes data become available in ways you don't anticipate. Throughout the course of our research we benefited from an informal, extremely generous group of current and former administrators, faculty, and alumni from schools throughout the United States and across the globe. These informants regularly shared their ranking stories, described their meetings (and sometimes even took field notes), recommended contacts, forwarded helpful emails and memos, and vouched for us to wary administrators. Our international colleagues have also provided invaluable insight into the ways rankings are changing education outside of the United States. We treated the informal and illuminating data that our discreet and discerning sources provided differently from the material we collected ourselves. We used it as a source of hypotheses or ideas to refine our interview questions, to help us make sense of our own findings, or to corroborate what we thought we knew. We did not quote from these sources or incorporate them directly into our analyses.

Law School Documents

Our final data source includes a broad range of law school documents. A research assistant performed a content analysis of the websites of every accredited law school during a full academic year. Searching the websites using a variety of relevant terms ("ranking," "rank," "tier," "U.S. News," "educational quality rankings," "Leiter," "deans speak out"), he collected all examples of ranking talk, indicating where and how it appeared on websites. During the same academic year this research assistant also requested and received (with the forbearance of his letter carrier) information from accredited law schools. We analyzed these materials for the ways rankings and reputation were presented in them.

In addition to these sources, we collected many other kinds of organizational documents. Our focus schools shared with us strategic plans, marketing plans and materials, surveys sent to current students, information on admitted students who selected other schools, data about recent graduates, copies of the surveys the schools supplied *USN*, and memos, emails, and other forms of internal communication. Faculty and students provided us with copies of emails and memos about rankings, including announcements and celebrations of improved rankings and elaborate explanations dissecting even small declines. One faculty member forwarded to us a long email that a dean sent to admitted students the day after a dramatic drop in that school's ranking. The email explained the drop as stemming from lower placement statistics, reflecting graduating students' lower response rates to inquiries about their employment. The email went on to reassure students that the director of career services had been replaced and that the drop did not reflect any significant change in quality of the law school or its placement success.

To better understand how schools market to each other, we asked a law school professor at a top-twenty school to save the marketing materials he received during the course of a school year. This pile of material included more than eighty brochures touting faculty achievements, announcing newly hired faculty, and publicizing their lecture series as well as less conventional materials such as videos about the school, bookmarks, a pen, and a paperweight. Even this large pile is smaller than the volume of such materials that land on the desks of the deans who fill out the *USN* reputational survey.

These organizational documents are especially valuable data for helping us to better understand a series of tricky relationships. They show in a concrete fashion how much effort and resources schools expend on efforts to improve rankings. Importantly, they allow us to better understand how rankings shape members' perceptions of their own and others' law schools and their fears about how rankings shape others' perceptions of them. So, for example, a carefully crafted memo sent by the dean of one elite school to all staff and faculty within days of the release of new rankings explained why two "rival" schools (as defined by rankings) had risen one or two notches while their law school had declined two notches. The memo concluded with an upbeat assessment about how this problem could be reversed. The memo demonstrated how carefully rankings are monitored, how demoralizing even a small drop can be, and how much effort must be expended on damage control.

Appendix B | *U.S. News' Methodology for Calculating Rankings, by Category*

Table B.1   *U.S. News'* Methodology for Calculating Rankings, by Category (Percents)

General Categories	Weight in Overall Score	Subcategories	Weight in General Category	Weight in Overall Score
Reputation	40	Assessment by academics (dean, associate dean, chair of recruitment, last tenured faculty member)	62.5	25.0
		Assessment by practitioners (two-year average)	37.5	15.0
Selectivity	25	Student LSAT scores	50.0	12.5
		Student GPA	40.0	10.0
		Acceptance rate	10.0	2.5
Placement success	20	Percentage employed at graduation	20.0	4.0
		Percentage employed nine months after graduation	70.0	14.0
		Bar passage rate	10.0	3.0
Faculty resources	15	Expenditure per student for instruction, library, and supporting services	65.0	9.75
		Student-to-faculty ratio	20.0	3.0
		Other per-student spending (for example, financial aid)	10.0	1.5
		Number of volumes in library	5.0	0.75

Source: "Best Graduate Schools," *U.S. News & World Report* 2014, 89.

Notes

ACKNOWLEDGMENTS

1. GR #26943, LSAC Research Grant Program.

CHAPTER ONE

1. Epigraph: Quoted in Gregory 2014.
2. U.S. Department of Veterans Affairs, Office of Inspector General 2014; Lowery and Hicks 2014.
3. U.S. Department of Veterans Affairs, Office of Inspector General 2014, iii.
4. Later reports estimated that over 63,000 veterans were waiting for care nationwide. In response to this crisis, the VA suspended all bonuses and salary increases tied to wait times.
5. Thomas 2014.
6. Ibid., A1.
7. Aviv 2014, 59.
8. See Rivera 2015.
9. On hospitals: Kim 2015; Pope 2009. On newspapers: Christin 2014. On corruption: Zaloznaya 2013.
10. See, for example, Arewa, Morriss, and Henderson 2014; Schworm 2014.
11. For example, Weber 1922/1978, 180–92; Bourdieu 1984; Lamont and Fournier 1992.
12. See Zerubavel 1991; Cerulo 2002.
13. Edelman 1992; Kalev, Dobbin, and Kelly 2006; Westphal and Zajac 2001.
14. Webster 1992a, 19.
15. Webster 1984.
16. Hughes 1925, 1934. For a detailed discussion of the history of college ratings and rankings before 1982, see Bogue and Hall 2003.
17. An early experiment in ranking law schools was conducted by the *Chicago Tribune* in 1958. Peter Blau and Rebecca Zames Margulies (1974) created

219

rankings of the top law schools from a survey of law school deans for the journal *Change* in 1973 and 1974. Other kinds of rankings had emerged earlier. Savvy consumers routinely consult *Consumer Reports*, the magazine that has evaluated products since 1936, before buying everything from peanut butter to automobiles. *Fortune* started ranking the five hundred largest companies in 1955. The National Research Council (part of the National Academy of Sciences) evaluated research-doctorate programs in the United States in three influential reports in 1982, 1995, and 2010. For more information on the history of college rankings see Webster 1992b; Bogue and Hall 2003.

18. Mel Elfin, author interview (telephone), November 14, 2006.
19. Van Dyne 1996. Once rankings were fully established, the sales of these issues were estimated at between 2.2 million and 2.3 million copies, reaching almost 11 million people, 40 percent more than sales for an average issue. See Dichev 2001; McDonough et al. 1998. Then there are the 8 million annual hits on *USN's* website. In 2013 *USN* reported an all-time record in web traffic due to the release of its "2014 Best Colleges." On September 10 of that year, 2.6 million unique visitors generated 18.9 million page views in a single day. See *U.S. News & World Report* 2013.
20. Law School Admission Council 1987.
21. Smith 2001. Several informants made the same or similar comments about Morse to us. In addition to his research activities, Morse is also a primary spokesperson for *USN* in explaining and defending the rankings. He regularly meets with deans and other educators to discuss rankings, appears at conferences and public forums to give speeches about rankings, and writes a blog at the magazine's website, entitled *Morse Code: Inside the College Rankings* (www.usnews.com/education/blogs/college-rankings-blog), that defends rankings, discusses rankings issues, and provides a forum for readers' comments.
22. Robert Morse, author interview, January 3, 2007.
23. Parloff 1998.
24. Morse 2008a.
25. Cohen, March, and Olsen 1972.
26. See Jencks and Riesman 1968; Thelin 2004.
27. Stevens 2007. In 1900, 6.3 percent of all seventeen-year-olds graduated from high school, and by the 1940s, about half did. By 1998, 83 percent of the population twenty-five years or older had completed high school. From 1980 to 2011 alone, the proportion of Americans twenty-five years and older who completed college rose from 17 to 33 percent. From 1971 to 1999 the percentage of those who completed some college rose from 44 to 66 percent. See Lemann 1999, 48.
28. Those who attend a selective college earn 52 percent more than those who attend an unselective college. Those who graduate from highly selective colleges earn an additional 32 percent. See Coleman, Rainwater, McClelland 1978, cited in McDonough 1994; see also Dale and Krueger 2002.
29. Lemann 1999.

30. Fitzsimmons 1991; *U.S. News & World Report* 2001.

31. Nicholas Lemann (2000) shows the crucial role that standardized testing played in propelling and mediating these trends. This pattern of increasing selectivity in admissions at top schools is further exacerbated by rankings.

32. For example, members of the Consortium for Financing Higher Education reported a 29 percent increase in applications to the most selective colleges from 1983 to 1989, which caused their acceptance rates to drop. See McDonough 1994, 432, citing Schurenberg 1989. This encouraged students, especially those from the middle class, to apply to more colleges. In 1968, half of all freshmen filled out just one college application. By 1990 this figure dropped to 33 percent. In that year, 37 percent of all full-time freshmen applied to four or more colleges. See McDonough 1994, 432, citing Dey, Astin, and Korn 1991.

33. McDonough 1994, 433. The cost of college is another factor that fuels anxieties over college admissions. As McDonough (1994, 434) notes, parents know that choosing a college for their child and paying for the child's college education could easily be one of their biggest and most important investments, up there with buying a house. Average annual college costs (tuition, room, and board) for 1998–1999 were over $7,000 at public colleges and over $19,000 at private colleges. Between 2000–2001 and 2010–2011, college costs rose 42 percent at public institutions and 31 percent at private ones. See National Center for Educational Statistics, "Fast Facts, Tuition Costs of Colleges and Universities," https://nces.ed.gov/fastfacts/display.asp?id=76 (accessed on November 21, 2015).

34. In 1995, just five years after annual rankings were created, a study based on a national survey of college freshman found that 60 percent of students surveyed reported that national magazine rankings were not important in their decision as to what college to attend, 30 percent said rankings were somewhat important, and 11 percent reported that they were very important in making their college choice. See McDonough et al. 1997.

35. Wright 1991. See also Schurenberg 1989; Winerip 1987.

36. One admissions director summarizes the trend: "College admission equals big business" (Wright 1991). The increase in demand for the best students has also led to some important changes. While the proportion of people going to college has increased, overall college enrollments have declined since the 1970s. To compete for students and their resources, colleges have vastly expanded college admissions staffs and have begun marketing their institutions vigorously. Marketing costs for colleges increased by 64 percent between 1980 and 1986, and schools spend on average $1,700 in marketing for each student enrolled. See McDonough 1994, 432. While information on marketing expenditures is difficult to obtain, surveys suggest that marketing and communications budgets have increased 60 to 100 percent for colleges of all types since 2001. See Education Portal 2010. The growth in the market for professional college admissions counselors prompted the founding of the Higher

Education Consultants Association in 1997; the organization now has over seven hundred members. The average cost of their services is over $3,000 per child. See Adams 2010.

37. Webster 1992a, 1992b.
38. Webster 1992b, 20.
39. Porter 1995.
40. Parloff 1998, 5.
41. Elfin author interview, November 2006. The success of *USN* and other rankings has propelled media rankings of all sorts. Magazines now rank everything from the best cities for walking (*Prevention*) to the best firms for working mothers (*Working Mother Magazine*) to the best doctors in town (*Chicago Magazine*). *Newsweek* and *USN* rank high schools, and *Princeton Review, Atlantic Monthly, Business Week,* the *Financial Times,* and the *Wall Street Journal* rank colleges and professional schools. *Princeton Review* also famously ranks the "best party schools," and *Money* ranks the colleges it considers the best "value." Even *Mother Jones* has succumbed, with rankings of the "best activist schools" in 2004. Outside the United States, prominent rankings of universities are published in Australia (*Australian Good University Guide*), Canada (*Maclean's*), Germany (*Der Spiegel, Stern, Focus*), the United Kingdom (*Times Higher Education Supplement*), and Asia (*Asiaweek*). Global rankings of universities are published by *Shanghai Jiao Tong Academic Ranking of World Universities, QS World University Rankings,* and the *Times Higher Education Supplement.*
42. For example, Lempert 2002; Seto 2007.
43. Klein and Hamilton 1998.
44. Stephen Klein and Laura Hamilton (1998) argue that the measure of reputation among lawyers and judges is deficient because *USN* provides no information about how the practitioner sample is derived and does not describe the difference between survey respondents and nonrespondents, despite the fact that the response rate is only 33 percent. In addition, the validity of the responses is questionable because lawyers and judges are likely to have little or no direct contact with graduates from most of the nation's law schools.
45. Klein and Hamilton 1998.
46. Leiter 2003.
47. McGuire 1995.
48. *USN* responded to this and similar critiques by including a diversity ranking for law schools in recent editions, but it is listed as a separate measure—not incorporated into the composite rankings of schools.
49. This letter, entitled "Deans Speak Out," was published on the Law School Admission Council's website until 2013 (www.lsac.org). The letter was sent to all law school applicants (about 70,000 annually) from 1997 to 2013, and until 2009 included signatures of support from the vast majority of law school deans.

50. Lempert 2002.
51. Rovella 1997.
52. Van Zandt 2007.

CHAPTER TWO

1. Von Dornum 1997, 1483.
2. In the fifth century BCE, the euthyna, meaning literally "straightening," entailed a rigorous examination of the accounts of officials on the expiration of their terms. In addition to the provisions for auditing financial records, it also required officials to publicly account for their conduct and permitted citizens to challenge their conduct and bring accusations against them that could result in criminal charges. The euthyna provided citizens with a powerful tool for policing their politicians. Deirdre Dionysia Von Dorrum (1997) sees the development of euthyna as an extension of an enduring, if informal, framework of accountability that is the precursor to, rather than the product of, early democracy.
3. *Oxford English Dictionary*, 2nd ed., s.v. "accountability." We do not know why the term first emerged in this context. According to the *OED*, "accountable" dates back to 1508, when it is used to describe an author's intended meaning. Its first published link to governance occurs in 1642, when a pamphlet written during the English Civil War, "Declaration of the Lords and Commons," asserts, "The Lord Lieutenant and Committee shall be accomptable [sic]." Neither "accountable" or "accountability" appears in the *Federalist Papers*, which suggests that the term was not yet widely associated with governance by the Framers of the Constitution. "Accounting" has a much older history, of course, but the move from verb to noun seems significant in the diffusion of the term.
4. Williams 1794, 139–40.
5. Espeland and Vannebo 2007.
6. Since the late 1980s there has been a dramatic increase in the number of laws introduced with the term "accountability" in the title. See Espeland and Vannebo 2007.
7. See, for example, Hacking 1990; Urla 1993; Porter 1995; Power 1997; Strathern 2000. For a sophisticated analysis of evaluation that does not rely on quantification, see Lamont 2009.
8. For Karl Marx and Georg Simmel, price is a distinctive form of measurement that powerfully mediates relations with self and others. See Weber 1922/1978; Simmel 1978; Starr 1987; Urla 1993; Poovey 1998; Igo 2009.
9. Carruthers and Espeland 1991.
10. The anthropologist Bernard S. Cohn (1987) was among the first to describe the role of the census in producing identities in colonial India. Sean Redding (2006, 17, 99) shows that the imposition of taxes was crucial to the establishment

and preservation of the colonial state in South Africa, and to the resistance of colonial subjects to the state. Before hut or poll taxes could be imposed, the state required a census. Colonial subjects were highly suspicious of efforts to conduct a census, partly because of prescient concerns about how this information might be used, as well as its potential use in witchcraft.

11. See Prewitt 1986; Hacking 1990; Ventresca 1995. On the reconstruction of Japan after World War 2 see Hein, Diefendorf, and Ishida 2003.

12. Faust 2008.

13. Foucault 1977; Hoskin 1996.

14. Porter 1995. Weber's (1922/1978) famous typology of authority permits him to analyze similar transformations. Unlike the authority that is vested in charismatic persons or ceded to patriarchs, rational legal authority is impersonal. Standardization and calculation are two tools for separating office from office holders; they turn persons or events into cases vetted by rules, creating the transcendence of bureaucracies that outlive and outperform the persons who make them up. This stripping away of the personal can be a means for redressing the problems of distrust that devolve from distance and difference. It is also a way of "leveling" social differences.

15. Historical work on the development of quantitative evaluation—for example, Porter 1995; Carson 2007; Igo 2009; Daston 1992; Desrosières 2002; Alonso and Starr 1987—is an exception to this, as is recent work in the field of social studies of finance. See Callon 1998; MacKenzie and Millo 2003; MacKenzie 2006.

16. Morse 2005.

17. Among the classic citations in this voluminous neo-institutional literature are Meyer and Rowan 1977; Zucker 1977; DiMaggio and Powell 1983; Dobbin 1997; Scott 2001.

18. Porter 1995.

19. Fourcade and Healy 2013.

20. This section relies on Espeland and Sauder 2007. For a classic discussion of reactivity as a methodological problem see Campbell 1957, 298.

21. See, for example, Campbell 1957; Reiss 1971; Webb et al. 1981; Katz 1983.

22. Desrosières 2002.

23. Strathern 1995, 4.

24. Schutz 1970, 137–45.

25. March and Simon 1958.

26. See Porac et al. 1995; Sauder 2006. We use the idea of a cognitive map simply to indicate the general mental representation of the field of legal education used to classify and evaluate the organizations and individuals within it.

27. Prominent social scientists who have argued for the importance of identifying mechanisms in social research include Merton 1967, 1968; Elster 1989; Hedstrom and Swedberg 1998; Stinchcombe 2005. For a detailed discussion of mechanisms and rankings, see also Espeland and Sauder 2007.

28. Ideas about commensuration are developed further in Espeland 1998; Espeland and Stevens 1998; Espeland 2000.

29. Simmel 1978, 443–45.

30. See Goody 1997.

31. The next sections draw on Espeland and Sauder 2007 and Espeland, forthcoming. The most influential analysis of self-fulfilling prophecy was conducted by the sociologist Robert Merton. For Merton (1968), a self-fulfilling prophecy is a "dynamic social mechanism" that is an "unintended consequence." This consequence arises when "confident error generates its own spurious confirmation," or from "a *false* definition of the situation evoking a new behavior which makes the originally false definition of the situation come *true*" (182–83, 477; emphasis in original). We do not restrict our definition of self-fulfilling prophecies to false beliefs; we include any behavior that conforms to predictions. Merton suggests that self-fulfilling prophecies create unique methodological problems for social science because subjects change their behavior in response to predictions, so that a prediction becomes a "*new and dynamic* factor" that changes the conditions that make it true. This observation harks back to W. I. Thomas's famous dictum, "If men define situations as real, they are real in their consequences" (Thomas and Thomas 1928, 572), a deceptively simple maxim that has informed the core of what has become known in sociology as labeling theory (Becker 1963). This characteristic of human behavior is one reason why many make sharp distinctions between natural and social science.

32. Robert Rosenthal and Lenore Jacobson's (1968) famous study of the effects of teachers' expectations on student performance exemplifies how measures confirm expectations. Similarly, the creation of categories of people (for example, "Hispanics") illustrates how the validity of measures increases over time (Porter 1995, 41–42). As a category acquires constituents who use it, those encompassed by the category develop shared interests and identities that make the category more meaningful and "real." See also Ian Hacking (1986) "on making up people."

33. For a contemporary example, see O'Keefe and Gold 2015.

34. For other examples of self-fulfilling prophecies, or "echo chamber effects," see Callon 1998; Ferraro, Pfeffer, and Sutton 2005; MacKenzie 2006.

35. Most informants believe that these effects are subtle or even subconscious. Only two people admitted to consulting the rankings as they filled out the survey. They did suggest that prior rankings contributed to their impressions of other schools, especially schools about which they knew little. See Jerry Kim (2015) for compelling evidence of the subconscious effects that ranking changes can have on individual decisions.

36. Stake 2006. Some deans dispute this effect, since they do not see immediate changes in their school's reputation following changes in rank. This is consistent with Richard Schmalbeck's (2001) analysis. Focusing on *USN* top-fifty law

schools, he finds that reputations are relatively durable, since rankings seem to have little effect on the perceptions of survey respondents: a drop in rank during one year does not harm a school's reputation score in the following year's survey. The effects of prior rankings may be more indirect than is captured in this study. As Jeffrey Evans Stake (2006) suggests, changes often take time to develop and may be most powerful for lower-ranked schools; they are less well known nationally and rankings may substitute for other information.

37. Frank and Cook 1996.
38. Many university administrators report that they use potential improvement in rank to justify claims on resources—reports confirmed by a quick survey of strategic plans and annual reports.
39. See Stabile 2000.
40. See Samuelson and Scotchmer 2002.
41. On auditing, Power 1994, 1997. On risk assessment, MacKenzie 1993; Power 2007. On governmentality, Foucault 1991; Miller and O'Leary 1987; Miller and Rose 1990. "Governmentality," a term coined by the philosopher Michel Foucault, refers to the way the state exercises control over, or governs, its populace.
42. For more on the narrative form in relation to rankings and other indicators, see Espeland 2015.
43. Burke 1966, 304.
44. Sauder and Espeland 2009.

CHAPTER THREE

1. The admissions cycle is annual for law schools. For applicants it usually lasts longer, if one includes the often-protracted decisions about applying to law school, studying for the LSAT, and taking test-prep classes. The LSAT, offered four times a year and administered by the Law School Admission Council, is required for nearly all applicants. Many take it several times to try to improve their scores. One likely effect of rankings has been to change how law schools treat multiple scores: now schools are encouraged to take the highest score of a student to improve the school's own selectivity factor, rather than averaging the scores, as was once common practice.
2. Player 30, "Waitlist craziness: BLS vs. Pace($) vs. PSU vs. Rutgers-C," *top-law-schools.com*, June 29, 2008, www.top-law-schools.com/forums/viewtopic.php?f=1&t=35864 (accessed August 22, 2014).
3. Experts in employment statistics estimate that in 2009 there were twice as many people who passed the bar as there were job openings for lawyers. All states except Nebraska and Wisconsin had a surplus of lawyers. See Rampell 2011.
4. Beginning in 2012, *USN* rankings no longer included tiers, instead assigning a rank to each of the top 145 law schools and then leaving the remaining 50

or so schools unranked. But students have continued to use tiers as a way to make distinctions among schools.

5. One YouTube clip features the "TTT Anthem Third Tier Toilet Law School Song": www.youtube.com/watch?v=jGQ4nT3_SiY. Other websites are devoted to elaborating TTT-ness. See Bitter Staff 2009; Burton 2011.

6. Hill and Lat 2010.

7. Rey 2010; Leonard and Israelsen-Hartley 2010.

8. Wellen 2003, 5.

9. Barron's, a test prep company founded in 1941, now produces many educational products. We thank Jeanette Colyvas for suggesting that we contrast the cognitive effects of guidebooks and rankings.

10. Cohen, March and Olsen 1972.

11. See Karabel 2005; Soares 2007; Stevens 2007.

12. For excellent analyses of the spread and effect of audits, see Power 1994, 1997; Strathern 2000; Vannebo 2010.

13. See Shore and Wright 1999; Strathern 2000.

14. Soares 1999; Vannebo 2010; Strathern 2000; Power 1994 1997; Hoskin and Macve 1986.

15. Ravitch 2010.

16. Mehta 2013.

17. For enlightening accounts of the history of admission practices see Stevens 2007; Steinberg 2002; Lemann 1999; Karabel 2005.

18. Owings et al. 1995.

19. The National Association for College Admissions Counseling reports that the number of students submitting seven or more applications increased from 8 percent in 1991 to 25 percent in 2010. During this same period the number of applicants submitting three or more applications rose from 60 to 77 percent. See Clinedinst, Hurley, and Hawkins 2012.

20. Stevens 2007.

21. U.S. Department of Education 2012, 66.

22. American Bar Association 2014.

23. On the continuing importance of the rankings in the post-recession legal environment, see Jones 2014 and Ryan 2015.

24. Morse 2009.

25. The appeal of law school has declined following the Great Recession that started in 2008, and this has had a profound effect on the volume of applications. According to the Law School Admission Council (2014a) applications have fallen at a consistent rate from 98,700 in 2004 to 58,400 in 2013, and a number of schools have reported that they are shrinking or considering shrinking the size of incoming cohorts as a way to slow the glut of lawyers. This response also has a rankings angle. Lower-tier schools are most likely to see applications and yields decline in a poor market as applicants decide that in tough times a degree from a "TTT" is not a good investment. For these

schools the pressure to maintain even mediocre selectivity statistics may mean accepting fewer students.

26. Prospective students apply to more law schools than they used to. In 1991 students applied on average to 4.8 schools; in 2014 this figure was 6.4 (Law School Admission Council 2014b). Students who apply to more selective schools usually apply to more schools.

27. In 2014, Yale, first in the *USN* rankings, admitted 9 percent of its applicants, whereas the University of Nebraska Law School, ranked fifty-fourth, accepted 64 percent of its applicants.

28. This section draws on Espeland and Sauder 2009.

29. Sauder and Lancaster 2006.

30. Schleef 2006.

31. Law School Admission Council 2006, 29, 62.

32. We asked four questions of ninety-three students who had registered to attend a free two-day admissions fair: (1) How serious are you about attending law school? (2) How important is a law school's reputation in your application decisions? (3) How influential are different resources in helping you decide where to apply and where to attend? (4) Which rankings, if any, have you consulted? Students reported that reputation was an important factor in determining where they apply: the average response was 3.82, with 5.0 indicating that reputation was a very important factor in their decision. They also reported that *USN* rankings were a bigger influence on where they chose to apply and attend law school—usually a much bigger influence than guidebooks, parents, friends, or pre-law advisers. On the same scale, rankings were 3.22, guidebooks 3.01, friends and acquaintances 2.35, parents 2.18, and advisers 1.57. When asked which materials about law school that they had consulted or planned to consult, forty-two cited *USN* rankings, ten cited *The Princeton Review* website, and six listed the ABA-LSAC's *Guide to Law Schools*. In addition, eighteen responded that they had consulted many unspecified sources and twenty stated that they had consulted none. Ours was a regionally biased sample of convenience so we don't know how representative these answers are, but they corroborate findings from interviews and other representative surveys.

33. Sauder and Lancaster 2006.

34. James Monks and Ronald G. Ehrenberg (1999) found similar patterns for undergraduate rankings.

35. Hansmann 1999.

CHAPTER FOUR

1. Goffman 1959, 99.

2. Weber 1922/1978, 956–98. Mitchell Stevens (2007) writes more about the "social machinery" that delivers applicants to schools in his analysis of selective undergraduate admissions.

3. The Harvard Law School website informs applicants, "Quantitative factors, while informative, do not play a decisive role in our selection process. We have no computational methods for making admission decisions, no mechanical shortcuts, no substitutes for careful assessment and good judgment. All completed applications are reviewed in their entirety with the LSAT as one factor in an overall assessment of academic promise, personal achievement, and potential contribution to the vitality of the student body." See "Admissions FAQ, How Important Is the Law School Admission Test," www.law.harvard.edu/prospective/jd/apply/the-application-process/jdfaq.html.

4. Schworm 2014.

5. Schudson 1972; Wechsler 1977; Lemann 1999; Carson 2007; Stevens 2007.

6. Stevens 2007, 21.

7. Simply calling the admission index a "magic number" mingles contrarian forces of reason and fate, the calculable and inexplicable. Both "magic" and "numbers" can be devices for deflecting responsibility. The mechanical objectivity that the index makes possible constrains the discretion of the deciders, while the "magic" that envelops outcomes invokes a mystery and fate that alleviates responsibility.

8. See Heimer 1992.

9. Heimer 2001.

10. Stevens 2007, 8. William LaPiana (2001) has said, "There is no doubt that there is a terrific and inescapable tension between the use of standardized tests and individualized decision making, and that tension has been part of American life since the transformation in the use of testing that occurred during the First World War" (7).

11. In 2003, in *Grutter v. Bollinger* (539 U.S. 306), the U.S. Supreme Court upheld the University of Michigan Law School's admissions policy, ruling that the narrowly tailored use of race in admissions was constitutional. In the *Gratz v. Bollinger* (539 U.S. 244) decision issued at the same time, the court ruled that the point system used in undergraduate admissions, which automatically awarded points to under-represented minorities, was too mechanical and therefore unconstitutional.

12. DeLeon 2006.

13. Stevens 2007, 16.

14. Some admissions staff suggest that students' responses have changed over time. Veterans say that in the early days of rankings more students would ask point-blank what you or your local competitors' rankings were. One described early student reaction to rankings as "frenzied." He said, "I think, for a time when these things were first out—ironically, when they were the worst—it was almost frenetic, the influence. I mean kids would . . . come up to visit the school with the [ranking] chart in their hands."

One indication that prospective students have learned to be more politic about rankings when talking to school representatives—among themselves, especially online, is another matter—is that they now use the same euphemisms that administrators do: "Tell me about your school's reputation and what you are doing to improve it." "Are you a nationally selective school?" "Which schools do you lose students to?" "How do you allocate scholarship money?" These questions sound innocent, but admissions officers can see rankings lurking behind them. Our research suggests they are right.

15. An associate dean at a top-ten school said, "I'm not sure what kind of service they do for that public out there that relies on them as gospel when it really is something that the kids should not be placing as much faith in as they do—they really shouldn't."

16. Korobkin 1998.

17. Although neither organization will confirm it, many believe that the ABA and LSAC began publishing their official ABA-approved *Guide to Law Schools* in 1999 in response to rankings. Rankings have also prompted changes in how the ABA reports its data. For example, instead of averaging scores of those who take the LSAT more than once, now schools are permitted to report the highest score.

18. See "Interview with Dean David E. Van Zandt of Northwestern University School of Law," September 2008, www.top-law-schools.com/van-zandt-interview.html (accessed November 22, 2015). Van Zandt offered similar arguments in addressing colleagues at an annual Association of American Law Schools meeting in 2006.

19. An approach known as actor-network theory, first developed by science and technology scholars, including Bruno Latour, Michel Callon, and Stephen Woolgar, explains the authority of knowledge as depending on how scientific ideas or programs link people and objects together in networks of users who creatively adopt and adapt this knowledge to new ends. As the network stabilizes and links more people, places, and things, the knowledge becomes more durable and taken for granted, becoming a "black box" whose contents no longer need to be scrutinized. See Callon, Law, and Rip 1986; Latour 1987, 2005.

20. See also Bialik 2005.

21. Henderson and Morriss 2006.

22. Although *USN* did not publish ordinal rankings of third-tier schools until the 2012 rankings, schools in the third or fourth tier could request their specific ranking from *USN* in the years prior to this.

23. Efrati 2008.

24. Henderson and Morriss 2006.

25. See Morse 2008b, 2008c. Note that the proposed change in the calculation of school admissions statistics made front-page news in the *Wall Street Journal,*

which suggests how dominant and newsworthy *USN* rankings had become by the late 2000s. See Efrati 2008.

26. Efrati 2008.

27. Some schools use revenue from LL.M. programs, a one-year master's degree, to replace lost revenue. The number and size of LL.M. programs have grown rapidly since the early 1990s, partly because of demand from international students (Silver 2006). A number of those we interviewed told us that the revenue from LL.M. programs helped fund merit scholarships, marketing, and other practices to affect rankings.

28. Brian Leiter, a professor of law at the University of Chicago Law School and an expert on rankings, posted a list of the ten schools with the highest rates of transfer students as a percentage of their first-year classes, derived from ABA data collected for 2006–2007. Florida State has the most transfers, with eleven students transferring out, and fifty-nine transferring in; this represented a net gain of forty-eight students or 24.62 percent of the 1L class. The list includes four top-fifteen schools, including Georgetown (14.82 percent of its 1L class coming from transfers), New York University (11.49 percent), Northwestern (10.30 percent), and Columbia (10.18 percent). See Leiter 2008.

29. http://www.elsblog.org/the_empirical_legal_studi/2007/10/transfers-us-ne.html#more (accessed December 16, 2015).

30. Henderson and Morriss 2006, 191.

31. Wightman 1998.

32. Henderson 2007.

33. The Law School Survey of Student Engagement (2005, 13–14), which surveys 28,000 students at seventy-three schools in the United States and Canada, found that transfer students, 3 percent of their sample, reported performing comparably with continuing students (transfer students are admitted because of their excellent records). However, they were less likely than continuing students to characterize their relations with other students as positive, work in clinical or field programs, participate in extracurricular activities, have serious conversations with students different from themselves, discuss reading, or work with others after class on an assignment outside of class. However, they were more likely to earn better grades and feel they had greater gains from attending law school than continuing students.

34. Droit Femme 2006.

35. Students have also changed how they respond to waitlists.

36. Lempert 2002.

37. LaPiana 2001.

38. For similar arguments about education more broadly, see Guinier 2003; Sacks 2000, 2007.

39. Jencks and Phillips 1998; Wightman 1996, 2003.

40. Diamond-Dalessandro, Stilwell, and Reese 2005. For statistics on the differences in average LSAT performance between racial and ethnic groups, see Wightman 1997, 2003; Wilder 2003. These score differences may sound small, but when you look at the small differences in the median LSAT scores that distinguish schools in the rankings, it's clear that the impact of these differences can loom large in admissions decisions. This is because so many of these decisions involve people with scores in the middle of the distribution and because law schools are so tightly bunched in the rankings. Median LSAT scores are even more compressed. For example, in 2014, twenty schools had median LSAT scores of 158, nine had median scores of 159, and ten had median scores of 160. See Internet Legal Research Group 2008.

41. Most law schools kept no records of minority enrollment before 1965 (Groves 1965, cited in Kidder 2003). Before 1968, about two hundred African Americans graduated from law school annually; there were fewer than twenty-five practicing Native American attorneys in the United States. Estimates for 1969 suggest that fewer than .006 percent of law students were "Spanish American," a category that included anyone who spoke Spanish or had a Spanish surname (Gellhorn 1968, cited in Kidder 2003). For histories of minority law school admissions, see Ramsey 1998; Kidder 2003.

42. Clancy 1998.

43. http://www2.law.columbia.edu/civilrights (accessed February 25, 2016). See also Longley 1998a, 1998b.

44. Roach 2009.

45. According to a former ABA president, Michael Greco, "The legal profession faces no greater challenge in the 21st century than the critical need to diversify its ranks. People of color continue to be woefully underrepresented in the bar and on the bench, while American society is becoming increasingly diverse" (quoted in Hynes and Armstead 2006). But according to Conrad Johnson (2009), declining enrollment among minorities is "not a pipeline problem" (quoted in Jones 2006). See also Law School Admission Council 2014c, 2014d.

46. Sturm and Guinier 1996; Wightman 1997; Longley 1998a, 1998b; Lempert 2002; Guinier 2003; Kidder 2003; Wilder 2003; Chambers et al. 2005; Ayres and Brooks 2005; Wilkins 2005; Johnson 2006.

47. Lempert 2002.

48. Wightman 1997; Wilder 2003; Diamond-Dalessandro, Stilwell, and Reese 2005.

49. Steele 1997; Steele and Aronson 1995.

50. When white male engineering students were told that Asian Americans typically did better on math exams than they did, the white males performed less well than the matched control group. See Aronson et al. 1999. Stereotypes related to class also harm performance. See Croizet and Claire 1998.

51. Schools with distributions skewed toward the ends of the overall distribution—schools that admit students with mostly high or low scores—are more sensitive to small changes.

CHAPTER FIVE

1. "College of Law Climbs Six Places in U.S. News Rankings," S. J. Quinney College of Law website, April 22, 2009, https://today.law.utah.edu/2009/04/college-of-law-climbs-six-places-in-u-s-news-rankings/ (accessed November 13, 2015).

2. http://law.utah.edu/news/college-of-law-rises-six-spots-in-the-2014-u-s-news-rankings/(accessed February 25, 2016).

3. "Rankings," University of California, Davis School of Law website, www.law.ucdavis.edu/about/rankings.html (accessed November 12, 2015).

4. Sauder 2008.

5. Rovella 1997.

6. Cotts 1998.

7. This letter is available at www.lsac.org/LSAC.asp?url=lsac/deans-speak-out-rankings.asp (accessed November 13, 2015). It is the most public of many attempts by law schools to resist or discredit the rankings, which included lobbying *USN* to eliminate or circumscribe the rankings of law schools early on, refusing to provide information to *USN,* and organizing panels at professional meetings designed to develop strategies to reduce the influence of rankings. All of these attempts failed.

8. See Klein and Hamilton 1998; Lempert 2002; Seto 2007.

9. As with most indicators, what gets included is what is easiest to measure. Although *USN* has stated that it would be willing to add teaching evaluations if a good measure were found, there is no shared teaching metric, and the cost of surveying students from every school would be very high.

10. Van Zandt 2010.

11. See Klim 2003; Stetson University, College of Law 2003.

12. Hyland 2012; *Chicago Tribune* 2012; Rezendes and Pazzanes 2013.

13. Mystal 2013a.

14. "Senators Chuck Grassley and Dick Durbin Call Out the Law School Pigs for Their Collective Greed in Issuing Worthless-Ass Law Degrees to Morons," *Third Tier Reality,* November 10, 2015, http://thirdtierreality.blogspot.de/ (accessed November 13, 2015).

15. Recently, an ABA task force called Task Force on the Future of Legal Education recommended making some of these changes and promoted greater heterogeneity among law schools. Law professors also write blogs critical of legal education. Paul Caron posts at his *TaxProf Blog* (http://taxprof.typepad.com/) and Paul Campos posts frequently at *Lawyers, Guns, & Money* (www.lawyersgunsmoneyblog.com).

16. A recent headline is representative of the blog's tone: "Why Do So Many People Detest the Reprehensible Law School Pigs and Cockroaches?!," *Third Tier Reality,* March 1, 2014, http://thirdtierreality.blogspot.com/2014/03/why-do-so-many-people-detest.html (accessed November 13, 2015).

17. See the websites *Temporary Attorney* (http://temporaryattorney.blogspot.de/), *The Law School Scam* (http://thelawschoolscam.com), and *Subprime JD* (http://subprimejd.blogspot.com/).

18. Mystal 2013b. This blog post also contains a similarly themed letter from a student at DePaul University asking what the law school intends to do about its decline in the rankings and questioning the dean's competence and honesty. See also "Students and Alumni of American University Washington College of Law: Remove Dean Grossman and Overhaul OCPD," *Change.org,* www.change.org/petitions/students-and-alumni-of-american-university-washington-college-of-law-remove-dean-grossman-and-overhaul-ocpd (accessed November 21, 2015).

19. Not only candidates respond to rankings during the recruitment and hiring process. Several respondents noted that rankings are also a consideration for schools during their job searches. As one dean told us, "There is still this general perception out there that the rankings make a difference in terms of faculty hiring and clearly we see that. . . . You make your school better if you hire faculty from a certain rank of school, and when you talk rank you can only talk *USN*." In addition, candidates are routinely discussed in terms of whether they will attract positive attention or "buzz" for the school or contribute to improving the school's reputation. Many assume that the reputation and visibility of faculty will influence *USN* reputation scores.

20. The effects of drops in the rankings are experienced by more schools than one might at first imagine: over 80 percent of law schools that have been ranked since 1993 have dropped in the rankings at least once during this time.

21. Given the dismal job market and the chorus of criticism over rising tuition, this response is no longer politically palatable and most schools are now looking to cut tuition or at least not raise it.

22. See Bell 2006.

23. One dean told us, "The difference between ten years ago and now in the volume of mail I get is astounding. The amount of money that law schools are spending . . . if you want to know, without question in my mind, the biggest impact that *USN* rankings have had, it's on the profits of printers."

24. Many deans reported that their schools spend well over $100,000 per year on such marketing, and estimates of annual spending ranged from the tens of thousands to over a million dollars. One dean told us, "If you look to see what the costs are of design — when you start looking at the competition for photography, for graphics and you multiply it by these huge amounts, we're talking in many cases millions of dollars, hundreds of thousands of dollars are spent by some institutions in order to get the design, the photography."

25. Not all marketing done by law schools is intended to influence rankings, and factors other than rankings contribute to an increased emphasis on marketing.

Some believe that marketing is a crucial tool for distinguishing one's school. Nevertheless, most respondents attribute the increase in marketing materials to efforts aimed at influencing rankings.

26. Christian Moos (2015) has argued that because rankings generate a variety of responses from schools, they do not produce the homogenizing effects that some scholars have suggested. As we show, law schools do respond to rankings differently depending on a variety of factors; however, given that all schools are responding to the same criteria, our data show that the overall trend is toward homogenization.

27. Espeland and Sauder 2007; Elsbach and Kramer 1996.

28. Cotts 1998. Alternatively, rankings successes are often publicly celebrated, through emails and press releases and sometimes even with receptions and parties. One such celebration, at Emory University Goizueta Business School, was filmed (www.youtube.com/watch?v=-R_eWfxADKM).

29. On Rapoport's resignation: Guzmán 2004; on Rapoport's blog post and reporter's comment: Edwards 2008.

30. Posgate 2013.

31. Our interviews confirm the changes in deans' attitudes according to age and number of years in the profession. Deans with eleven or more years of experience (N = 12) had a primarily negative opinion of rankings (an average score of 4.6), deans with 6 to 10 years of experience (N = 11) had a somewhat negative view (4.0), and relatively newer deans (N = 10) expressed an opinion in between mixed and somewhat negative (3.6). These results are only illustrative because ours was not a random sample, but they do indicate a clear trend: as more experienced deans are replaced by new ones, rankings become more naturalized. For a full discussion of this analysis and of our methodology, see Sauder 2008.

32. *U.S. World and News Report,* March 20, 1995.

33. Sloan 2012.

34. Bialik 2012; Olson 2013.

35. Whitman 2002, 1–3; Espeland and Sauder 2007.

36. Robert is referring here to the fact that these top schools do not receive a score of 5.0 in their reputational ranking. The implication of this is that a portion of people who filled out the reputational survey thought that some schools (such as Yale, Harvard, and Stanford) that are considered by nearly everyone in the law school community to be the very best in the country are not even in the top 20 percent of law schools in the United States. Robert and others believe only those who are trying to game the rankings or who are not providing honest assessments of reputation would make such off-base assessments.

37. For a detailed discussion of these effects see Sauder and Espeland 2009.

38. Burawoy 1979.

CHAPTER SIX

1. The rankings in this quote were changed slightly to protect the identity of the school.

2. Until the 2014 rankings, "employed graduates" included those reported as working or pursuing graduate degrees. For the nine-month rate only, 25 percent of those whose status was unknown were also counted as working; the 75 percent who were presumed not to be working fed the tracking frenzy. Those not seeking jobs were excluded. The placement factor also included the rate of bar passage (worth 2 percent of the overall ranking), which called for a more diffused culpability. Beginning in 2014, *USN* developed a more complex measurement of employment success based on the types of jobs graduates were able to attain. The employment score is still 20 percent of the ranking formula, but *USN* has not made public the weights it assigns to these various employment statuses. See Flanigan and Morse 2014.

3. See Morriss and Henderson (2008, 797–813) for a close examination of how *USN* has changed its methodology for measuring career-services success over time and how these changes have influenced the overall rankings. The changes discussed here are too recent to be included in their useful survey.

4. Mystal 2013b.

5. American Bar Association 2014; Segal 2011a.

6. Weber 1922/1978.

7. The classic source for this point is Thompson 1967. It has been creatively elaborated within the neo-institutional approach to organizations. Here, important contributions include Weick 1976; Meyer and Rowan 1977; DiMaggio and Powell 1983.

8. Those arguing for the existence of a crisis include Henderson and Zahorsky 2011; Campos 2012; Schlunk 2009; Tamanaha 2012. For rebuttals, see Garth 2013; Dinovitzer, Garth, and Sterling 2013; Lempert 2002. See also Elie Mystal (2013c) for a story about the heated exchange between Brian Leiter and Paul Campos on this issue. Leiter's debunking of Campos's views have appeared frequently on his blog *Brian Leiter's Law School Reports*. See, for example, Leiter 2012.

9. Seto 2007, 34.

10. "Students and Alumni of American University Washington College of Law: Remove Dean Grossman and Overhaul OCPD," www.change.org/p/students-and-alumni-of-american-university-washington-college-of-law-remove-dean-grossman-and-overhaul-ocpd (accessed November 17, 2015); 134 signed the petition.

11. See also Segal 2011b.

12. See also Matasar 2005.

13. See also Whitman 2002; Matasar 2005; Wellen 2005.

14. One Ivy League school adopted a related strategy, requesting that firms that had traditionally donated money to the school might instead hire their unemployed graduates on a temporary basis.
15. Morriss and Henderson 2008.
16. Andrew P. Morriss and William D. Henderson (2007), not harsh critics of rankings, come to a similar conclusion, writing, "What has emerged among *U.S. News*, the law schools and the ABA is a ranking system [that] underserves prospective students by failing to facilitate meaningful competition on what matters a great deal to students: post-graduation outcomes" (21).
17. National Association for Law Placement 2013.
18. In 2011–2012, the average amount students who went to public schools borrowed was $84,600; the figure was $122,158 for students who attended private school. The figures for 2001 were $46,499 and $70,147, respectively. See American Bar Association 2014.
19. Segal 2011a, 2011b.
20. The schools that have been sued include New York Law School, Thomas Jefferson School of Law, Thomas M. Cooley Law School, Southwestern Law School, Golden State University Law School, and the University of San Francisco School of Law, among others. See Mangan 2012a. The first of these suits, against New York Law School, was dismissed by Judge Melvin L. Schweitzer of the Manhattan Supreme Court, who found that the plaintiffs failed to prove that law schools misled them "in a material way." See Mangan 2012b. This ruling will likely lead to dismissals of the other lawsuits.
21. See also Jones 2005.
22. Jones 2005.
23. Seto 2007, 34.
24. Brooks 1998.
25. Chandler 2010.
26. We heard many stories of the tricks career-services personnel use to boost their response rates. One school withholds diplomas until students fill out surveys about their job status and contact information. Another told us that whenever she was contacted by a law firm looking for an employee, she would "contact every single graduated student who didn't have a job in the book. So I tell them this is a wonderful opportunity and I would love to give them your résumé. Please send me an updated résumé, and please send me an updated email address, ... And, of course, I forwarded those résumés on, but I also knew that for most of them, the firm wasn't going to be interested in them. I was using something that existed to get other information that we needed."
27. An administrator at a first-tier school noted that his school gets employment information for most of their students quickly, "but we still have to spend a lot of time tracking people down. And a lot of times these are people who don't necessarily want to be tracked down. A lot of times they didn't have a

good experience or they haven't quite found a job yet and they don't want to respond until they have."

28. Rivera 2015, 36.

29. Because they are medians, these statistics mask the wide variation in salaries. There are slight differences among sources for some of these numbers, but the trends described are consistent. The ones reported here are from the U.S. Department of Labor, Bureau of Labor Statistics (2015).

30. National Association for Law Placement 2015a. For discussions of post-recession employment trends, see Leipold 2011; Friedman and Schulze 2012. After the recent mergers of large firms, the biggest firms now have thousands of employees spread around the globe. For perspective, in 2015, Baker McKenzie LLP was the largest law firm in the United States. Founded in Chicago in 1949, it now has 77 offices in 47 countries. Currently, it employs 4,245 lawyers; of these, 1,431 are partners (750 equity partners) and 2,814 are associates. See Internet Legal Research Group 2015.

31. *National Law Journal* 2011; National Association for Law Placement 2015b. In 2007, there was a record high employment rate of 91.9 percent, the largest in twenty-five years. Keep in mind that these statistics were reported before new ABA rules that changed how law schools would calculate employment and are not directly comparable given these changes in how schools report their numbers and the likely decline in the once-rampant gaming of employment numbers.

32. See Bryant Garth (2013) for an interesting discussion of how "crisis" has been regularly invoked and interpreted historically. He finds a surprising consistency in how "crisis" in the profession and in legal education is depicted.

33. Matt Leichter (2012, cited in Garth 2013), who is on the radical reform end of the spectrum in debates about legal education, jobs, and student debt, argues that prospective students should be prevented from getting federal student loans or other public subsidies if they do not attend an elite law school. In other words, they must be protected from their poor judgment by withdrawal of their financial support, which is paid by taxpayers. This policy should force poorly performing schools to close. Those espousing more moderate positions call for reforms such as reducing the time needed to get a law degree, reducing the number of required classes, drastically cutting tuition, and increasing faculty teaching loads. These strategies aim either to reduce the oversupply of lawyers or to cut costs for law students. Garth 2013 points out that reforms directed at culling law schools would likely penalize those who provide traditionally under-represented groups with legal education.

34. Brian Z. Tamanaha's proposals (2012) include eliminating the third year of law school and eliminating tenure for faculty. For empirical and normative rebuttals to Tamanaha, see Lempert 2014; Garth 2013.

35. Leichter 2012. Needless to say, critics who call for fundamental reform in legal education are controversial, especially with many law faculty and administrators. Such critics often enjoy strong support from lawyers who are unemployed or underemployed in law, as well as many sympathetic faculty. The emergence of "scam blogs" that issue warnings to prospective law students about the perils of law school, often attacking law schools or even individual professors, shows how deep the frustration goes among former law students who feel badly served by law schools. Nevertheless the most common perspectives among legal scholars include supporting the current model, calling for more modest reforms, or for interpreting the contemporary crisis with historical sensibilities. Despite some occasional heated rhetoric, those on both sides of this debate generally argue that students can and should profit from some reform, that there is room for pluralism in legal education, and that a standardized law school catering to a presumably standardized student is not the ideal vision for legal education.

36. There are many well-edited sites for tracking this debate. Blogs are especially good for observing arguments in process, although debates are also featured prominently in published scholarship, media, and at conferences. There are too many sources to list them exhaustively, but some of the more prominent include an edited network of legal blogs organized by topic at *The Law Professor Blogs Network* (www.lawprofessorblogs.com/#), where one can find links to *Law Deans on Legal Education Blog*, *Legal Profession Blog*, and *Leiter's Law School Rankings*, among others.

37. See, for example, Weissman 2012.

38. National Association for Law Placement 2004.

39. Droit Femme 2006.

40. We interviewed ten employers in national and various regional labor markets. More informally, we talked with dozens of employers ranging from equity partners at international firms to associates at boutique firms in cities large and small to staff attorneys at legal clinics serving the poor. Our original data on employers' points of view are less systematic and exhaustive than our data from our sources within legal education. For this part of our analysis we rely more on secondary and media sources (including newspapers, magazines, websites, and blogs), in addition to formal interviews and informal conversations.

41. See, for example, the March 2013 letter "The Economics of Legal Education: A Concern of Colleagues," sent to the American Bar Association Section on Legal Education, www.americanbar.org/content/dam/aba/administrative/professional_responsibility/taskforcecomments/032013_coalition_revcomment.authcheckdam.pdf (accessed November 17, 2013).

42. Opinions, sometimes heated, about the faculty composition that best serves students vary. This is an old debate that flares up often, and is especially prevalent in economic downturns. Many faculty members and current and

former students believe that the proportion of those with practical experience is too small and that those with Ph.D.'s are over-represented. This view has been particularly prominent since the recession, especially among those in legal education who argue for more radical reforms. Having some practical experience is still widely regarded as a valuable credential. Moreover, many schools have expanded the number of adjunct professors who work in different parts of the bench and bar so that they can share their more practical experiences with students, and schools have expanded their career-services staff, legal clinics, and practice-based training to help students get jobs.

Even in schools whose educational model is more that of the law as an academic discipline, faculty members usually keep a keen eye on at least some part of the job market. Most care whether their schools' reputations with employers, and hence their students' job prospects, are affected by rankings. In fact, this subject came up among faculty from the entire range of schools where we interviewed, including at schools in the very top and bottom ranks: faculty members with Ph.D.s, J.D.s, LL.M.s, M.A.s, or any combination thereof, and those whose careers were devoted to disciplinary-based scholarship in fields such as history, economics, sociology, philosophy, and business. Regardless of the diversity of opinion on the subject of rankings and prospective employment of graduates, many in law schools do monitor the market and work hard to help students find jobs. And this means that they must be attentive to whether and how rankings might affect their students. Depictions of law professors as callous and unconcerned about the job prospects of their students, a prominent feature of scam blogs and the opinions of some inside legal education, were not supported by our data.

43. Henderson and Zahorsky 2011.
44. Rivera 2015, 44. Lauren A. Rivera analyzes recruitment at elite banks, consulting firms, and law firms. The pattern for law firms is very similar to that for the other professions, and she is careful to note when there are differences. This section draws extensively on her research of those who help hire at eleven elite law firms. In addition to participant observation for about nine months during 2006 and 2007, she interviewed forty professionals involved with hiring law students as interns and new associates. She asked most of them to screen résumés of fictive candidates whose résumés varied according to race, gender, undergraduate institutions, and law school attended. She also interviewed seven job candidates who were applying to these and other elite firms.
45. Ibid., 3–5.
46. The desire for sameness—what Kanter (1977) called "homo-social reproduction"—and how it leads to self-reproduction at the top of organizations and professions is an old and durable pattern, even as the mechanisms for producing it have evolved. This phenomenon is now labeled "homophily"; for a review, see McPherson, Smith-Lovin, and Cook 2001.

47. Rivera 2015, 136–37. Rivera uses the concepts of social and cultural capital of the French sociologist Pierre Bourdieu to theorize these qualities and the advantage or disadvantage they confer. Scholars too numerous to count analyze the reproduction of economic and social advantage using cultural approaches. A few exemplars of this approach include Lamont 2009; Lareau 2003; Stevens 2007.

48. Rivera 2015, 29.

49. Interestingly, the creation of the top fourteen as a category is a good example of the decommensuration of a powerful cultural classification. "Top ten" has become a common way of highlighting features of social life. "Top fourteen" is a way of "talking back to" or reclaiming the power to distinguish in order to reassert the excellence of influential schools that are excluded from or aspire to being considered among the elite. The ranking terms are still defined by *USN* but represent a clumping near the top ten that seems stable enough to be worthy of such demarcation.

50. If one of these schools were to fall precipitously in the rankings, however, the importance of its ranking might quickly become much more salient. Even those among the very top ranks agreed that the "luxury" of not needing to focus on rankings too closely was provisional.

51. Theodore P. Seto (2007) provides evidence of the strength of regional networks in an examination of partners at the five largest law firms in Los Angeles. He shows that local schools, even those not ranked in the first tier, were better represented than elite law schools with the exception of Harvard. Here is a good example of how region can be more important than rank.

52. Sauder 2006.

53. But an administrator at a school ranked between fifty and one hundred, describing the school's relationship to local employers, said, "I think that if we were a tier-one school, those schools would be much more willing to go deeper into our class. Instead of those schools looking at only the top 10 percent of our class—that's really where the focus is—they might be willing to accept anybody in the top 25 percent. So even in our own backyard, I definitely see an impact."

54. "Law School Numbers," University of Mississippi Law School website, http://mississippi.lawschoolnumbers.com/ (accessed November 15, 2015).

55. See also National Association for Law Placement 2004.

CHAPTER SEVEN

1. Epigraph: This adage is known as Campbell's Law. See Campbell 1979, 85. Thanks to Sam Carruthers for suggesting it. On "evaluative culture": Michael Power (1994, 1997) was among the first to document what he called the "audit explosion." See also Espeland and Sauder 2012; Shore 2008; Shore and Wright 2000; Strathern 1995, 2000.

2. On human rights, development, and governance, see Merry 2011; Davis, Kingsbury, and Merry 2012; Rottenburg 2000; Rottenburg et al. 2015.
3. For a similar approach, see Jeanette Colyvas's (2012, 167–68) framework for investigating performance metrics. She understands such measures as distinctive forms of data whose power rests on their formalized abstractions of classificatory systems and the social mechanisms such as "reactivity" that shape their use.
4. Miller and Rose 1990, 9.
5. Porter 1995.
6. It is important to note that the rankings and the accountability they entail did not emerge in response to an outpouring of skepticism about law schools but were part of a complex broader array of institutional changes, including increases in the number of both law schools and law students, the nationalization of demand, and a broader pressure for increased transparency and accountability. This pressure has many sources and its impetus varies across fields. In the United States, pressure for more participatory governance was part of the liberalizing social movements of the 1960s. Conversely, some see pressure for accountability in education in the conservative backlash in the United States against the educational reforms of the same period. Others link quantification to global neoliberal politics (Power 2003, 191). Cris Shore and Susan Wright (1999) trace the audit explosion in Britain to the Thatcher government's efforts to shrink the welfare state by replacing public services with private ones. Proponents of this shrinking assumed that market controls were superior to bureaucratic ones. After privatizing a broad array of public services, the shrunken public sector was subjected to techniques of accountability, sometimes referred to as New Public Management, that were adopted from the private sector. Accountancy and audits became vehicles for inserting the practices and norms of the private sector into the public realm. Efforts to integrate economies or governments also spur quantification, as states must find ways to standardize and monitor one another. The formation of the EU has created an explosion of new statistics as members and potential members must document their standing and standardize their practices. International financial institutions such as the World Bank and the International Monetary Fund, in pressuring member countries for transparency and accountability, have also contributed to the proliferation of quantitative measures. These shifts in institutional sectors, national policies, and global politics all have contributed to the success of rankings in becoming defined as helpful technologies of evaluation.
7. "Research Interests & Papers," Walter W. Powell's website, http://woody powell.com/research-interests (accessed November 17, 2015).
8. According to Reed College's president, Colin Diver, when Reed first boycotted the *USN* rankings in 1995, *USN* "estimated" low values for the missing data

and the college's ranking plummeted to the bottom quintile. See Diver 2005. The estimation of data may also have played a role in Howard University's recent plunge in the rankings. Howard fell 22 spots, to 142, in the 2013 *USN* rankings. Some of the decline may be due to conflict among trustees, declining budgets, and lower selection statistics, but, writes Robert Morse, "Howard's decline in the most recent rankings was mainly due to its administrative inability or refusal to report its most recent data about itself to *U.S. News*." See Morse 2013.

9. Foucault 1977.

10. Michel Foucault (1977) depicts rankings as a key disciplinary practice: "In discipline, the elements are interchangeable, since each is defined by the place it occupies in a series, and by the gap that separates it from the others. The unit is, therefore, neither the territory (unit of domination), nor the place (unit of residence), but the *rank:* the place one occupies in a classification, the point at which a line and a column intersect, the interval in a series of intervals that one may traverse one after the other. Discipline is an art of rank, a technique for the transformation of arrangements. It individualizes bodies by a location that does not give them a fixed position, but distributes them and circulates them in a network of relations" (145–46; original italics). For more on rankings, discipline, and organizational change see Sauder and Espeland 2009.

11. "Legal compliance": Edelman 1992; "implement ineffective programs": Kalev, Dobbin, and Kelly 2006; "may never have to be implemented": Westphal and Zajac 2001.

12. Porter 1995.

13. An organizational field consists of "those organizations that, in the aggregate, constitute a recognized area of institutional life: key suppliers, resource and product consumers, regulatory agencies, and other organizations that produce similar services and products." See DiMaggio and Powell 1983, 64–65; Bourdieu and Wacquant 1992; Martin 2003; Fligstein and McAdam 2012. For law schools, the organizational field includes the colleges that produce law applicants and employ the pre-law advisers; professional and regulating institutions such as the Law School Admission Council, which creates and administers the LSAT and coordinates admissions practices; the Association of American Law Schools; the Society of American Law Teachers; the National Association for Law Placement; the American Bar Association; the student editors at law reviews around the country; the state bar associations and the boards that create and administer state bar exams and generate the "bar passage" statistics included in rankings; and the law firms, companies, courts, and government agencies that employ lawyers. For further discussion of the role of rankings in the legal education field, see Sauder 2008. Moos (2015) argues for the importance of field-level analyses for understanding the effects of rankings on organizations.

14. Sauder 2006.

15. Craig Tutterow and James Evans (forthcoming) provide evidence that the rankings have played an important role in the rise of enrollment management and educational consultants across higher education in the United States. They argue, "In an effort to improve rankings, universities solicit more applications from students to reduce their acceptance rate. Lower acceptance rates lead to more uncertainty for students about acceptance, leading them to apply to more schools, which decreases the probability that accepted students will attend. This leads to greater uncertainty about enrollment for students and universities and generates demand for new services to manage it" (1–2). Exactly these dynamics obtain in legal education.

16. See Arewa, Morriss, and Henderson 2014.

17. On global rankings, see Espeland and Sauder 2012. On business schools, see Sauder and Espeland 2006.

18. The effects of *USN* rankings have been felt worldwide, and global rankings are the most recent evidence of this impact. When the first American college rankings were published in 1981, other media soon launched their own rankings of universities and graduate programs. *Business Week* started ranking American business schools in 1988. *Maclean's* magazine began ranking Canadian universities in 1991. In the UK, *The Times* created its rankings in 1992, the *Sunday Times* in 1998, and *The Guardian* in 1999. Today there are over forty countries in which national magazines publish rankings of their universities, and scholars in these countries have identified many of the same consequences that we discovered in the case of law schools. See, for example, Hazelkorn 2009, 2011; Wedlin 2006; Labi 2008; Marginson and van der Wende 2007; Münch 2014.

19. For more detailed discussions of the history and effects of global rankings, see Hazelkorn 2008, 2011; Usher and Savino 2006; Salmi and Saroyan 2007; Dill and Soo 2005; Espeland and Sauder 2012; Münch 2014. This section relies in part on Espeland and Sauder 2012.

20. On "the backbone of research governance": Osterloh and Frey 2010, 2, quoted in Jensen 2011; on promotion of competition: Wedlin 2014.

21. The first regional rankings in east Asia were published by *Asiaweek,* which began ranking Pacific Rim universities in 1997. The Academic Rankings of World Universities, also sometimes referred to as the Shanghai Rankings, were created in 2003 by Professors N. C. Liu and Y. Cheng (2005) at Shanghai Jiao Tong University to determine "the gap between Chinese Universities and world-class universities." According to Mayumi Ishikawa (2009), one reason the Chinese government was concerned about this gap was that many of its best students were opting to get their graduate degrees abroad. The ARWU made a big splash as media around the world reported on how universities in their countries measured up. Published annually since then, these rankings

of some twelve hundred universities include factors such as the number of Nobel Prize and Field Medal winners associated with a university and citation counts in top science journals. Just as in the case of U.S. law schools, scholars have pointed out the limitations and biases of the ARWU ranking: they strongly favor natural science, English-language journals, and older and wealthier universities. They ignore teaching quality.

The World University Rankings and QS World University Rankings have a complicated and intertwined history. In 2004, the *Times Higher Education Supplement* joined with Quacquarelli Symonds to produce the QS World University Rankings. These rankings included a reputation factor derived from surveys that, as critics pointed out, were strongly biased in favor of Western and English-speaking countries. The partnership between the *Times Higher Education Supplement* and QS came to an end in 2009, with each firm creating its own global rankings: the World University Rankings and the QS World University Rankings.

22. See Morse 2009; *University Ranking Watch*, http://rankingwatch.blogspot.com/ (accessed November 17, 2015). Global rankings have also inspired new twists on rankings. For example, beginning in 2004, Webometrics Rankings of World Universities was created by the Cybermetrics Lab, a branch of the National Research Council of Spain (Centro de Ciencias Humanas y Sociales). This ranking of twenty thousand universities is based on the size and visibility of their websites as measured by the number of pages and inward links (*Ranking Web of World Universities*, www.webometrics.info/en; accessed November 17, 2015).

23. See, for example, Hazelkorn 2007a, 2008, 2009, 2011. A recent report published by the European University Association (Rauhvargers 2011) concludes: "There is no doubt that the arrival on the scene of global classifications and rankings of universities has galvanized the world of higher education. Since the emergence of global rankings, universities have been unable to avoid national and international comparisons, and this has caused changes in the way universities function" (68). The report sees potential benefits in these rankings systems in that they make universities more transparent, but also warns that there is a lack of transparency in the methodologies used to construct the rankings that makes the validity of these rankings difficult to assess.

24. Hazelkorn 2007b, 1.

25. Hazelkorn 2009, 2011.

26. Institute for Higher Education Policy 2009; Hazelkorn 2011, 112.

27. Hazelkorn 2009.

28. Salmi and Saroyan 2007; Hazelkorn 2009.

29. Luxbacher 2013.

30. Hazelkorn 2010.

31. Labi 2008; Münch 2014.

32. See Hazelkorn 2011, 25.
33. Staley 2014.
34. Labi 2008, 2010.
35. Münch 2014, 183.
36. Hazelkorn 2011, 173.
37. Hazelkorn 2009.
38. Hazelkorn 2011, 173
39. Hazelkorn 2008.
40. Institute for Higher Education Policy 2009.
41. Healy 2010.
42. Labi 2008.
43. Hazelkorn 2008, 2011.
44. Guttenplan 2013.
45. Ishikawa 2009.
46. Ibid., 165.
47. See Wedlin 2014.
48. Staley 2014.
49. See Ronald G. Ehrenberg (2002) for a convincing argument about how *USN*'s emphasis on money spent per student in their ranking formula encourages budget, and therefore tuition, increases.
50. Perez-Pena and Slotnik 2012.
51. Most of the people with whom we spoke would agree that this is likely just the tip of the iceberg, and that "the number of universities and colleges caught misreporting data remains a tiny fraction of the total." See Marcus 2013; see also Perez-Pena and Slotnik 2012; O'Shaughnessy 2012.
52. Tutterow 2015.
53. The business school rankings that matter most according to our interviewees are those published by *Business Week, USN*, the *Wall Street Journal*, the *Financial Times, The Economist*, and *Forbes*. For more detail on the comparison between law school and business school rankings, see Sauder and Espeland 2006.
54. Linda Wedlin (2006, 99–100) documents these inconsistent results in a variety of business school rankings in the 2000s. For example, MIT ranked sixth in *Business Week* and thirtieth in the *Wall Street Journal*; Michigan was ranked second in the *Wall Street Journal* but twenty-sixth in *Forbes*.
55. This factor includes two statistics: the number of faculty publications on this list and the number of publications weighted on the basis of the size of the faculty. Two features of the list are notable. First, with its emphasis on "international" journals and those catering to "management," it excludes the top journals from numerous disciplines represented within business schools, including those in economics, organizations, and sociology. So the favored journals of elite schools are under-represented.

56. It is important to note that because there are fewer dental schools, they form a smaller market for *USN*. This fact likely shaped the magazine's response to the boycott.

57. See "Reed and the Rankings Game," https://www.reed.edu/apply/college-rankings.html (accessed December 16, 2016).

58. Diver 2005.

59. There have been other collective efforts to limit the effects of rankings. In the early 2000s a group of 130 liberal arts colleges, dubbed "the Annapolis Group," led efforts to convince schools to stop filling out *USN*'s reputation surveys and to stop using rankings to promote schools to the general public (for the letter that they wrote to schools, see *The Education Conservancy*, www.educationconservancy.org/presidents_letter.html; accessed November 22, 2015). A number of schools signed the letter in support of these measures, but the highest-ranking liberal arts schools did not. In any event, these measures have had no discernible effect on the rankings nor on how they are used.

60. Colin Diver, then the president of Reed, pointed out in 2005 that even if complaints about rankings are nearly universal, so is compliance. Despite concerted efforts that have been made to convince schools to boycott the undergraduate rankings, in 2005 only 5 percent of colleges and universities failed to submit data to *USN*. See Diver 2005.

61. Halliday 2012.

62. Gallagher and Chuang 2012.

63. For a recent and somewhat more sympathetic account of indicators as a mechanism of visibility and accountability, see Merry, Davis, and Kingsbury 2015.

64. For a thoughtful critique of corruption indicators see Zaloznaya 2013.

65. For Transparency International's "Corruptions Perceptions Index," see http://en.wikipedia.org/wiki/Corruption_Perceptions_Index (accessed November 23, 2015). For the Heritage Foundation's "2015 Index of Economic Freedom," see www.heritage.org/index/ (accessed November 23, 2015).

66. Jacobs 2012.

67. Wills 2012.

68. Eterno and Silverman 2012.

69. Kemp 2010.

70. Eterno and Silverman 2012; see also Jones-Brown, Gill, and Trone 2010.

71. Rosenfeld and Fornango 2014, 99.

72. See Rayman 2010a, 2010b, 2010c.

73. Didier 2011.

74. Fogelman 2010.

75. On the proliferation of accountability measures and their influence in health care, see Cutler, Huckman, and Landrum 2004; Jin and Sorenson 2006; Dafny and Dranove 2008; Pope 2009; Kim 2015.

76. Dixon-Woods and Perencevich 2013, 556.
77. Narins et al. 2005, 83.
78. Dranove et al. 2003.
79. McGivern and Fischer 2012, 295.
80. See Waring 2009.
81. Bevan and Hood 2006, 534.
82. Merry 2011, S52.
83. Gates 2013, 39; Gawande 2007, 254.
84. Morse 2009.
85. Shore and Wright 1997; Miller 2001.
86. Hazelkorn 2011.
87. See Lamont 2009.

APPENDIX A

1. Stevens 2007; Schleef 2006.
2. See, for example, Denzin 1978; Jick 1979.
3. Sauder and Lancaster 2006.
4. See Glaser and Strauss 1967: 45–55; Denzin 1978.
5. McCall and Simmons 1969.
6. Glaser and Strauss 1967, 61.
7. On one occasion, a boss sat in on our interview with a new director, and our impression was that this was for reasons of oversight as well as clarification. By contrast, another dean did not hesitate to grant us access to any employee, including an assistant dean who had just been fired.
8. After the second iteration of coding, we had seventeen general codes, including the topics "admissions," "student reactions," "changes in rank," "problems of quantification," and "positive effects." Each of these general codes contained numerous subthemes. For example, the general category "problems of quantification" comprised twenty-six subthemes (such as "exaggeration of small differences," "nonexperts defining criteria of excellence," and "a single rubric evaluating all schools"); "the positive effects" category contained twelve subthemes (such as "increased accountability," "improved career services," and "more information for constituents").
9. For additional methodological details see Sauder and Lancaster 2006.
10. Our role was mainly that of observer, but we contributed one post in October and one in April asking visitors their opinions of rankings as a source of information in making their decisions about where to apply to law school and where to attend law school. We received twenty-one posted responses to the first question, which ranged from "I'm only applying to top-twenty-five schools" to "I probably won't worry too much about them since I want to stay in Alabama." To the second question we received eleven responses over

two weeks, ranging from "I'm going to best school I get into" (using rankings to define best) to "I only got into one school so they don't matter." During this period, students seemed understandably more concerned with getting practical advice about their particular decisions ("Should I go to a top-thirty school and pay full tuition or take a good scholarship and go to a second-tier school") than with responding to a general query about rankings.

11. For a succinct summary of these issues, see DiMaggio 2014; see also Jerolmack and Khan 2014.

References |

Adams, Caralee. 2010. "Complexity and Competition Drive Demand for Consultants." *Education Week—College Bound,* June 8, 2010. Available at: http://blogs. edweek.org/edweek/college_bound/2010/06/rising_college_costs_and_competition_fuel_demand_for_consultants.html?cmp=SOC-SHR-FB (accessed July 24, 2014).

Alonso, William, and Paul Starr. 1987. *The Politics of Numbers.* New York: Russell Sage Foundation.

American Bar Association. 2014. "2014 Employment Questionnaire (For 2013 Graduates): Definitions and Instructions." *ABA Section of Legal Education and Admissions to the Bar.* Available at: http://employmentsummary.abaquestion naire.org/ (accessed November 22, 2015).

Arewa, Olufunmilayo B., Andrew P. Morriss, and William D. Henderson. 2014. "Enduring Hierarchies in American Legal Education." *Indiana Law Journal* 89(3): 941–1068.

Aronson, Joshua, Michael J. Lustina, Catherine Good, Kellie Keough, Claude M. Steele, and Joseph Brown. 1999. "When White Men Can't Do Math: Necessary and Sufficient Factors in Stereotype Threat." *Journal of Experimental Social Psychology* 35(1): 29–46.

Aviv, Rachel. 2014. "Wrong Answer: In an Era of High-Stakes Testing, a Struggling School Made a Shocking Choice." *New Yorker,* July 21.

Ayres, Ian, and Richard Brooks. 2005. "Does Affirmative Action Reduce the Number of Black Lawyers?" *Stanford Law Review* 57(6): 1807–54.

Becker, Howard S. 1963. *Outsiders: Studies in the Sociology of Deviance.* Glencoe, Ill.: Free Press of Glencoe.

Bell, Tom W. 2006. "Baylor's Score in the USN&WR Law School Rankings." *Agoraphilia: The Center for Blurbs in the Public Interest,* June 18, 2006. Available at: http://agoraphilia.blogspot.de/search?q=baylor+rankings (accessed August 3, 2014).

Bevan, Gwyn, and Christopher Hood. 2006. "What's Measured Is What Matters: Targets and Gaming in the English Public Health Care System." *Public Administration* 84(3): 517–38.

Bialik, Carl. 2005. "Small Change by U.S. News Leads to New Controversy in Rankings." *Wall Street Journal*, April 7. Available at: http://online.wsj.com/article/SB111279937006999640.html?publicf=yes (accessed August 3, 2014).

———. 2012. "Law-School Jobs Data Under Review." *Wall Street Journal*, March 16. Available at: http://blogs.wsj.com/numbers/law-school-jobs-data-under-review-1126/ (accessed August 3, 2014).

Bitter Staff. 2009. "Eight Hallmarks of a TTT Law School." *Bitter Lawyer* blog, April 10. Available at www.bitterlawyer.com/eight-hallmarks-of-a-ttt-school/ (accessed November 21, 2015).

Blau, Peter M., and Rebecca Zames Margulies. 1974. "A Research Replication: The Reputations of American Professional Schools." *Change: The Magazine of Higher Learning* 6(10): 42–47.

Bogue, Ernest Grady, and Kimberely Bingham Hall. 2003. *Quality and Accountability in Higher Education: Improving Policy, Enhancing Performance.* Westport, Conn.: Praeger.

Bourdieu, Pierre. 1984. *Distinction: A Social Critique of the Judgment of Taste.* Translated by Richard Nice. Cambridge, Mass.: Harvard University Press.

Bourdieu, Pierre, and Loic Wacquant. 1992. *An Invitation to Reflexive Sociology.* Chicago: University of Chicago Press.

Brooks, A. Phillips. 1998. "UT Law School Falls from Top 25; Officials Will Appeal U.S. News." *Austin American-Statesman*, February 20, p. A1.

Burke, Kenneth. 1966. *Language as Symbolic Action: Essays on Life, Literature, and Method.* Berkeley: University of California Press.

Burton, Daniel. 2011. "No More 'Third-Tier Toilet' for You to Worry about?" *Publius Online*, March 15. Available at: www.publiusonline.com/no-more-third-tier-toilet-for-you-to-worry-about/ (accessed July 26, 2014).

Burawoy, Michael. 1979. *Manufacturing Consent: Changes in the Labor Process under Monopoly Capitalism.* Chicago: University of Chicago Press.

Callon, Michel. 1998. "Introduction: The Embeddedness of Economic Markets in Economics." *Sociological Review* 46(S1): 1–57.

Callon, Michel, John Law, and Arie Rip, eds. 1986. *Mapping the Dynamics of Science and Technology: Sociology of Science in the Real World.* New York: Palgrave Macmillan.

Campbell, Donald T. 1957. "Factors Relevant to the Validity of Experiments in Social Settings." *Psychological Bulletin* 54(4): 297–312.

———. 1979. "Assessing the Impact of Planned Social Change." Report. *Evaluation and Program Planning* 2(1): 67–90.

Campos, Paul. 2012. *Don't Go to Law School (Unless): A Law Professor's Inside Guide to Maximizing Opportunity and Minimizing Risk.* Las Vegas: CreateSpace Independent Publishing Platform.

Carruthers, Bruce G., and Wendy Nelson Espeland. 1991. "Accounting for Rationality: Double-Entry Bookkeeping and the Rhetoric of Economic Rationality." *American Journal of Sociology* 97(1): 31–69.

Carson, John. 2007. *The Measure of Merit: Talents, Intelligence, and Inequality in the French and American Republics, 1750–1940*. Princeton: Princeton University Press.

Cerulo, Karen A. 2002. "Establishing a Sociology of Culture and Cognition." In *Culture in Mind: Toward a Sociology of Culture and Cognition*. New York: Routledge.

Chambers, David L., Timothy T. Clydesdale, William C. Kidder, and Richard O. Lempert. 2005. "The Real Impact of Eliminating Affirmative Action in American Law Schools: An Empirical Critique of Richard Sander's Study." *Stanford Law Review* 57(6): 1855–98.

Chandler, Matt. 2010. "Mutua Shares Vision for UB Law." *Buffalo Law Journal*, April 29, 2010. Available at: www.bizjournals.com/buffalo/blog/buffalo-law-journal/2010/04/mutua-shares-vision-for-ub-law.html?page=all (accessed August 4, 2014).

Chicago Tribune. 2012. "University of Chicago Law School Beats Northwestern in U.S. News Rankings Again." March 13.

Christin, Angele. 2014. "Clicks or Pulitzers? Web Journalists and Their Work in the United States and France." Ph.D. diss., Princeton University.

Clancy, Kevin Finian. 1998. "The Question of Group Rights: With Special Reference to Affirmative Action." Ph.D. diss., Trinity College, Dublin.

Clinedinst, Melissa E., Sarah F. Hurley, and David A. Hawkins. 2012. "2011 State of College Admissions." Arlington, Va.: National Association for College Admissions Counseling. Available at: www.nacacnet.org/research/PublicationsResources/Marketplace/Documents/SOCA2011.pdf (accessed November 21, 2015).

Cohen, Michael D., James G. March, and Johan P. Olsen. 1972. "A Garbage Can Model of Organizational Choice." *Administrative Science Quarterly* 17(1): 1–25.

Cohn, Bernard S. 1987. *An Anthropologist Among the Historians and Other Essays*. Delhi: Oxford University Press.

Coleman, Richard Patrick, Lee Rainwater, and Kent A. McClelland. 1978. *Social Standing in American: New Dimensions of Class*. New York: Basic Books.

Colyvas, Jeanette A. 2012. "Performance Measures as Formal Structures and through the Lens of Social Mechanisms: When Do They Work and How Do They Influence?" *American Journal of Education* 118(2): 167–97.

Cotts, Cynthia. 1998. "Deans and Watchdogs Flunk U.S. News Law School Rankings." *National Law Journal*, March 2, p. A13.

Croizet, Jean-Claude, and Theresa Claire. 1998. "Extending the Concept of Stereotype Threat to Social Class: The Intellectual Underperformance of Students from Low Socioeconomic Backgrounds." *Personality and Social Psychology Bulletin* 24(6): 588–94.

Cutler, David, Robert Huckman, and Mary Beth Landrum. 2004. "The Role of Information in Medical Markets: An Analysis of Publicly Reported Outcomes in Cardiac Surgery." *American Economic Review* 94(2): 342–46.

Dafny, Leenore, and David Dranove. 2008. "Do Report Cards Tell Consumers Anything They Don't Already Know? The Case of Medicare HMOs." *Rand Journal of Economics* 39(3): 790–821.

Dale, Stacy Berg, and Alan B. Krueger. 2002. "Estimating the Payoff to Attending a More Selective College: An Application of Selection on Observables and Unobservables." *Quarterly Journal of Economics* 107(4): 1491–27.

Daston, Lorraine. 1992. "Objectivity and Escape from Perspective." *Representations* 40(4): 81–128.

Davis, Kevin E., Benedict Kingsbury, and Sally Engle Merry, eds. 2012. *Governance by Indicators: Global Power Through Quantification and Rankings.* New York: Oxford University Press.

DeLeon, Ken. 2006. "Interview with Edward Tom, Dean of Admissions U.C. Berkeley Boalt Hall School." *Top Law Schools.* Available at: www.top-law-schools. com/tom-interview.html (accessed November 22, 2015).

Denzin, Norman. 1978. *Sociological Methods: A Sourcebook.* 2nd ed. New York: McGraw Hill.

Desrosières, Alain. 2002. *The Politics of Large Numbers: A History of Statistical Reasoning.* Cambridge, Mass.: Harvard University Press.

Dey, Eric L., Alexander W. Astin, and William S. Korn. 1991. *The American Freshman: Twenty-Five Year Trends, 1966–1990.* Los Angeles: Higher Education Research Institute.

Diamond-Dalessandro, Susan P., Lisa A. Stilwell, and Lynda M. Reese. 2005. "LSAT Performance with Regional, Gender, and Racial/Ethnic Breakdowns: 1997–1998 through 2003–2004 Testing Years." LSAT Technical Report 04-01. Newtown, Penn.: Law School Admission Council.

Dichev, Ilia D. 2001. "News or Noise? Estimating the Noise in the *U.S. News* University Rankings." *Research in Higher Education* 42(3): 237–66.

Didier, Emmanuel. 2011. "L'État Néolibéral Ment-il? 'Chanstique' et Statistiques de Dolice." *Terrain* 57: 66–81.

Dill, David D., and Maarja Soo. 2005. "Academic Quality, League Tables, and Public Policy: A Cross-National Analysis of University Ranking Systems." *Higher Education* 49(4): 495–534.

DiMaggio, Paul J. 2014. "Comment on Jerolmack and Khan, 'Talk Is Cheap': Ethnography and the Attitudinal Fallacy." *Sociological Methods & Research* 43(2): 232–37.

DiMaggio, Paul J., and Walter W. Powell. 1983. "The Iron Cage Revisited: Institutional Isomorphism and Collective Rationality in Organizational Fields." *American Sociological Review* 48(2): 147–60.

Dinovitzer, Ronit, Bryant G. Garth, and Joyce S. Sterling. 2013. "Buyers' Remorse: An Empirical Assessment of the Desirability of a Lawyer Career." *Journal of Legal Education* 63(2): 211–34.

Diver, Colin. 2005. "Is There Life After Rankings?" *The Atlantic*, November 1. Available at: www.theatlantic.com/magazine/archive/2005/11/is-there-life-after-rankings/304308/ (accessed August 31, 2014).

Dixon-Woods, Mary, and Eli N. Perencevich. 2013. "When Counting Central Line Infections Counts." *Infection Control and Hospital Epidemiology* 34(6): 555–57.

Dobbin, Frank. 1997. *Forging Industrial Policy: The United States, Britain and France in the Railway Age.* New York: Cambridge University Press.

Dranove, David, Daniel Kessler, Mark McClellan, and Mark Satterthwaite. 2003. "Is More Information Better? The Effects of 'Report Cards' on Health Care Providers." *Journal of Political Economy* 111(3): 555–88.

Droit Femme. 2006. "Should You Transfer Law Schools?" May 12. *Droit Femme* blog. Available at: http://droitfemme.blogspot.com/2006/05/should-you-transfer-law-schools.html (accessed July 30, 2014).

Edelman, Lauren B. 1992. "Legal Ambiguity and Symbolic Structures: Organizational Mediation of the Civil Rights Law." *American Journal of Sociology* 97(6): 1531–76.

Education Portal. 2010. "Study Explores Marketing Trends in Higher Education." July 10. Available at: http://education-portal.com/articles/Study_Explores_Marketing_Trends_in_Higher_Education.html (accessed August 31, 2014).

Edwards, Lynda. 2008. "The Rankings Czar." *American Bar Association Journal,* April 1. Available at: www.abajournal.com/magazine/article/the_rankings_czar (accessed November 22, 2015).

Efrati, Amir. 2008. "Law School Rankings Reviewed to Deter 'Gaming.'" *Wall Street Journal,* August 27. Available at: http://online.wsj.com/news/articles/SB121971712700771731 (accessed July 30, 2014).

Ehrenberg, Ronald G. 2002. *Tuition Rising: Why College Costs So Much.* Cambridge, Mass.: Harvard University Press.

Ehrenreich, Barbara. 1989. *Fear of Falling: The Inner Life of the Middle Classic.* New York: Pantheon.

Elsbach, Kimberly D., and Roderick M. Kramer. 1996. "Members' Responses to Organizational Identity Threats: Encountering and Countering the Business Week Rankings." *Administrative Science Quarterly* 41(3): 442–76.

Elster, Jon. 1989. *Nuts and Bolts for the Social Sciences.* New York: Cambridge University Press.

Espeland, Wendy Nelson. 1998. *The Struggle for Water: Politics, Identity and Rationality in the American Southwest.* Chicago: University of Chicago Press.

———. 2000. "Bureaucratizing Democracy, Democratizing Bureaucracy." *Law and Social Inquiry* 24(4): 1077–1109.

———. 2015. "Narrating Numbers." In *The World of Indicators: The Making of Government Knowledge Through Quantification,* edited by Richard Rottenburg, Sally E. Merry, Sung Joon-Park, and Johanna Mugler. Cambridge: Cambridge University Press.

———. Forthcoming. "Reverse Engineering and Emotional Attachments as Mechanisms Mediating the Effects of Quantification." *Historical Social Research* 41(2).

Espeland, Wendy Nelson, and Michael Sauder. 2007. "Rankings and Reactivity: How Public Measures Recreate Social Worlds." *American Journal of Sociology* 113(1): 1–40.

———. 2009. "Rankings and Diversity." *Southern California Review of Law and Social Justice* 18(3): 587–610.

———. 2012. "The Dynamism of Indicators." In *Governance by Indicators: Global Power Through Quantification and Rankings,* edited by Kevin E. Davis, Benedict Kingsbury, and Sally Engle Merry. New York: Oxford University Press.

Espeland, Wendy Nelson, and Mitchell Stevens. 1998. "Commensuration as a Social Process." *Annual Review of Sociology* 24: 312–43.

Espeland, Wendy Nelson, and Berit Irene Vannebo. 2007. "Accountability, Quantification, and Law." *Annual Review of Law and Social Science* 3: 21–43.

Eterno, John A., and Eli B. Silverman. 2012. *The Crime Numbers Game: Management by Manipulation.* Boca Raton, Fla.: CRC Press.

Faust, Drew Gilpin. 2008. *The Republic of Suffering: Death and the American Civil War.* New York: Alfred A. Knopf.

Ferraro, Fabrizio, Jeffrey Pfeffer, and Robert Sutton. 2005. "Economics Language and Assumptions: How Theories Can Become Self-Fulfilling." *Academy of Management Review* 30(1): 8–24.

Fitzsimmons, William. 1991. "Risky Business." *Harvard Magazine,* January–February, p. 23–29.

Flanigan, Sam, and Robert Morse. 2014. "Methodology: 2014 Best Law School Rankings." *U.S. News & World Report—Education,* March 10. Available at: www.usnews.com/education/best-graduate-schools/top-law-schools/articles/2014/03/10/methodology-2015-best-law-schools-rankings (accessed August 4, 2014).

Fligstein, Neil, and Doug McAdam. 2012. *A Theory of Fields.* New York: Oxford University Press.

Fogelman, Shay. 2010. "Winning on Points." *Haaretz.com,* July 9. Available at: www.haaretz.com/weekend/magazine/winning-on-points-1.300971 (accessed August 13, 2014).

Foucault, Michel. 1977. *Discipline and Punish: The Birth of the Prison.* London: Allen Lane.

———. 1991. "Governmentality." In *The Foucault Effect: Studies in Governmentality with Two Lectures by and an Interview with Michel Foucault,* edited by Graham Bruchell, Colin Gordon, and Peter Miller. Chicago: University of Chicago Press.

Fourcade, Marion, and Kieran Healy. 2013. "Classification Situations: Life-Chances in the Neoliberal Era." *Accounting, Organizations and Society* 38(00): 559–72.

Frank, Robert H., and Philip J. Cook. 1996. *The Winner-Take-All Society: Why the Few at the Top Get So Much More Than the Rest of Us.* New York: Penguin Books.

Friedman, Lawrence, and Louis Schulze. 2012. "Not Everyone Works in Biglaw: A Response to Neil J. Dilloff." *Maryland Law Review Endnotes* 71: 41–50.

Gallagher, Anne, and Janie A. Chuang. 2012. "The Use of Indicators to Measure Government Responses to Human Trafficking." In *Governance by Indicators: Global Power Through Quantification and Rankings,* edited by Kevin E. Davis, Benedict Kingsbury, and Sally Engle Merry. New York: Oxford University Press.

Garth, Bryant. 2013. "Crises, Crisis Rhetoric, and Competition in Legal Education: A Sociological Perspective on the (Latest) Crisis of the Legal Profession and Legal Education." *Stanford Law & Policy Review* 24(2): 503–32.

Gates, Bill. 2013. "In the War on Disease, Measurement Matters." *Time,* September 30, p. 39.

Gawande, Atul. 2007. *Better: A Surgeon's Notes on Performance.* New York: Picador.

Gellhorn, Ernest. 1968. "The Law Schools and the Negro." *Duke Law Journal* 17(6): 1069–99.

Glaser, Barney G., and Anselm L. Strauss. 1967. *The Discovery of Grounded Theory: Strategies for Qualitative Research.* New Brunswick, N.J.: Aldine Transaction.

Goffman, Erving. 1959. *The Presentation of Self in Everyday Life.* New York: Doubleday.

Goody, Jack. 1997. *Representations and Contradictions: Ambivalence Towards Images, Theatre, Fiction, Relics, and Sexuality.* Malden, Mass.: Blackwell Publishers.

Gregory, Alice. 2014. "Pictures from an Institution." *The New Yorker,* September 29.

Groves, Harry. 1965. "Report on the Minority Groups Project." In *Association of American Law Schools 1965 Annual Meeting Proceedings, Part 1.* Washington, D.C.: Association of American Law Schools.

Guinier, Lani. 2003. "Admissions Rituals as Political Acts: Guardians at the Gates of Our Democratic Ideals." *Harvard Law Review* 117(1): 133–224.

Guttenplan, D.D. 2013. "Vying for a Spot on the World's A List." *New York Times,* April 14, ED12.

Guzmán, Mónica. 2006. "Dean of UH Law Center Resigning." *Houston Chronicle,* April 18. Available at: www.chron.com/news/houston-texas/article/Dean-of-UH-Law-Center-resigning-1901006.php (accessed August 3, 2014).

Hacking, Ian. 1986. "Making Up People." In *Reconstructing Individualism,* edited by Thomas Heller, Morton Sosna, and David E. Wellbery. Stanford: Stanford University Press.

———. 1990. *The Taming of Chance.* New York: Cambridge University Press.

Halliday, Terence C. 2012. "Legal Yardsticks: International Financial Institutions as Diagnosticians and Designers of the Laws of Nations." In *Governance by Indicators: Global Power through Quantification and Rankings,* edited by Kevin E. Davis, Benedict Kingsbury, and Sally Engle Merry. New York: Oxford University Press.

Hansmann, Henry. 1999. "Higher Education as an Associative Good." In *Forum Futures: 1999 Papers,* edited by Maureen Devlin and Joel Meyerson. Washington, D.C.: Foundation for the Future of Higher Education.

Hazelkorn, Ellen. 2007a. "The Impact of League Tables and Ranking Systems on Higher Education Decision Making." *Higher Education Management and Policy* 19(2): 87–110.

———. 2007b. "How Do Rankings Impact on Higher Education?" *Institutional Management in Higher Education Info,* December, p. 1–2.

———. 2008. "Learning to Live with League Tables and Ranking: The Experiences of Institutional Leaders." *Higher Education Policy* 21(2): 193–215.

———. 2009. "Rankings and the Battle for World-Class Excellence: Institutional Strategies and Policy Choices." *Higher Education Management and Policy* 21(1): 1–22.

———. 2010. "Handle with Care." *Times Higher Education*, July 8. Available at: www.timeshighereducation.co.uk/412342.article (accessed August 31, 2014).

———. 2011. *Rankings and the Reshaping of Higher Education.* New York: Palgrave Macmillan.

Healy, Guy. 2010. "Ranking Shock Has No Impact." *The Australian*, September 15. Available at: http://theaustralian.com.au/higher-education/ (accessed August 31, 2014).

Hedstrom, Peter, and Richard Swedberg, eds. 1998. *Social Mechanisms: An Analytic Approach to Social Theory.* New York: Cambridge University Press.

Hein, Carola, Jeffrey Diefendorf, and Yorifusa Ishida, eds. 2003. *Rebuilding Urban Japan After 1945.* New York: Palgrave Macmillan.

Heimer, Carol. A. 1992. "Doing Your Job and Helping Your Friends: Universalistic Norms About Obligations to Particular Others in Networks." In *Networks and Organizations: Structure, Form and Action,* edited by Nitin Nohria and Robert G. Eccles. Boston: Harvard Business School Press.

———. 2001. "Cases and Biographies: An Essay on Routinization and the Nature of Comparison." *Annual Review of Sociology* 27: 47–76.

Henderson, William D. 2007. "Transfers, US News Gaming, and Brand Dilution." *Empirical Legal Studies* blog, October 18. Available at: http://www.elsblog.org/the_empirical_legal_studi/2007/10/transfers-us-ne.html#more (accessed July 30, 2014).

Henderson, William D., and Andrew P. Morriss. 2006. "Student Quality as Measured by LSAT Scores: Migration Patterns in the US News Rankings Era." *Indiana Law Journal* 81(1): 163–204.

Henderson, William D., and Rachel M. Zahorsky. 2011. "Law Job Stagnation May Have Started Before the Recession—And It May Be a Sign of Lasting Change." *ABA Journal* 97(7): 2–3.

Hill, Kashmir, and David Lat. 2010. "Clarence Thomas Clarifies: His Clerks Aren't 'TTT.'" *Above the Law*, February 6. Available at: http://abovethelaw.com/2010/02/clarence-thomas-clarifies-his-clerks-arent-ttt/ (accessed July 26, 2014).

Hoskin, Keith W. 1996. "The 'Awful Idea of Accountability': Inscribing People into the Measurement of Objects." In *Accountability, Power, Ethos and the Technologies of Managing,* edited by Rolland Munro and Jan Mouritsen. London: International Thomson Business Press.

Hoskin, Keith W., and Richard H. Macve. 1986. "Accounting and the Examination: A Genealogy of Disciplinary Power." *Accounting, Organizations and Society* 11(2): 105–36.

Hughes, Raymond M. 1925. *A Study of the Graduate Schools of America.* Oxford, Ohio: Miami University Press.

———. 1934. *Report of Committee on Graduate Instruction.* Washington, D.C.: American Council on Education.

Hyland, Andy. 2012. "KU's Law School Drops Again in National Rankings, While 12 Programs Make Top 10." *Lawrence (Kansas) Journal-World,* March 13. Available at: www2.ljworld.com/news/2012/mar/13/kus-law-school-drops-again-national-rankings-while/ (accessed August 3, 2014).

Hynes, Mary Ann, and Cie B. Armstead. 2006. "Where Are They? The Legal Profession Reaches Out for Future Minority Lawyers." *ABA Business Law Section Newsletter,* September–October. Available at: http://apps.americanbar.org/buslaw/blt/2006-09-10/armstead.shtml (accessed August 31, 2014).

Igo, Sarah E. 2009. *The Averaged American: Surveys, Citizens, and the Making of a Mass Public.* Cambridge, Mass.: Harvard University Press.

Institute for Higher Education Policy. 2009. "Impact of College Rankings on Institutional Decision-Making: Four Country Case Studies." *Institute for Higher Education Policy Issue Brief,* May, p. 1–28.

Internet Legal Research Group. 2008. "2008 Raw Data Law School Rankings." Available at: www.ilrg.com/rankings/law/index.php/2/desc/LawSchool/2008 (accessed July 31, 2014).

———. 2015. "America's Largest 350 Law Firms." Available at: www.ilrg.com/nlj250 (accessed November 15, 2015).

Ishikawa, Mayumi. 2009. "University Rankings, Global Models, and Emerging Hegemony: Critical Analysis from Japan." *Journal of Studies in International Education* 13(2): 159–73.

Jacobs, Ryan. 2012. "Just Like in 'The Wire': Real FBI Crime Stats Are 'Juked.'" *Mother Jones* magazine's website, June 19. Available at: www.motherjones.com/mojo/2012/06/fbi-crime-stats-fudged-the-wire-nypd (accessed December 17, 2015).

Jencks, Christopher, and Meredith Phillips. 1998. *The Black-White Test Score Gap.* Washington, D.C.: Brookings Institution Press.

Jencks, Christopher, and David Riesman. 1968. *The Academic Revolution.* New York: Doubleday.

Jensen, Casper Bruun. 2011. "Making Lists, Enlisting Scientists: The Bibliometric Indicator, Uncertainty, and Emergent Agency." *Science Studies* 24(2): 64–84.

Jerolmack, Colin, and Shamus Khan. 2014. "Talk Is Cheap: Ethnography and the Attitudinal Fallacy." *Sociological Methods & Research* 43(2): 178–209.

Jick, Todd D. 1979. "Mixing Qualitative and Quantitative Methods: Triangulation in Action." *Administrative Science Quarterly* 24(4): 602–11.

Jin, Ginger Z., and Alan T. Sorensen. 2006 "Information and Consumer Choice: The Value of Publicized Health Plan Ratings." *Journal of Health Economics* 25(2): 248–75.

Johnson, Alex M. 2006. "The Destruction of the Holistic Approach to Admissions: The Pernicious Effects of Rankings." *Indiana Law Journal* 81(1): 309–58.

Johnson, Conrad. 2009. "A Disturbing Trend in Law School Diversity." *Lawyering in the Digital Age, Columbia University School of Law.* Available at: http://www2. law.columbia.edu/civilrights (accessed July 31, 2014).

Jones, Leigh. 2005. "Law Schools Play the Rank Game." *National Law Journal* 26(80): 1.

———. 2006. "Law School Deans Feel Heat from Rankings." *National Law Journal* 27(6): 6.

Jones, Robert L. 2014. "A Longitudinal Analysis of the U.S. News Law School Academic Reputation Scores between 1998 and 2013." *Florida State University Law Review* 40(Summer): 722–90.

Jones-Brown, Delores, Jaspreet Gill, and Jennifer Trone. 2010. *Stop, Question, and Frisk Policing Practices in New York City: A Primer.* New York: John Jay College of Criminal Justice.

Kalev, Alexandra, Frank Dobbin, and Erin Kelly. 2006. "Best Practices or Best Guesses? Assessing the Efficacy of Corporate Affirmative Action and Diversity Policies." *American Sociological Review* 71(4): 589–627.

Kanter, Rosabeth Moss. 1977. *Men and Women of the Corporation.* New York: Basic Books.

Karabel, Jerome. 2005. *The Chosen: The Hidden History of Admission and Exclusion at Harvard, Yale, and Princeton.* Boston, Mass.: Houghton Mifflin Harcourt.

Katz, Jack. 1983. "A Theory of Qualitative Methodology: The Social System of Analytical Fieldwork." In *Contemporary Field Research,* edited by Robert Emerson. Prospect Heights, Ill.: Waveland.

Kemp, Joe. 2010. "NYPD Brass Pressuring Cops to Keep Down Crime Stats: Report." *New York Daily News,* August 27. Available at: www.nydailynews.com/ new-york/nypd-brass-pressuring-cops-crime-stats-report-article-1.204618 (accessed December 17, 2015).

Kidder, William C. 2003. "The Struggle for Access from Sweatt to Grutter: A History of African American, Latino, and American Indian Law School Admissions, 1950–2000." *Harvard Blackletter Law Journal* 19: 1–42.

Kim, Jerry W. 2015. "Halos or Egos? External Rankings and Internal Collaboration in Multi-Specialty U.S. Hospitals 2002–2011." Working Paper. New York: Columbia University.

Klein, Stephen, and Laura Hamilton. 1998. "The Validity of the U.S. News and World Report Rankings of the ABA Law Schools." Study commissioned by the American Association of Law Schools.

Klim, Frank. 2003. "May 9—Gary Vause, Stetson University College of Law Dean, Dies." Press release, May 9. Available at: www.stetson.edu/law/news/index. php/2003/05/09/may-9-gary-vause-stetson-university-college-of-law-dean-dies/#.VkYWV1JUFpk (accessed November 13, 2015).

Korobkin, Russell. 1998. "In Praise of Law School Rankings: Solutions to Coordination and Collective Action Problems." *Texas Law Review* 77(2): 403–28.

Labi, Aisha. 2008. "Obsession with Rankings Goes Global." *Chronicle of Higher Education,* October 17, p. A27.

———. 2010. "Germany Pursues Excellence over Egalitarianism." *Chronicle of Higher Education,* June 27. Available at: http://chronicle.com/article/Germany-Pursues-Excellence/66048/ (accessed August 14, 2014).

Lamont, Michèle. 2009. *How Professors Think: Inside the Curious World of Academic Judgment.* Cambridge, Mass.: Harvard University Press.

Lamont, Michèle, and Marcel Fournier, eds. 1992. *Cultivating Differences: Symbolic Boundaries and the Making of Inequality.* Chicago: University of Chicago Press.

LaPiana, William P. 2001. "A History of the Law School Admission Council and the LSAT." Keynote address, Law School Admission Council 1998 annual meeting. Available at: www.lsac.org/docs/default-source/publications-(lsac-resources)/history-lsac-lsat.pdf (accessed November 24, 2015).

Lareau, Annette. 2003. *Unequal Childhoods: Race, Class, and Family Life.* Berkeley: University of California Press.

Latour, Bruno. 1987. *Science in Action.* Cambridge, Mass.: Harvard University Press.

———. 2005. *Reassembling the Social: An Introduction to Actor-Network Theory.* New York: Oxford University Press.

Law School Admission Council. 1987. *The Official Guide to U.S. Law Schools.* Newton, Pa.: Law School Admission Council.

———. 2006. "Law School Applicant Study." Newton, Pa.: Law School Admission Council.

———. 2014a. "End of Year Summary: ABA Applicant, Applications, Admissions, Enrollments, LSATS, CAS." Available at: www.lsac.org/lsacresources/data/lsac-volume-summary (accessed July 26, 2014).

———. 2014b. "Three-Year Applicant Volume Graphs." Available at: www.lsac.org/lsacresources/data/three-year-volume (accessed August 31, 2014).

———. 2014c. "Cautionary Policies Concerning LSAT Scores and Related Services." Available at: www.lsac.org/docs/default-source/publications-%28lsac-resources%29/cautionarypolicies.pdf (accessed November 21, 2015).

———. 2014d. "LSAC Statement of Good Admission and Financial Aid Practices—JD Programs." Available at: www.lsac.org/docs/default-source/publications-%28lsac-resources%29/statementofgoodadm.pdf (accessed November 21, 2015).

Law School Survey of Student Engagement. 2005. "Student Engagement in Law School: A First Look." Available at: http://eric.ed.gov/?id=ED528392 (accessed November 21, 2015).

Leichter, Matt. 2012. "The Juris Doctor Is 'Versatile' Thanks Mainly to Numerous Logical Fallacies." *American Law Daily,* August 14. Available at: www.rocketnews.com/2012/08/the-juris-doctor-is-versatile-thanks-mainly-to-numerous-logical-fallacies/ (accessed November 21, 2015).

Leipold, James. 2011. "The Legal Job Market for New Graduates Looks a Lot like It Did 15 Years Ago (Only Worse)." National Association for Law Placement website, June. Available at: www.nalp.org/perspectives2011commentary (accessed November 22, 2015).

Leiter, Brian. 2003. "The U.S. News Law School Rankings: A Guide for the Perplexed." *Brian Leiter's Law School Rankings*, May. Available at: www.leiter rankings.com/usnews/guide.shtml (accessed July 30, 2014).

———. 2008. "Schools That Take the Largest Number of Transfers (Relative to the Size of Their 1L Class)." *Brian Leiter's Law School Reports*, June 3. Available at: http://leiterlawschool.typepad.com/leiter/2008/06/schools-that-ta.html (accessed July 30, 2014).

———. 2012. "Post-Tenure Review Moves Slowly at Colorado … or Whatever Happened to Paul Campos." *Brian Leiter's Law School Reports*, October 11. Available at: http://leiterlawschool.typepad.com/leiter/2012/10/post-tenure-review-moves-slowly-at-coloradoor-whatever-happened-to-paul-campos.html (accessed August 4, 2014).

Lemann, Nicholas. 1999. *The Big Test: The Secret History of the American Meritocracy.* New York: Farrar, Straus and Giroux.

———. 2000. "The Empathy Defense: Can the University of Michigan Save Affirmative Action?" *The New Yorker,* December 12, 46–51.

Lempert, Richard. 2002. "Pseudo Science as News: Ranking the Nation's Law Schools." Paper presented at the Annual Meeting of the American Association of Law Schools, New Orleans (January 3–5).

———. 2014. "Failing Law Schools, by Brian. Z. Tamanaha: A Review." *Contemporary Sociology* 43(2): 269–71.

Leonard, Wendy, and Sara Israelsen-Hartley. 2010. "BYU, Utah Tie in U.S. News Law School Rankings." *Deseret News,* April 17. Available at: www.deseretnews.com/article/705377768/BYU-Utah-tie-in-US-News-law-school-rankings.html?pg=all (accessed July 26, 2014).

Liu, Nian C., and Ying Cheng. 2005. "The Academic Ranking of World Universities." *Higher Education in Europe* 30(2): 127–36.

Longley, Charles. 1998a. *Law School Admissions, 1985 to 1995: Assessing the Effect of Application Volume.* LSAC Research Report Series. Newtown, Pa.: Law School Admission Council.

———. 1998b. *Who Gets the App? Explaining Law School Application Volume, 1993 to 1996.* LSAC Research Report Series. Newtown, Pa.: Law School Admission Council.

Lowery, Wesley, and Josh Hicks. 2014. "Troubling Report Sparks New Wave of Calls for VA Chief's Resignation" *Washington Post,* May 28.

Luxbacher, Great. 2013. "World University Rankings: How Much Influence Do They Really Have?" *The Guardian,* September 10. Available at: www.theguardian.com/higher-education-network/blog/2013/sep/10/university-rankings-influence-government-policy (accessed August 13, 2014).

MacKenzie, Donald A. 1993. *Inventing Accuracy: A Historical Sociology of Nuclear Missile Guidance.* Cambridge, Mass.: MIT Press.

———. 2006. "Is Economics Performative? Option Theory and the Construction of Derivatives Markets." *Journal of the History of Economic Thought* 28(1): 29–55.

MacKenzie, Donald, and Yuval Millo. 2003. "Constructing a Market, Performing Theory: The Historical Sociology of a Financial Derivatives Exchange." *American Journal of Sociology* 109(1): 107–45.

Mangan, Katherine. 2012a. "Lawsuits over Job Placement Rates Threaten 20 More." *Chronicle of Higher Education,* March 14. Available at http://chronicle.com/article/Lawsuits-Over-Job-Placement/131163/ (accessed August 31, 2014).

———. 2012b. "Judge Dismisses Lawsuit Accusing Law School of Inflating Job and Salary Data." *Chronicle of Higher Education,* March 21. Available at: http://chronicle.com/article/Judge-Dismisses-Lawsuit/131266/ (accessed August 4, 2014).

March, James G., and Herbert A. Simon. 1958. *Organizations.* New York: Wiley.

Marcus, Jon. 2013. "Caught Cheating: Colleges Falsify Admissions Data for Higher Rankings." *NBC News,* March 20. Available at: http://investigations.nbcnews.com/_news/2013/03/20/17376664-caught-cheating-colleges-falsify-admissions-data-for-higher-rankings (accessed December 17, 2015).

Marginson, Simon, and Marijk van der Wende. 2007. "To Rank or to Be Ranked: The Impact of Global Rankings in Higher Education." *Journal of Studies in International Education* 11(3/4): 306–29.

Martin, John Levi. 2003. "What Is Field Theory?" *American Journal of Sociology* 109(1): 1–49.

Matasar, Richard A. 2005. "The Rise and Fall of American Legal Education." *New York Law School Law Review* 49(2): 465–504.

McCall, George J., and Jerry L. Simmons. 1969. *Issues in Participant Observation.* Reading, Mass.: Addison-Wesley.

McDonough, Patricia. 1994. "Buying and Selling Higher Education: The Social Construction of the College Applicant." *Journal of Higher Education* 65(4): 427–46.

McDonough, Patricia, Anthony Lising Antonio, MaryBeth Walpole, and Leonor Perez. 1997. "College Rankings: Who Uses Them and with What Impact." Paper presented at the Annual Meeting of the American Educational Research Association, Chicago (March).

———. 1998. "College Rankings: Democratized College Knowledge for Whom?" *Research in Higher Education* 39(5): 513–37.

McGivern, Gerry, and Michael D. Fischer. 2012. "Reactivity and Reactions to Regulatory Transparency in Medicine, Psychotherapy, and Counselling." *Social Science & Medicine* 74(3): 289–96.

McGuire, Michael D. 1995. "Validity Issues for Reputational Studies." *New Directions for Institutional Research* 88: 45–59.

McPherson, Miller, Lynn Smith-Lovin, and James M. Cook. 2001. "Birds of a Feather: Homophily in Social Networks." *Annual Review of Sociology* 27: 415–44.

Mehta, Jal. 2013. *The Allure of Order: High Hopes, Dashed Expectations, and the Troubled Quest to Remake American Schooling.* New York: Oxford University Press.

Merry, Sally. 2011. "Measuring the World: Indicators, Human Rights, and Global Governance." *Current Anthropology* 52(S3): S83–S95.

Merry, Sally, Kevin E. Davis, and Benedict Kingsbury. 2015. *The Quiet Power of Indicators: Measuring Governance, Corruption, and Rule of Law.* Cambridge: Cambridge University Press.

Merton, Robert K. 1967. *On Theoretical Sociology.* New York: Free Press.

———. 1968. *Social Theory and Social Structure.* New York: Free Press.

Meyer, John W., and Brian Rowan. 1977. "Institutionalized Organizations: Formal Structure as Myth and Ceremony." *American Journal of Sociology* 83(2): 340–63.

Miller, Peter. 2001. "Governing by Numbers: Why Calculative Practices Matter." *Social Research* 68(2): 379–96.

Miller, Peter, and Ted O'Leary. 1987. "Accounting the Construction of the Governable Person." *Accounting, Organizations and Society* 12(3): 235–65.

Miller, Peter, and Nikolas Rose. 1990. "Governing Economic Life." *Economy and Society* 19(1): 1–31.

Monks, James, and Ronald G. Ehrenberg. 1999. "The Impact of U.S. News and World Report College Rankings on Admissions Outcomes and Pricing Policies at Selective Private Institutions." NBER Working Paper No. 7227. Cambridge, Mass.: National Bureau of Economic Research. Available at: www.nber.org/papers/w7227 (accessed November 22, 2015).

Moos, Christian. 2015. "A Sociology of Rankings: A Longitudinal Examination of the *Financial Times* MBA Rankings." Ph.D. diss., London School of Economics.

Morriss, Andrew P., and William D. Henderson. 2008. "Measuring Outcomes: Post-Graduation Measures of Success in the US News & World Report Law School Rankings." *Indiana Law Journal* 83(3): 791–834.

Morse, Robert J. 2005. "U.S. News and World Report's Law School Rankings: How and Why U.S. News Does Them." Paper presented at the annual meeting of the Law School Admission Council, San Diego, California (June 2005).

———. 2008a. "What Secretary Spellings Thinks of the College Rankings." *Morse Code: Inside the College Rankings,* July 9. Available at: www.usnews.com/education/blogs/college-rankings-blog/2008/01/09/what-secretary-spellings-thinks-of-the-college-rankings (accessed July 23, 2014).

———. 2008b. "Changing the Law School Ranking Formula." *Morse Code: Inside the College Rankings,* June 26. Available at: www.usnews.com/education/blogs/college-rankings-blog/2008/06/26/changing-the-law-school-ranking-formula (accessed July 30, 2014).

———. 2008c. "The Law School Rankings Debate, Part 2." *Morse Code: Inside the College Rankings,* July 2. Available at: www.usnews.com/education/blogs/

college-rankings-blog/2008/07/02/the-law-school-rankings-debate-part-2 (accessed July 30, 2014).

———. 2009. "Do the Rankings 'Punish' Law Schools?" *Morse Code: Inside the College Rankings,* February 2. Available at: www.usnews.com/education/blogs/college-rankings-blog/2009/02/02/do-the-rankings-punish-law-schools (accessed July 26, 2014).

———. 2013. "Why Howard University Fell in the Best Colleges Rankings." *Morse Code: Inside College Rankings,* October 7. Available at: www.usnews.com/education/blogs/college-rankings-blog/2013/10/07/why-howard-university-fell-in-the-best-colleges-rankings (accessed July 24, 2014).

Münch, Richard. 2014. *Academic Capitalism: Universities in the Global Struggle for Excellence.* London: Routledge.

Mystal, Elie. 2013a. "Responding to the U.S. News Rankings: The Parade of Butthurt Deans Begins Now." *Above the Law,* March 12. Available at: http://abovethelaw.com/2013/03/responding-to-the-new-u-s-news-rankings-the-parade-of-butthurt-deans-begins (accessed August 3, 2014).

———. 2013b. "Some Students Want Their Deans Fired After Poor Showing in the U.S. News Rankings (and One Head That's Already Rolled)." *Above the Law,* March 14. Available at: http://abovethelaw.com/2013/03/some-students-want-their-deans-fired-after-poor-showing-in-the-u-s-news-rankings-and-one-head-thats-already-rolled/2/ (accessed August 3, 2014).

———. 2013c. "Celebrity Law Pro Death Match: Paul Campos v. Brian Leiter." *Above the Law,* March 8. Available at: http://abovethelaw.com/2013/03/celebrity-law-prof-death-match-paul-campos-v-brian-leiter/ (accessed August 4, 2014).

Narins, Craig R., Ann M. Dozier, Frederick Ling, and Wojciech Zareba. 2005. "The Influence of Public Reporting of Outcome Data on Medical Decision Making by Physicians." *Archives of Internal Medicine* 165(1): 83–87.

National Association for Law Placement. 2004. "The Use and Influence of School Informational Resources." Washington, D.C.: National Association of Law Placement.

———. 2013. "Law School Class of 2012 Finds More Jobs, Starting Salaries Rise—But Large Class Size Hurts Overall Employment Rate." National Association of Law Placement website, "Employment for the Class of 2012—Selected Findings." Available at: www.nalp.org/uploads/Classof2012SelectedFindings.pdf (accessed August 4, 2014).

———. 2015a. "Employment Rate for New Law Graduates Rises by More Than Two Percentage Points—but Overall Number of Jobs Falls as the Size of the Graduating Class Shrinks." Press release, July 30. Available at: www.nalp.org/uploads/PressReleases/Classof2014SelectedFindingsPressRelease.pdf (accessed December 17, 2015).

————. 2015b. "Employment Rate of New Law Grads Up for the First Time Since 2007, Helped by Smaller Class Size." *NALP Bulletin*, August. Available at: www. nalp.org/0815research (accessed December 17, 2015).

National Law Journal. 2011. "The National Law Review 250." April 25. Available at: www.nationallawjournal.com/id=1202546887393?slreturn=20150806182746 (accessed December 17, 2015).

O'Keefe, Ed, and Matea Gold. 2015. "It's Make or Break Time for Jeb Bush." *Washington Post*, September 27. Available at: https://www.washingtonpost. com/politics/its-make-or-break-time-for-jeb-bush/2015/09/27/73d5f6fa-63c0-11e5-b38e-06883aacba64_story.html (accessed September 30, 2015).

O'Shaugnessy, Lynn. 2012. "4 Reasons to Ignore U.S. News' College Rankings." *CBS Moneywatch*. Available at: www.cbsnews.com/news/4-reasons-to-ignore-us-news-college-rankings/ (accessed August 31, 2014).

Olson, Elizabeth G. 2013. "Law Schools: Still Hiding the Sad Truth from Students?" *Fortune*. March 20. Available at: http://fortune.com/2013/03/20/law-schools-still-hiding-the-sad-truth-from-students/ (accessed August 3, 2014).

Osterloh, Margit, and Bruno S. Frey. 2010. "Academic Rankings and Research Governance." Institute for Empirical Research in Economics Working Paper Series 482. Available at: https://ideas.repec.org/p/cra/wpaper/2010-04.html (accessed December 17, 2015).

Owings, Jeffrey, Marilyn McMillen, John Burkett, and Bruce Daniel. 1995. "Making the Cut: Who Meets Highly Selective College Entrance Criteria?" NCES 95-732. Washington, D.C.: National Center for Education Statistics.

Parloff, Roger. 1998. "Who's Number One? And Who's Number 52, 91, and 137?" *American Lawyer*, April, p. 5.

Perez-Pena, Richard, and Daniel E. Slotnik. 2012. "Gaming the College Rankings." *New York Times*, January 31. Available at: www.nytimes.com/2012/02/01/education/gaming-the-college-rankings.html?pagewanted=all&_r=0 (accessed August 31, 2014).

Poovey, Mary. 1998. *A History of the Modern Fact: Problems of Knowledge in the Sciences of Wealth and Society.* Chicago: University of Chicago Press.

Pope, Devin G. 2009. "Reacting to Rankings: Evidence from 'America's Best Hospitals.'" *Journal of Health Economics* 28(6): 1154–65.

Porac, Joseph F., Howard Thomas, Fiona Wilson, Douglas Paton, and Alaina Kanfer. 1995. "Rivalry and the Industry of Scottish Knitwear Producers." *Administrative Science Quarterly* 40(2): 203–27.

Porter, Theodore M. 1995. *Trust in Numbers.* Princeton: Princeton University Press.

Posgate, Natalie. 2013. "Search for SMU Law Dean Will Shape School's Future." *Dallas Morning News*, February 8. Available at: www.dallasnews.com/business/headlines/20130206-search-for-smu-law-dean-will-shape-schools-future.ece (accessed August 3, 2014).

Power, Michael K. 1994. *The Audit Explosion*. London: Demos.

———. 1997. *The Audit Society: Rituals of Verification*. New York: Oxford University Press.

———. 2003. "Evaluating the Audit Explosion." *Law & Policy* 25(3): 185–202.

———. 2007. *Organized Uncertainty: Designing A World of Risk Management*. New York: Oxford University Press.

Prewitt, Kenneth. 1986. "Public Statistics and Democratic Politics." In *Behavioral and Social Science: 50 Years of Discovery*, edited by Neil Smelser and Dean R. Gerstein. Washington, D.C.: National Academy Press.

Rampell, Catherine. 2011. "The Lawyer Surplus, State by State." *Economix*, June 27. Available at: http://economix.blogs.nytimes.com/2011/06/27/the-lawyer-surplus-state-by-state/?_php=true&_type=blogs&_r=0 (accessed July 26, 2014).

Ramsey, Henry, Jr. 1998. "Historical Introduction." In "LSAC National Longitudinal Bar Passage Study," by Linda Wightman. LSAC Research Report Series. Newtown, Pa.: Law School Admission Council.

Rauhvargers, Andrejs. 2011. "Global University Rankings and Their Impacts." Report prepared for EUA. Brussels: European University Association.

Ravitch, Diane. 2010. *The Death and Life of the Great American School System*. New York: Basic Books.

Rayman, Graham. 2010a. "The NYPD Tapes: Inside Bed-Stuy's 81st Precinct." *Village Voice*, May 4. Available at: www.villagevoice.com/2010-05-04/news/the-nypd-tapes-inside-bed-stuy-s-81st-precinct/ (accessed August 31, 2014).

———. 2010b. "The NYPD Tapes, Part 2." *Village Voice*, May 11. Available at: www.villagevoice.com/2010-05-11/news/nypd-tapes-part-2-bed-stuy/ (accessed August 31, 2014).

———. 2010c. "The NYPD Tapes 3: A Detective Comes Forward About Downgraded Sexual Assaults." *Village Voice*, June 8. Available at: www.villagevoice.com/2010-06-08/news/nypd-tapes-3-detective-comes-forward-downgrading-rape/ (accessed August 31, 2014).

Redding, Sean. 2006. *Sorcery and Sovereignty Taxation, Power and Rebellion in South Africa, 1880–1963*. Athens, Ohio: Ohio University Press.

Reiss, Albert J., Jr. 1971. "Systematic Observation of Natural Science Phenomena." In *Sociological Methodology 1971*, edited by Herbert Costner. San Francisco: Jossey-Bass.

Rey, Jay. 2010. "UB Law School Slips out of Top Tier." *Buffalo News*, April 18. Available at: www.buffalonews.com/cgi-bin/print_this.cgi (accessed August 31, 2014).

Rezendes, Michael, and Christina Pazzanes. 2013. "New England Law Head Draws Scrutiny for His Pay: A Princely Paycheck for Dean of Unheralded School." *Boston Globe*, January 13. Available at: www.bostonglobe.com/metro/2013/01/13/law-school-dean-salary-may-nation-highest/r59QMPRZANUkeJOkxhne1K/story.html (accessed August 3, 2014).

Rivera, Lauren A. 2015. *Pedigree: How Elite Students Get Elite Jobs*. Princeton: Princeton University Press.

Roach, Ronald. 2009. "Shut Out." *Diverse,* April 16. Available at: http://diverse education.com/article/12481/ (accessed July 31, 2014).

Rosenfeld, Richard, and Robert Fornango. 2014, "The Impact of Police Stops on Precinct Robbery and Burglary Rates in New York City, 2003–2010." *Justice Quarterly* 31(1): 96–122.

Rosenthal, Robert, and Lenore Jacobson. 1968. *Pygmalion in the Classroom: Teacher Expectation and Pupils' Intellectual Development.* New York: Holt, Rinehart & Winston.

Rottenburg, Richard. 2000. "Accountability for Development Aid." In *Facts and Figures: Economic Representations and Practices,* edited by Herbert Kalthoff, Richard Rottenburg, and Hans-Jürgen Wagener. Marburg: Metropolis-Verlag.

Rottenburg, Richard, Sally Merry, Sung-Joon Park, and Johanna Mugler, eds. 2015. *A World of Indicators: The Making of Governmental Knowledge Through Quantification.* Cambridge: Cambridge University Press.

Rovella, David E. 1997. "A Survey of Surveys Ranks the Top U.S. Law Schools." *National Law Journal,* June 2, p. A-1.

Ryan, Christopher J. 2015. "Crunching the Numbers: Rethinking Measures of Quality and Value in National Law School Rankings." Available at: http://ssrn. com/abstract=2623728 (accessed December 17, 2015).

Sacks, Peter. 2000. "Predictable Losers in Testing Schemes." *School Administrator* 57(11): 6–9.

———. 2007. *Tearing Down the Gates: Confronting the Class Divide in American Education.* Berkeley: University of California Press.

Salmi, Jamil, and Alenoush Saroyan. 2007. "League Tables as Policy Instruments: Uses and Misuses." *Higher Education Management and Policy* 19(2): 31–68.

Samuelson, Pamela, and Suzanne Scotchmer. 2002. "The Law and Economics of Reverse Engineering." *Yale Law Journal* 111(7): 1575–1663.

Sauder, Michael. 2006. "Third Parties and Status Systems: How the Structures of Status Systems Matter." *Theory & Society* 35(3): 299–321.

———. 2008. "Interlopers and Field Change: The Entry of U.S. News into the Field of Legal Education." *Administrative Science Quarterly* 53(2): 209–34.

Sauder, Michael, and Wendy Nelson Espeland. 2006. "Strength in Numbers: The Advantages of Multiple Rankings." *Indiana Law Journal* 81(1): 205–27.

———. 2009. "The Discipline of Rankings: Tight Coupling and Organizational Change." *American Sociological Review* 74(1): 63–82.

Sauder, Michael, and Ryon Lancaster. 2006. "Do Rankings Matter? The Effects of U.S. News and World Report Rankings on the Admission Process of Law Schools." *Law and Society Review* 40(1): 105–34.

Schleef, Debra J. 2006. *Managing Elites: Professional Socialization in Law and Business Schools.* New York: Rowman & Littlefield.

Schlunk, Herwig J. 2009. "Mamas Don't Let Your Babies Grow Up to Be ... Lawyers." Law and Economics Working Paper No. 09-29. Nashville: Vanderbilt University. Available at: http://ssrn.com/abstract=1497044 (accessed August 4, 2014).

Schmalbeck, Richard. 2001. "The Durability of Law School Reputation." *Journal of Legal Education* 48(4): 568–90.

Schudson, Michael S. 1972. "Organizing the 'Meritocracy': A History of the College Entrance Examination Board." *Harvard Educational Review* 42(1): 34–69.

Schurenberg, Eric. 1989. "The Agony of College Admissions." *Money Magazine,* May 1989, p. 142–45.

Schutz, Alfred. 1970. *On Phenomenology and Social Relations.* Edited by Helmut R. Wagner. Chicago: University of Chicago Press.

Schworm, Peter. 2014. "Waning Ranks at Law Schools: Institutions Fear Recession's Effect Could Be Lasting." *Boston Globe* July 6. Available at: https://www.bostonglobe.com/metro/2014/07/05/law-school-enrollment-fails-rebound-after-recession-local-colleges-make-cuts/fR7dYqwBsrOeXPbS9ibqtN/story.html (accessed December 17, 2015).

Scott, W. Richard. 2001. *Institutions and Organizations.* Thousand Oaks, Calif.: Sage.

Segal, David. 2011a. "Law School Economics: Ka-Ching!" *New York Times,* July 16. Available at: www.nytimes.com/2011/07/17/business/law-school-economics-job-market-weakens-tuition-rises.html?pagewanted=all&_r=0 (accessed August 4, 2014).

———. 2011b. "Is Law School a Losing Game?" *New York Times,* January 8. Available at: www.nytimes.com/2011/01/09/business/09law.html?pagewanted=all (accessed August 4, 2014).

Seto, Theodore P. 2007. "Understanding the U.S. News Law School Rankings." *SMU Law Review* 60(2): 493–576.

Shore, Cris. 2008. "Audit Culture and Illiberal Governance: Universities and the Politics of Accountability." *Anthropological Theory* 8(3): 278–99.

Shore, Cris, and Susan Wright. 1997. "Policy: A New Field of Anthropology." In *Anthropology of Policy: Critical Perspective on Governance and Power,* edited by Cris Shore and Susan Wright. London: Routledge.

———. 1999. "Audit Culture and Anthropology: Neo-liberalism in British Higher Education." *Journal of the Royal Anthropological Institute* 5(4): 557–75.

———. 2000. "Coercive Accountability: The Rise of Audit Culture in Higher Education." In *Audit Cultures: Anthropological Studies in Accountability, Ethics and the Academy,* edited by Marilyn Strathern. London: Routledge.

Silver, Carole. 2006. "Internationalizing U.S. Legal Education: A Report on the Education of Transnational Lawyers." *Cardozo Journal of International & Comparative Law* 14(1): 143–75.

Simmel, Georg. 1978. *The Philosophy of Money.* Translated by Tom Bottomore and David Frisby. Chicago: Routledge & Kegan Paul.

Sloan, Karen. 2012. "Ill. Law School Fined $250K for Inflating GPA, LSAT Data." *Legal Intelligencer,* July 26. Available at: www.thelegalintelligencer.com/

id=1342974975259/Ill.-Law-School-Fined-250K-for-Inflating-GPA,-LSAT-Data?slreturn=20140703164834 (accessed August 3, 2014).

Smith, Chris. 2001. "News You Can Abuse." *University of Chicago Magazine* 94(1): 18–25.

Soares, Joseph A. 1999. *The Decline of Privilege: The Modernization of Oxford University.* Stanford: Stanford University Press.

———. 2007. *The Power of Privilege: Yale and America's Elite Colleges.* Stanford: Stanford University Press.

Stabile, Tom. 2000. "How to Beat U.S. News: A Law School Tries to Manufacture a Better Ranking." *National Jurist* 10(2): 19.

Stake, Jeffrey Evans. 2006. "The Interplay Between Law School Rankings, Reputations, and Resource Allocations: Ways Rankings Mislead." *Indiana Law Journal* 81(1): 229–70.

Staley, Oliver. 2014. "Nations Chasing Harvard Merge Colleges to Ascend Rankings." *Bloomberg News,* March 13. Available at www.bloomberg.com/news/2014-03-13/nations-chasing-harvard-merge-universities-to-ascend-rankings.html (accessed August 13, 2014).

Starr, Paul. 1987. *The Limits of Privatization.* Washington, D.C.: Economic Policy Institute.

Steele, Claude M. 1997. "A Threat in the Air: How Stereotypes Shape Intellectual Identity and Performance." *American Psychologist* 52(6): 613–29.

Steele, Claude M., and Joshua Aronson. 1995. "Stereotype Threat and the Intellectual Test Performance of African Americans." *Journal of Personality and Social Psychology* 69(5): 797–811.

Steinberg, Jacques. 2002. *The Gatekeepers: Inside the Admissions Process of a Premier College.* New York: Penguin.

Stetson University, College of Law. 2003. "Gary Vause, Stetson University College of Law Dean, Dies." *Stetson Law,* May 9. Available at: www.stetson.edu/law/news/index.php/2003/05/09/may-9-gary-vause-stetson-university-college-of-law-dean-dies/#.U96AqxDaJ1A (accessed November 22, 2015).

Stevens, Mitchell. 2007. *Creating a Class.* Cambridge, Mass.: Harvard University Press.

Stinchcombe, Arthur L. 2005. *The Logic of Social Science Research.* Chicago: University of Chicago Press.

Strathern, Marilyn, ed. 1995. *Shifting Context: Transformations in Anthropological Knowledge.* New York: Routledge.

———. 2000. *Audit Cultures: Anthropological Studies in Accountability, Ethics, and the Academy.* New York: Routledge.

Sturm, Susan, and Lani Guinier. 1996. "The Future of Affirmative Action: Reclaiming the Innovative Idea." *California Law Review* 84(4): 953–1036.

Tamanaha, Brian Z. 2012. *Failing Law Schools.* Chicago: University of Chicago Press.

Thelin, John R. 2004. *A History of American Higher Education.* Baltimore: Johns Hopkins University Press.

Thomas, Katie. 2014. "Ratings Allow Nursing Homes to Game the System." *New York Times*, August 25, A1.

Thomas, William Isaac, and Dorothy Swaine Thomas. 1928. *The Child in America: Behavior Problems and Programs.* New York: Alfred A. Knopf.

Thompson, James D. 1967. *Organizations in Action: Social Science Bases of Administrative Theory.* New York: McGraw-Hill.

Tutterow, Craig. 2015. "Complying with Commensuration: How Ranking Monopolies Redistribute Resources in U.S. Higher Education." Paper presented at the American Sociological Association Annual Meeting, Chicago (August 22–25).

Tutterow, Craig, and James Evans. Forthcoming. "Reconciling the Small Effects of Rankings on University Performance with the Transformational Cost of Conformity." In *Research in the Sociology of Organizations*, edited by Elizabeth Popp Berman and Catherine Paradeise.

Urla, Jacqueline. 1993. "Cultural Politics in an Age of Statistics: Numbers, Nations, and the Making of Basque Identity." *American Ethnologist* 20(4): 818–43.

Usher, Alex, and Massimo Savino. 2006. "A World of Difference: A Global Survey of University League Tables." Canadian Education Report Series. Toronto: Education Policy Institute.

U.S. Department of Education. 2012. *Digest of Education Statistics, 2011.* NCES 2012-001. Washington, D.C.: National Center for Education Statistics.

U.S. Department of Labor, Bureau of Labor Statistics. 2015. "Lawyers." *Occupational Outlook Handbook, 2014–15 Edition.* Available at: http://www.bls.gov/ooh/legal/lawyers.htm (accessed December 17, 2015).

U.S. Department of Veterans Affairs, Office of Inspector General. 2014. "Review of Patient Wait Times, Scheduling Practices, and Alleged Patient Deaths at the Phoenix Health Care System." *Veterans Health Administration Interim Report.* May 28. Available at: http://www.va.gov/oig/pubs/VAOIG-14-02603-178.pdf (accessed August 31, 2014).

U.S. News & World Report. 2001. *College Guidebook.* Washington, D.C.: U.S. News and World Report.

———. 2013. "U.S. News Breaks Online Traffic Record." Available at: www.usnews.com/info/blogs/press-room/2013/09/12/us-news-breaks-online-traffic-record (accessed August 22, 2014).

———. 2014. *America's Best Graduate Schools.* Washington, D.C.: U.S. News and World Report.

Van Dyne, Larry. 1996. "Who's Number One?" *The Washingtonian*, September 1, p. 60.

Van Zandt, David. 2007. "This Isn't Going Away." Paper presented at workshop on the ratings game, Association of American Law Schools annual meeting, Washington D.C. (January 3).

———. 2010. "Rankings Are Valuable (and Here to Stay) So Let's Focus on Making Them Better." *Above the Law*, April 13. Available at: http://abovethelaw.

com/2010/04/rankings-are-valuable-and-here-to-stay-so-let%E2%80%99s-focus-on-making-them-better/ (accessed August 3, 2014).

Vannebo, Berit Irene. 2010. "Contested Authorities: Accountability Reform and the Changing Nature of Relations of Authority in Academia." Ph.D. diss., Northwestern University.

Ventresca, Marc Joseph. 1995. "When States Count: Institutional and Political Dynamics in Modern Census Establishment, 1800–1993." Ph.D. diss., Stanford University.

Von Dornum, Deirdre Dionysia. 1997. "The Straight and the Crooked: Legal Accountability in Ancient Greece." *Columbia Law Review* 97(5): 1483–518.

Waring, Justin. 2009. "Constructing and Reconstructing Narratives of Patient Safety." *Social Science & Medicine* 69(2): 1722–31.

Webb, Eugene J., Donald T. Campbell, Richard D. Schwartz, Lee Sechrest, and Jane B. Grove. 1981. *Nonreactive Measures in the Social Sciences.* 2nd ed. Boston: Houghton Mifflin.

Weber, Max. 1922/1978. *Economy and Society.* Edited by Guenther Roth and Claus Wittich. Berkeley: University of California Press.

Webster, David S. 1984. "The Bureau of Education's Suppressed Rating of Colleges, 1911–1912." *History of Education Quarterly* 24(4): 499–511.

———. 1992a. "Academic Rankings: First on a List of One." *Academe* 78(5): 19–22.

———. 1992b. "Rankings of Undergraduate Education in US News & World Report and Money: Are They Any Good?" *Change: The Magazine of Higher Learning* 24(2): 19–31.

Wechsler, Harold S. 1977. *The Qualified Student: A History of Selective College Admission in America.* New York: Wiley.

Wedlin, Linda. 2006. *Ranking Business Schools: Forming Fields, Identities and Boundaries in International Management Education.* Northampton, Mass.: Edwin Elgar.

———. 2014. "How Global Comparisons Matter: The 'Truths' of International Rankings." In *Bibliometrics: Issues and Contexts,* edited by Lars Engwall, Wim Blockmans, and Denis Weaire. London: Portland Press Limited.

Weick, Karl E. 1976. "Educational Organizations as Loosely Coupled Systems." *Administrative Science Quarterly* 21(1): 1–19.

Weissman, Jordan. 2012. "Pop Goes the Law School Bubble." *The Atlantic,* March 20. Available at: www.theatlantic.com/business/archive/2012/03/pop-goes-the-law-school-bubble/254792/ (accessed November 22, 2015).

Wellen, Alex. 2003. *Barman: Ping-Pong, Pathos, and Passing the Bar.* New York: Crown.

———. 2005. "The $8.78 Million Maneuver." *New York Times,* July 31. Available at: www.nytimes.com/2005/07/31/education/edlife/wellen31.html?pagewanted=all (accessed August 4, 2014).

Westphal, James D., and Edward J. Zajac. 2001. "Decoupling Policy from Practice: The Case of Stock Repurchase Programs." *Administrative Science Quarterly* 46(2): 202–28.

Whitman, Dale. 2002. "Doing the Right Thing." *Newsletter of the Association of American Law Schools,* April, p. 1–4.

Wightman, Linda. 1996. "Women in Legal Education: A Comparison of the Law School Performance and Law School Experiences of Women and Men." LSAC Research Report Series. Newtown, Pa.: Law School Admission Council.

———. 1997. "The Threat to Diversity in Legal Education: An Empirical Analysis of the Consequences of Abandoning Race as a Factor in Law School Admission Decisions." *New York University Law Review* 72(1): 1–53.

———. 1998. "LSAC National Longitudinal Bar Passage Study." Law School Admissions Council Research Report Series. Available at: http://lawschool transparency.com/reform/projects/investigations/2015/documents/NLBPS. pdf (accessed December 17, 2015).

———. 2003. "The Consequences of Race-Blindness: Revisiting Prediction Models with Current Law School Data." *Journal of Legal Education* 53(2): 229–53.

Wilder, Gita. 2003. "The Road to Law School and Beyond: Examining Challenges to Racial and Ethnic Diversity in the Legal Profession." LSAC Research Report 02-01. Newtown, Pa.: Law School Admission Council.

Wilkins, David B. 2005. "A Systematic Response to Systemic Disadvantage: A Response to Sander." *Stanford Law Review* 57(6): 1915–61.

Williams, Samuel. 1794. *The Natural and Civil History of Vermont.* Early American Imprints, Series 1, no. 28094. Worcester, Mass.: Isaiah Thomas and David Carlisle.

Wills, Kerry. 2012. "COMPSTAT Critic Eli Silverman of John Jay College Says City Seems to Be Paying Mind to Stop-and-Frisk Outcry." *Daily News,* October 12. Available at: www.nydailynews.com/new-york/bronx/compstat-critic-eli-silverman-sees-efforts-curb-stop-and-frisk-article-1.1180795#ixzz2VqY4XH9R (accessed November 22, 2015).

Winerip, Michael. 1987. "The Hardest Thing You'll Ever Have to Write: College Admissions Essays." *New York Times,* January 4, p. 38.

Wright, B. Ann. 1991. "The Rating Game: How the Media Affect College Admission." *College Board Review* 158(Winter): 12–33.

Zaloznaya, Marina. 2013. "Beyond Anti-Corruptionism: Sociological Imagination and Comparative Study of Corruption." *Comparative Sociology* 12(5): 1–47.

Zerubavel, Eviatar. 1991. *The Fine Line: Making Distinctions in Everyday Life.* Chicago: University of Chicago Press.

Zucker, Lynn. 1977. "The Role of Institutionalization in Cultural Persistence." *American Sociological Review* 42(5): 726–43.

Index

Boldface numbers refer to figures and tables.

273

Cohen, Michael D., 12, 44
Cohn, Bernard S., 223*n*10
Columbia Law School, 231*n*28
Colyvas, Jeanette, 242*n*3
commensuration, 28–30, 37, 99
CompStat, 193–95
Council of Deans of the American
    Association of Dental Schools, 191
crime statistics, 193–96
Curtis, Karmari, 196

data for this study. *See* methods and
    data
deans, 100; accountability, rankings
    and, 108–18, 174–75; alumni and,
    110–11; the faculty, rankings and
    relations with, 114–16, 118; gaming
    the rankings, 129–32; governing bod-
    ies and, 108–10; hiring, rankings and,
    128; internalizing judgments implied
    by rankings, 127–28; the job of, rank-
    ings and, 101–4, 128–29, 132–33;
    managing the rankings, 118–23; the
    media and, 111–12; rankings, views
    of, 16–17, 104–8, 149, 235*n*31; school
    identity, ranking criteria and, 123–27;
    skepticism about statements made
    by, 204; students, rankings and rela-
    tions with, 113–14
dental schools, 190–91
DePaul University College of Law,
    234*n*18
Desrosières, Alain, 27
Didier, Emmanuel, 196
discipline, 177–78, 243*n*10
Diver, Colin, 242–43*n*8, 247*n*60
diversity: as a challenge to the legal
    profession, 232*n*45; standardized
    tests and, 89–94; *U.S. News and World
    Report* law school rankings and, 93,
    222*n*48
Dixon-Woods, Mary, 196–97

Drucker, Peter, 198
Du Chao-Hui, 184

education: high school and college
    completion, trends in, 220*n*27; mar-
    ket logic and neoliberal reforms,
    emergence of, 45–47
Education, U.S. Bureau of, 9
Education, U.S. Department of, 46
"Educational Quality Rankings of U.S.
    Law Schools," 16
educational rankings: American col-
    leges and universities, 186–88; busi-
    ness schools, 188–90; dynamics of
    non-law school, 181–82; global uni-
    versity rankings, 182–86; popularity
    and influence of, 5; resistance to,
    190–92, 247*n*59
Educational Testing Service, 48
Ehrenreich, Barbara, 47
Elfin, Mel, 10–11, 14, 211
Emory University, 188
employers: elite firms and elite schools,
    relationship of, 158–60, 163–64; geog-
    raphy and rankings effects, 167–68;
    hierarchy of schools and rankings
    effects, 160–61, 164–67; school
    reputation as decisive factor for,
    169; status differences and, 152–53;
    unfamiliarity of schools, rankings
    and, 168–69; use of rankings, 155–57,
    169–70; use of rankings, understand-
    ing inside law schools of, 157–58;
    variations in rankings effects,
    163–70. *See also* career services; legal
    labor market
Eterno, John, 194–95
ethical dilemmas posed by rankings,
    199–201
European Bank for Reconstruction and
    Development, 193
Evans, James, 244*n*15

effect of rankings on, 54–56; guides to law schools for, 43–44 (see also *U.S. News and World Report* (*USN*) law school rankings); identities of, rankings and, 58; paths taken by, rankings and, 49–56; questions confronting, 41; rankings, characteristics of those less/more concerned about, 56; rankings as concern/guidance for, 49, 58–59, 72–73, 204–5, 229–30n14; tier talk among, 40–43

QS World University Rankings, 182, 185, 245n21

quantification: accountability and, 19, 23–24; in admissions, 65–66; alternative forms of valuation imperiled by, 201; crime statistics, 193–96; cultural authority of, 8, 24–25; descriptive and proscriptive purposes of, tension between, 27; ethical dilemmas created by, 8, 199–201; health care, 196–98; history of modern embrace of, 21; narratives and, opposition between, 37; numbers, impact of making and using, 21–25; numbers, opportunities and challenges in interpreting, 30; objectivity, patina of, 1; paradox of, 200; populism and, 13–14, 21; selective accountability from, 7–8, 26; ubiquity of, 3, 172, 192–93; unintended consequences of, 1–3. *See also* measures/measurement

Randall, Kenneth, 110
rankings: as accountability measures, 4, 175–76; admissions and (see admissions; admissions officers); Americans' mania for, 13–14; career services and (see career services); clarity in response to informational problems, 24; clerkships and, 161–63; cognitive maps, shaping of, 27–28;

commensuration and, 28–30; competing, impact of, 189–90; deans and (see deans); demand for, trends leading to, 44–49; demoralization associated with a drop in, 127–28; diversity and, 89–94; of education beyond American law schools (see educational rankings); employers and (see employers); ethical dilemmas created by, 199–201; examples of early, 219–20n17; fee waivers and, 51; financial resources and, 118–19; history of, 9–14; institutionalization of, 72–73; international, geopolitics over students in, 186; of law schools by *U.S. News and World Report* (see *U.S. News and World Report* (*USN*) law school rankings); legal education, patterns of change in (see legal education, rankings and patterns of change in); mechanisms generating the consequences of, 28–39; methods and data for this study of (see methods and data); narratives and, 36–38; popularity and legitimacy of, 4–5; proliferation of, 3, 172, 222n41; prospective law students and (see prospective law students); reactivity of, 27–28; reverse engineering and, 33–36; self-fulfilling prophecies and, 31–33, 57–58; top-ten lists, 14; users/ uses of, 28

Rapoport, Nancy, 128
reactivity: cognitive maps and, 26–28; in health care performance measures, 196–98; of rankings and social measures, 7, 17; self-fulfilling prophecies and, 31–33
Reagan, Ronald, 45
Redding, Sean, 223n10
Reed College, 192, 242–43n8
reverse engineering, 33–36

University of Houston Law Center, 128
University of Illinois School of Law, 130
University of Michigan Law School, 91, 229*n*11
University of Mississippi School of Law, 168
University of Nebraska Law School, 228*n*27
University of Pittsburgh School of Law, 127
University of San Francisco School of Law, 237*n*20
University of Texas Law School, 149
University of Toledo College of Law, 80–81, 83
University of Utah, S.J. Quinney College of Law, 103
U.S. News and World Report (*USN*): history of rankings by, 10–12; rankings as the "brand"/franchise of, 14
U.S. News and World Report (*USN*) law school rankings: accountability, as instrument of, 23; admissions officers' views of, 69–73; *Barron's Guide to Law Schools* and, contrast between, 43–44; biases requiring deconstruction of, 26; boycott of, attempted, 191; coercion associated with, 177; deans' views of, 16–17, 104–8, 149, 235*n*31; definition of good law school, homogenizing effect of, 124–25, 179–80; diversity not factored into, 93, 222*n*48; future rankings, effect of current on, 55; gaming of, 130–32, 187–88; marketing of, 49; praise for, 72; reputation ranking, efforts to manipulate, 119–20, 131; reverse engineering of, 34–35; self-fulfilling prophecies and, 31–33, 57; study of, 4; tiers, discontinuation of, 226–27*n*4; unintended consequences/perverse incentives of, 98–99, 127, 144–45, 148. *See also* rankings

U.S. News and World Report (*USN*) law school rankings, methodology of: the calculations, 14–16, **218;** criticisms of, 16–17, 105–6; employment statistics, 136–37, 143–47, **218,** 236*n*2; impact of changes in, 83; the reputational surveys, 35, 106, 120, **218,** 222*n*44; selectivity factor, calculation of, 60, 75–76, **218**
USN. See U.S. News and World Report

Valparaiso University School of Law, 84
Van Zandt, David, 17, 72, 107–8, 230*n*18
Vernay, Dominique, 183
Veterans Affairs Health Care System, 1–2, 196
Villanova University School of Law, 130
Von Dornum, Deirdre Dionysia, 20, 223*n*2

Walk Free Foundation, 193
Washington University School of Law, 84
Weber, Max, 21, 65, 136, 224*n*14
Webometrics Rankings of World Universities, 245*n*22
Webster, David, 13
Wedlin, Linda, 246*n*54
Wegner, Judith, 17, 105
Weissman, Sam, 50–53
Wellen, Alex, 42–43
Wightman, Linda, 91
Williams, Samuel, 20
Woolgar, Stephen, 230*n*19
World University Rankings (WUR), 182, 184, 245*n*21
Wright, Susan, 242*n*6
WUR. *See* World University Rankings

Yale Law School, 57, 111, 228*n*27

Zahorsky, Rachel M., 158
Zuckerman, Mort, 10, 14, 44